D1125985

DISMANTLING THE STATE

DISMANTLING THE STATE

Downsizing to Disaster

WALTER STEWART

Stoddart

Published in 1998 by Stoddart Publishing Co. Limited
34 Lesmill Road, Toronto, Ontario M3B 2T6
180 Varick Street, 9th Floor, New York, New York 10014

Distributed in Canada by:
General Distribution Services Ltd.
325 Humber College Blvd., Toronto, Ontario M9W 7C3
Tel. (416) 213-1919   Fax (416) 213-1917
Email customer.service@ccmailgw.genpub.com

Distributed in the United States by:
General Distribution Services Inc.
85 River Rock Drive, Suite 202, Buffalo, New York 14207
Toll-free Tel.1-800-805-1083   Toll-free Fax 1-800-481-6207
Email gdsinc@genpub.com

02 01 00 99 98 1 2 3 4 5

Canadian Cataloguing in Publication Data

Stewart, Walter, 1931–
Dismantling the state : downsizing to disaster

ISBN 0-7737-3130-X

1. Canada — Economic policy — 1945– .
2. Business and politics — Canada.
3. Canada —Politics and government — 1984–1993.
4. Canada — Politics and government — 1993– .
I. Title.

JL86.P64S73 1998   338.971   C98-931468-5

Cover Design: Angel Guerra
Text Design: Kinetics Design & Illustration

Printed and bound in Canada

We gratefully acknowledge the Canada Council for the Arts and the Ontario Arts Council for their support of our publishing program.

This one is for

John and Pat Kennedy

of Cut-Pig Hill, Algarve, Portugal,

just in case the other one

never gets finished

Contents

The Axeman Cometh

It's as if we looked up one day and saw that
we had too much debt on our credit cards, so we
decided to save money by cancelling the
education of our children.
— Dr. John C. Hardy, August 1997

This part reminds us of the background against which the dismantling of government is taking place, through the history of the growth of government as a social intermediator, and the disdain in which it has come to be held.

The Slow Rise and Swift Fall

of the Responsive State

**Due to financial restraints, the light at the
end of the tunnel has been turned off.**
—Sign in a window, Calgary, November 1996

*They've taken away the hospital in Radville, Saskatchewan; closed it
down, turned it into a long-term care facility — and even that was
kept only because the locals raised one hell of a noise. What makes it
kind of funny, or not, depending on your point of view, is that the
Radville and District Hospital, a twenty-bed facility that has won its
share of awards over the years, was opened in the first place by
Premier T.C. Douglas, the father of Canadian medicare, whose ghost
must be whirling in its grave.*

*Made a pretty good speech, did Tommy, to a crowd of 1,200 people
— which is about one-and-a-half times the current population of this
dusty little town about 100 kilometres south of Regina. That was
on October 8, 1947, more than half a century ago. Tommy told them
why he had led the fight for public hospital care in this country. As a
boy, he had been struck by the devastation that follows when the
quality of health is left up to the fatness of the wallets of the people or
the whims of the doctors. He told the gathering — it was a line he
used in most of his speeches, back then — that a nation's greatness*

was not measured by its wealth or its armies, but by how it treated its unfortunates, including its ill, indigent, and elderly. He made a couple of jokes, too, for the little bantam with the large forehead and waving arms liked his jokes. And then he told them how proud he was of them, proud of the way they had dug down and chipped in to get the hospital built. He knew that a good many of those in the crowd had been born at home, in kitchens, or bedrooms, or even on a couch in the living room, and that it had been a painful, dangerous, and sometimes tragic business. Now they had a hospital nearby, their very own, which they had built, and which they could count on the government to help them keep going and up to date.

On October 1, 1993, the government of Roy Romanow, another Saskatchewan premier and Tommy's political, but not spiritual, descendant, closed down Radville's hospital. His government tried to slam the doors entirely, while it was in the process of winding up fifty-one hospitals around the province, but after the townspeople got up petitions and complained to the media, the folks in charge allowed them to keep the facility for extended care, and even to maintain a tiny emergency department. But they couldn't afford to have the hospital itself any more; there just wasn't any money. For some reason, the locals don't appreciate the kindness of the government in postponing the ultimate execution, possibly because there is no longer any ambulance service here, and now, for routine medical needs, you either drive to Weyburn, about three-quarters of an hour away over some of the lousiest roads in the province, or call Weyburn and hope the ambulance gets here before you pass on.

If you're in serious trouble, you should probably head for Regina, which is twice as far away as Weyburn but has better facilities. You are advised that if you are really going to need medical care, for a heart attack, say, or because you got your arm caught in a threshing machine, you want to allow a little extra time for passing out or nearly bleeding to death on account of the longer trip.

Saskatchewan, in 1947, was about the poorest province in the country, and Canada was a good deal poorer than it is today. Yet Saskatchewan, back then, could afford a hospital insurance plan, which would be copied by the federal government ten years later and which guaranteed the financing of institutions like this one. Now, apparently, it can no longer afford the luxury of a full medical facility. Instead, in the little town huddled among the wheat fields, we have a liquor store and a drugstore and a swimming pool and even a motel, but no hospital. To be sure, it was argued that the province had too many hospitals — 129, more than half the number in Ontario (223), for about one-tenth the population — but most of them were small, and the folks who built them and used them argued that closing them down now, when the demand for hospital care is about to go bounding up with the aging of Canada's population, made no sense. No one in authority paid the slightest attention; it is the characteristic quality of our age.

You can live here quite happily, but it is a hell of a place in which to get sick or die.

I arrived in Ottawa on April 22, 1963, along with Lester B. Pearson. He was taking over the reins of government, as our new Liberal prime minister. I was taking over a battle-scarred desk halfway down a hallway on the third floor of the House of Commons, as the new Parliamentary Press Gallery correspondent for the *Star Weekly*. The nation was, in many ways, much as it is today: divided and cantankerous, on the one hand, but, on the other, moderately prosperous, peaceable, and, at times, complacent.

There was one huge difference from today: at that time most Canadians believed that their lot, and the lot of the nation, had improved, was improving, and would continue to improve. Now we are sure we have sunk, are sinking, and will sink further. We are, in fact, much better off economically than we were then, but we don't believe it; our pockets — at least some of them — are bulging, but our spirit is bereft. Curious, really. Overhanging us at that time were the dangers of nuclear annihilation, threatened by the Soviet Union; and economic malaise, threatened by the United States, which was just about to impose a crippling Interest Equalization Tax. Quebec, newly energized by the Quiet Revolution, was prodding to have a new version of Confederation drawn up, and, in Western Canada, the usual disciples of disorder were complaining about French on the cereal boxes. I don't say we were a nation without travails, but we were a nation, and thought ourselves one of the better models available. We believed we were a people unique in the world; we believed we had discovered a way to sort out the competing claims of personal rights, private enterprise, and the public purpose.

Most of us had a high regard for the notion that the state, responsive to a democratic electorate, had a right and a duty to establish the rules, support the structures, and nourish the culture that made us a Canadian people, rather than Americans without the passport. We were in favour of our particular brand of capitalism, which we recognized as a mixed economy; we weren't as rich as the Americans, but we had something far more valuable — we were better off. Pearson remarked that Canadians paid about 25 per cent extra for the privilege of being Canadians and were proud to do so.[1] That figure seemed about right; we all knew it was cheaper to live in the United States, but the fact raised no envy within us.

Very few of us found it extraordinary that government owned the major elements of transport and communications. It seemed natural that we had a federal marketing board to move our wheat over the rails of our national railroad, through public ports, down the St. Lawrence Seaway, or that we had a federal broadcasting system to move our ideas and dreams to fruition. Ontario Hydro had been created early in the century to keep the cost of power, on which so much of our manufacturing depended, from being dictated by American entrepreneurs, and the corporation still held the monopoly, with our approval.

The usual pejoratives were hurled about, as we laboriously moved into place the planks that would fashion a modern state. We were "collectivists," "socialists," even "communists" — but it was hard to make such labels stick to the slick sides of men like R.B. Bennett, who had given us a national bank and broadcaster; Mackenzie King, who had established Trans-Canada Airlines; and Sir Adam Beck, who had given Ontario Hydro a motto that would strike horror in any boardroom today: *Dona Naturae Pro Populo Sunt*, the gifts of nature are for the people.

By the early 1960s, these matters had been pretty well thrashed out, and it was no more than a platitude to observe that, in Canada, we endured a higher level of government activity than did the Americans. Without it, we would not be Canada; it was the bulwark of a land with too few people and too much geography, in the cliché of the time. We were in the midst of a wholesale expansion of that activity, a process that began with the passage of the Unemployment Assistance Act of 1956, and continued with the series of laws that turned us, almost unconsciously — and briefly — into a welfare state.

We convinced ourselves that we had always been a kinder, gentler people and that it was in our nature to look out for each other. Even if we shied away from the phrase welfare state because it made some of us edgy, we knew what we meant: we had a social safety net and were proud of it. We did not have food banks because we didn't need them. It was not until we were much richer that this proof of our poverty became commonplace in Canadian cities.

In the past few years we have managed to create a nation in which the following oddities obtain:

- We have more than twice as many private police as public ones.
- We are convinced that we are broke, although we are far richer than ever in our history, and far richer than almost any other nation in the world.
- We have managed to accumulate a monstrous national debt, almost entirely by charging ourselves high interest rates. More than 85 cents out of every dollar of our collective indebtedness was put there not by government spending on welfare, medicare and pensions, but by the magic of compound interest. This interest is paid to our banks and other moneyed interests, which have ordered us to stop all other spending.
- The Canadian bureaucracy has been steadily declining for years, both in costs and in numbers, and the average pay of a federal civil servant has been around the poverty line.
- We can no longer afford to look after our people because of the cuts in social spending, but every year we are giving our chartered banks a bonus of $3.5 billion in public funds, simply by transferring more of our public debt away from the Bank of Canada, which we own, to the chartered banks, which we do not.
- Our new welfare rules, and especially our new "workfare"

rules, are not new at all. They are based on the principles of the Elizabethan Poor Law, written in England in 1601.

- Scores of mental patients are being put into jails, quite illegally, because we have closed so many psychiatric hospitals. We have no place to house them when they become a danger to themselves and others, except behind bars.
- In Ontario, the cathedral of the new economic religion, we have, at one and the same time, fired most of the inspectors of mines, whose job it was to protect us from abuses, and changed the law to allow mine owners, stuck with environmental messes of their own creation, to transfer the mines, and the costs of restoring the minesites, to the public purse. One estimate of the cleanup cost is $3 billion.
- Although we are so broke that we had to cut $7 billion out of social transfers to the provinces, we will be spending $12 billion, or much more, to correct the Millennium Bug, an entirely private blunder that afflicts our computer programs. The costs are legitimate business expenses and will all be written off against taxes.
- People who are terminally ill, but refuse to die in time for their beds to be used by others on schedule, should be prepared for the medical authorities to charge them for every day they linger on.
- Having failed to meet any of the deadlines we accepted to curb global warming, we are now setting up a system under which corporations can buy a licence to pollute.
- To save money, the Canada Health Protection Branch is being reduced by more than half, and much of the work of protecting the public turned over to private entrepreneurs. Many investigative projects formerly under the aegis of the branch have been dropped; among them, studies of the presence of "extraneous" matter in food, such as rat hair and insect dung.
- While our leaders constantly call for more research to allow us to compete effectively abroad, our scientific community is being gutted by cuts. In one outstanding act of inanity, we have abandoned a unique scientific instrument, the Tandem Accelerator Super-Conducting Cyclotron, which cost $100 million and kept us at the leading edge of research in the field.

- Thanks to the downsizing of environmental protection, Canada today has fewer stations to monitor acid rain than Croatia.
- Part of the frenzy to privatize government facilities is explained by the fact that they are carried on the books at a value of $1, even if they cost hundreds of millions to establish.

Enter, on tiptoes, the welfare state

All of these bizarre decisions are based on a compulsion to rid ourselves of the alleged inefficiencies, or, even worse, "market distortions" that were imposed when we gradually, reluctantly, embraced the welfare state. We did this only after a series of depressions of increasing severity cast the first doubt on the capacity of the market to correct itself, in the late nineteenth and early twentieth centuries. Although the lesson was slow to penetrate the circles of power, it was driven home to most ordinary Canadians in the late 1920s, with the onset of the Great Depression.

Our political masters in Ottawa thought they knew where the blame for all that tribulation lay. Prime Minister R.B. Bennett, a wealthy corporate lawyer, was fearless in laying down the root cause:

> The people are not bearing their share of the load. Half a century ago people would work their way out of their difficulties rather than look to a government to take care of them. The fibre of some of our people has grown softer and they are not willing to turn in and save themselves.[2]

When Bennett was finally moved to take some action by the certainty that he would be defeated in the next election if he did nothing, he borrowed elements of U.S. president Franklin D. Roosevelt's New Deal, which he heard about through his brother-in-law W.D. Herridge, the minister in charge of the Canadian legation in Washington. Bennett actually introduced sweeping legislation, including a Prices Commission, the Bank of Canada Act, the Wheat Board Act, the Companies Act, and an Employment and Social Insurance Act. Unemployment insurance was backed by a number of major banks as a means of keeping the rabble in line. Sir Charles Gordon, president of both the Bank of Montreal and Dominion Textiles, wrote a letter to Bennett in early 1934 deploring the "waste" of municipal spending on relief and worrying that these costs might lead to bankruptcies. To restore stability to the system and "for our own general self-preservation," he recommended a scheme of unemployment insurance that would not only steady the working classes but remove some of the strain on the relief rolls before the whole system collapsed.[3]

Bennett was impressed; he believed, as did many business leaders of the time, that workers, unlike corporations, did not have the sense to save against a rainy day, and a contributory scheme would, in effect, be a forced savings plan and would save everybody money in the long run.[4] Alas, the legislation, along with many other reforms, was declared *ultra vires* by the Judicial Committee of the Privy Council in England. Bennett was defeated in October 1935 by Mackenzie King, on a promise of "fiscal restraint" and a balanced budget "within a reasonable time."[5] For King, charity was the cardinal Christian virtue, so there was no need to take government action until public agitation reached the point where his own political survival hung in the balance.

That condition was met when a new depression struck in the late 1940s and Canada was in much the same position to deal with it as it had been in the 1930s. A 1947 study for the Department of Health and Welfare reported that "most of Canada had not advanced beyond the local poor relief stage of public aid for needy persons": "The provisions for general assistance are limited, mean and inadequate . . . They are literally disgraceful and unworthy of a nation of Canada's status." Until 1949 there was no provision whatever to pay relief to the "employable unemployed"; their plight, as everyone knew, was their own fault. In Nova Scotia and New Brunswick, "overseers of the poor" would refuse relief to paupers in their own homes "if accommodation in the local almshouse was available."[6]

However, the world was now beginning to be swept with the radical notions that had come out of Europe, through England, and even into crannies of the United States and our own provinces. A copy of the Beveridge Report of 1942 was brought over from England. It proposed a social security system that would cover every British citizen "from the cradle to the grave." It would be funded in the main from taxes, and would provide a "social minimum" of income, health, housing, and education for all.[7] It would be both a mechanism for government intervention in the economy and a redistributor of wealth. In 1943 Dr. Leonard Marsh, a social science professor at McGill, was commissioned to prepare a document on "Social Security for Canada," which he did, recommending many of the same reforms. The only one that survived was the Family Allowance Act, introduced in 1944.

King kept the rest of the benefits on hand for the next election. He had the Cockfield Brown advertising agency produce a series of pamphlets offering "womb-to-tomb" security — old age pensions, health insurance, unemployment aid, and housing subsidies. All these promises did their magic and he won the 1945 election handily.[8] Then he put the entire program away and forgot about it.

In Saskatchewan, however, the CCF under Tommy Douglas had been elected and in 1947 had introduced hospital insurance. The Ottawa Liberals, and even some Conservatives, began to shift their positions to forestall the left-wingers, advancing just enough to convince mainstream voters that capitalism could accommodate change. We didn't need socialism.

Still, when the government passed the first Unemployment Insurance Act in 1949, it was not because Ottawa had embraced the welfare state; rather, it was inspired mainly by a federal strategy to bully the provinces into giving up, permanently, the tax powers they had surrendered during wartime. In return for provincial support for a constitutional amendment that made unemployment a federal responsibility, Ottawa agreed to provide a minimum, limited payment to workers who had been laid off through no fault of their own and could prove it. They and their employers paid into an insurance fund; for the first time, Canadians did not have to be entirely destitute — only out of work — to receive relief.

The winter of 1949 brought the highest level of unemployment since the Great Depression. In a series of conferences, federal and provincial officials met to discuss what could and should be done, but they could not agree on a common policy. With the outbreak of war in Korea, the problem was solved, temporarily, as the workless went back to the factories to build bombs.

Still, the notion that there should be another war every time economic malaise became too much for the private social assistance system did not recommend itself to the more thoughtful of our bureaucrats and politicians. Thus, when another "recession" struck in early 1954, the apostles of discontent began to find a ready audience within the councils of the mainline parties. At the same time, public servants, allied with the Canadian Welfare Council, began to press for comprehensive welfare "rights," including a legal right to assistance for health and welfare anywhere in the country.

The guardians of conventional wisdom were appalled. A legal right to relief constituted "a doctrinaire formula forming part of the Marxist canon," which could only come about "in a socialist state."[9] Nothing was done.

The reluctant birth of the welfare state

By March 1954 a record 570,000 Canadians were out of work and "people were actually suffering hunger because of unemployment."* At this time, the unemployment insurance fund, by restricting access to the funds, had accumulated almost one billion dollars in funds surplus to any estimated need.† The government of Louis St. Laurent, who had replaced King, responded that "unemployment was mostly seasonal," and that helping the victims was "not beyond the capacity of local communities." But the local communities would pay relief only "to those who are starving." The soup kitchens that had appeared in the Great Depression and then shut down were reopening, vagrants were being shipped out of town by train, and fathers were again deserting families so the mothers and children could

---

*We were astounded at this at the time: Could people actually go hungry in a nation as rich as our own? Nowadays, of course, it is commonplace.

†Again, the same patterns are being repeated today; by late 1997, what is now "Employment Insurance" was accumulating a surplus of $13 billion, with more than a million Canadians out of work. We hung onto it; let the buggers try harder for a job.

collect relief. In Vancouver, Premier W.A.C. Bennett told St. Laurent that the charitable organizations "had exhausted their funds," and the same was true in most major cities.

When the Liberals refused to call a federal-provincial conference to discuss the situation, Finance Minister Walter Harris explained: "If the federal government took such an initiative the other governments would immediately expect it to bear a share of the cost of any solution."[10] That was true, too.

The Canadian Welfare Council, made up of social workers, academics, and other troublemakers, launched a publicity campaign of its own, with pamphlets outlining the suffering in the cities and the inability of private charities to meet the emergency. It then called the conference Ottawa had refused to call. Embarrassed, St. Laurent finally agreed to a series of meetings that resulted in the Unemployment Assistance Act of 1956. As historian James Struthers notes, the act "marked the first permanent federal commitment to social assistance for employables on welfare and provided a crucial bridgehead into the wider welfare reforms of the 1960s."[11] Government assistance was no longer a matter for shame; it was part of the package of civilization. This concept led, as all the Right Thinkers had said it would, to a massive extension of government programs at every level.

In an astonishingly short time — between 1956 and 1975 — Canada became a modern welfare state. We had the Unemployment Assistance Act in 1956; federal hospital insurance in 1957; Saskatchewan's Medical Care Insurance Act in 1962; the Canada Pension Plan in 1965; the Canada Assistance Plan in 1966, and the Guaranteed Income Supplement a year later; federal aid to education in 1967; federal medicare in 1968; major changes to unemployment insurance in 1970; provincial supplements to the elderly, beginning in British Columbia in 1972; major changes to family allowances and the Canada and Quebec Pension plans in 1973; and spouse's allowances in 1975.

The Canada Assistance Plan was perhaps the key to escaping the claims of Lady Bountiful; it came into effect on April 1, 1966, after a federal-provincial conference.[12] It was intended to bring together a patchwork of federal and provincial programs into a general plan to assist anyone who needed help. The provinces would administer the funds, with the federal government sharing the cost. Coverage would be by way of a "needs test," rather than a "means test." The distinction is that, with a means test, the eligibility of an applicant is determined by how much he or she has in assets and income from other sources. For claimants with other money, public support is either reduced or eliminated according to an exact scale.[13] With a needs test, the issue is whether claimants must have the money to maintain a decent standard of living, and the preamble to the act states that the assistance must be "adequate." It was a vague term, but it clearly meant that how people got to be poor was no one's concern; if people needed help, people were to get it, and on a scale that was related to needs, whether the claimant was a pensioner, disabled, or simply out of work.

When the Guaranteed Income Supplement was added, it meant that any Canadian living on a pension was assured of a minimum income, no matter what. The rest of the package ensured that Canadians would have a job when they could work and a benefit when they could not,[14] and, by 1975, that is roughly what we had.

By that time, the notion that poverty was a sin had received some hard — but not, it would turn out, fatal — knocks. Most Canadians believed that it was normal and natural for the state to alleviate some of the damage caused by an economic system which, whatever its other virtues, makes no pretence at fairness. We had become, and proudly so, a modern welfare state. I quote the best definition I have read of this vague term:

> A Welfare State is a state in which organized power is deliberately used, through policies and administration, in an effort to modify the play of market forces in three directions — first, by guaranteeing individuals and families a minimum income irrespective of the market value of their work or their property; second, by narrowing the extent of insecurity by enabling individuals and families to meet certain social contingencies (for example, sickness, old age and unemployment), which would otherwise lead to individual and family crises; and third, by ensuring that all citizens, without distinction of status or class, are offered the best standards available in relation to a certain agreed range of social services.[15]

For some Canadians, this period was our Camelot, our one brief shining moment; for others, it was the road to dusty hell, the slippery slope to deficits, debts, and despair. For the latter, the notion that collective responsibilities ought to outweigh individual rights, from time to time, seemed anathema. John Wayne didn't need anybody to pay his hospital bills, why should Joe Blow?

However, there was a flaw in the Keynesian argument on which the expansive and responsive state had been built. British economist John Maynard Keynes had not foreseen the huge inflationary pressures that could be built up by full employment and government spending. He said, in effect, that governments should spend when that was necessary and save as soon as spending was no longer necessary, so as to balance the books.[16] He did not see anything wrong with deficit financing, but he understood as well as anyone that governments could not go on spending in good years and bad without a grim reckoning. He had no idea how hard it would be to impose the necessary discipline on governments.

We built the welfare state for reasons of defence against the faults and failures of an economic system that created huge wealth for some of our people and unendurable poverty for others. We did not build a counter-balancing check on government spending. In economic terms, it did not matter, as we shall see, that much of the excessive spending that was creating debt was going to pay interest charges; all that mattered was that we were, in the classic phrase, "living beyond our means." Faced with large — albeit misstated — long-term debts amounting by the mid-1990s to $18,435 for every Canadian man, woman, and child,[17] we reacted with panic. We decided, with the highly subsidized aid of our corporations, academics, and think-tanks, which churned out vast volumes of propaganda, that we had gone too far, that we could not afford this approach any more.

Three levels of dismantling

Typical of this new wisdom was a brief from the Canadian Manufacturers Association in 1990 calling for more and harsher spending cuts: "The reality is that deficit reduction must be the top national priority." Not the looming crisis in health care, not the state of our schools, not public transport, not the dismaying continued existence of child poverty, but deficit reduction was the big issue. The *Financial Post* chimed in with the argument that, while lineups at the food banks grew longer, and the emergency rooms of our hospitals turned into chaos, we were really just a bunch of spoiled whiners: "Two generations of Canadians have become spoiled, thanks to spendthrift politicians at all levels of government."[18]

The ghost of R.B. Bennett nodded in affirmation. Instead of looking to see what had put us in this pickle, we decided to punish those groups in society on whom we felt we had lavished too much money: the spoiled bunch. We rediscovered the invisible hand and renamed it the "free market." Don't mess with the free market, folks, you will only make trouble. Besides, if government spends money to stimulate employment, it will interfere with the "natural" rate of unemployment, invented by our very own Bank of Canada. Briefly, the natural rate of unemployment — more formally, the "Non-Accelerating Inflationary Rate of Unemployment," or NAIRU — is that rate of joblessness that will take the heat off the job market.[19] Keep enough suckers lined up for every job, and they won't be so fussy about the pay. The NAIRU is now considered to be about 9 per cent — it's usually about 1 per cent below whatever the current unemployment rate is, proving that this weird stuff works. A few years ago, a 9 per cent unemployment rate would get a government turned out of office; today it is natural.

Were we kidding ourselves back in the 1960s, before we received the new market wisdom? Possibly, probably; things are never exactly what they seem. Yet I believe that our natural optimism during that brief Camelot in Canada was better, healthier, and more productive for the nation and for ourselves than today's sour cant that the government is our enemy and the bureaucracy our betrayers.

The purpose of this book is to examine the dismantling of the state that has taken place over the past fifteen or so years, to look at how it came about, what it has done to us, and how we can work our way back to a state of grace. The future of this nation depends on rediscovering what we knew two decades ago — that we must have a government active enough and muscular enough to right the imbalances created by our marvellously efficient, monumentally unfair economic system.

"Globalism" is the catch-word of our time. It appears to mean that unless we dismantle all the apparatus of intervention we have put in place to protect our people and our nation, we are doomed. But who says so, and why?

It is now an article of faith that we are overgoverned and overregulated, and that we ought to throw off all the panoply of strictures and services, from environmental protection to minimum wages, before we are stifled entirely. I am as opposed as anyone to the insolence of office, but I can't help reflecting that one man's dead hand of bureaucracy is another man's cop-on-the-beat. We have taken most of the cops off the beat, in the corporate world, and the result has been a disaster for all but a very few of us.

Finally, we have been convinced that all these changes are necessary because we went too far, spent too much, got ourselves too deeply in debt. Even if we regret some of the damage done when we set out to correct the flaws, we must accept that it was only done for the greater good of all. What we are observing now is a huge transfer of wealth from some sectors of society — most of us — to a few at the top. We bear the pain; they take the gain. We have also been convinced of the most monstrous lie of all — that the suffering we went through and continue to go through was necessary because we are now emerging from our trials with balanced budgets and new hopes. If the trials were based on faked evidence, as we shall see they were, it is little comfort to be told that the worst is behind us. What is really meant is that the next time we begin to restore some balance to the distribution of our wealth, we will be hit on the head again. Furthermore, the many choirs assembled to sing the hymns of redemption forget that the destruction of the state still goes on, and, because of budget provisions already in place, will continue in even harsher terms long after we celebrate the return to normalcy.

Three levels of dismantling are going on at once — at the federal, provincial, and municipal levels — but the process began in Ottawa. In every case, whether we are discussing the demolition of medicare, the emasculation of education, the privatization of our regulatory system, or the abandonment of environmental protection, the process began with Ottawa — Tory and then Liberal Ottawa — pulling up its skirts and passing by on the other side of the road, and then lamenting that the provinces can no longer get the job done.

It is no coincidence that Ottawa's massive retreat has been accompanied by an increasing hostility and selfishness on the part of the well-to-do provinces on any matters that have to do with national goals. The balkanization of the nation and its bankruptcy are joined at the hip, and the fact that the shortage of funds is largely illusory doesn't seem to matter much, now that we have been persuaded to digest the market myth by our opinion leaders.

We are in the process of revising, if not reversing, the concept of "responsible government" which it took us so many painful, bloody centuries of English, French, and Canadian history to fashion. We still have a government that is responsible, all right, but not to us — not to the great majority of Canadians. We have given up all that old-fashioned nonsense about the will of the people and put in its place responsibility to the market, to the corporations that make and control the economy on which the market depends. In a few short years we have gone from a political economy that was spread over an increasing number of citizens, that responded to the will of the nation, to one that is focused on an ever smaller segment of the population, and that responds to nothing more than the needs and the will of the market.

We have not voted to destroy the welfare system of which we were once so proud. Indeed, the people we keep returning to office must assure us during the election period that preserving that system is uppermost in their minds, that they wouldn't have it any other way, and that, in the words of former prime minister Brian Mulroney, it is a "sacred trust." These solemn rituals are performed by every party that offers its candidates for office. They are symbolic reassurances offered to the notion of a past that is recalled with great fondness even as it slips from memory. Many of us put up Christmas trees because they carry the nostalgic sense of happy days gone by. We forget where they actually came from and what they mean, but we take comfort in the tradition.

So with our politicians, who pander to our yearning for a simpler time when we could afford to care for each other, but have no intention of indulging our foolish fancies. Once the election is over and they are back in the seat of power, they announce that they are helpless. That rascally market is on the loose again, and its demands must be met first, before they can get around to the agenda that we all agreed on before the ballots were counted.

Enough of that! We still have the capacity to bring our politicians to heel, to reach out for compassion, to restore the social safety net we fashioned with such care over the years. Sam Slick, that colourful creation of Thomas Haliburton, once noted that "nothin' improves a man's manners like an election," and we still retain the power to command politeness, if we choose to use it. What we require is a government that is responsible to the people, not the cosmocorporations, and a system that places the market where it belongs, as part of the economic landscape, not its centre of gravity.

What we must do is look at what has actually happened to our system over the recent past and sort out those parts of the pruning operation that have been useful and worthwhile from those that have put the entire process in jeopardy. There is nothing wrong with this nation that cannot be fixed by an application of will, by drawing on the lessons of the past, by re-establishing a responsive state at the centre of our civil life, and restoring the nation we once were, and deserve to be again.

Goddam Guvmint

The irony is that the public service of Canada
is among the best in the world by any standard of
measurement. International comparative studies only
confirm what travelling Canadians and visitors to
Canada know from their own observation — Canada
is an extraordinarily well-run country, and it has its
public servants to thank for it.

— Paul Chapin, *Optimum*, 1996

*The television camera swings across an empty room piled with boxes.
Some cartons are neatly taped shut; others bulge with papers, letters,
forms, and booklets. There are dozens of these boxes, shoved into corners, placed on overflowing desks, and pushed into the corridor, from
where the camera records the scene in an early morning raid on the
offices of the Ontario government's Family Support Plan on Yonge
Street in Toronto. The boxes contain the forms, documents, and, yes,
the cheques that make the system work. But it doesn't work any more.
All the camera picks up are the barren desks, buried with paper and
bereft of bureaucrats.*

*A couple of years ago, the province became alarmed because, in
many cases, once a divorce court had ordered family support payments,
the payer — almost always the husband — either neglected or refused
to send along the money. The unpaid balance owed by deadbeat*

parents passed the $1 billion mark in 1995, and that staggering figure spurred the province to take over the collecting itself. It was more persuasive, somehow, to have an officer in blue with a writ in hand parked on the doorstep than to receive another phone call from a former loved one asking what happened to the monthly cheque. When the province became the collector, everyone agreed, the money moved faster and better. Then, in the name of downsizing, the doors slammed shut on eight of the regional offices that handle the work across the province, and more than one-third of the civil servants responsible were discharged. Most of the cases handled through these closed offices were transferred to Toronto, where the workload was already too much to handle. At the same time, the experts installed a new computer system that was going to streamline the process and allow the firing of still more civil servants — but that didn't seem to work, either. What the ex-spouses got when they called to find out why the money flow had ceased was a four- or five-hour battle with a telephone answering machine that thanked them for waiting and told them to buzz off. The former spouses were still disgorging, but the money was not getting through because there was no one to push it down the pipeline, and no one to explain what had happened.

So mothers are dodging the landlord, paying penalties on bounced cheques, and putting everything they can on credit cards all because they can't get the cash that has already been paid into court on their behalf. Now, two New Democratic Party members of the legislature have staged this raid; they knew it was going to be embarrassing for somebody, and it was. The MPPs, Peter Kormos and Shelley Martel, were initially charged with mischief and trespass but, by trial date, Kormos faced a single charge of assault for allegedly having pushed a guard during the fracas. The charge was dismissed on January 28, 1998.[1]

The newspapers climbed onto the story and wrote about Pamela Addison waiting six months to get a payment made on behalf of her son, Omar, aged 5, under a court order,[2] and Ruby White having to put $400 on her VISA card to pay for drugs to treat her cancer,[3] and dozens of other heartbreaking cases.

And the province said, Ain't it a shame?

A chap I know, an accountant, worked for a large, profitable company for a few years and then decided to try the civil service. "I never intended to stay," he remembers. "I just thought I would get to know the new Income Tax Act really well and then go back to the private sector. I joined Revenue Canada in 1973. It was a revelation to me. The people I worked with were bright, well motivated, it was a pleasure to go to work in the morning. I decided to forget the corporation; I was staying in government." Now he's getting out, and glad to go: "The morale is the pits; everyone is suspicious of everyone else; anyone who has employable skills has bailed out long ago unless, like me, they are on the verge of retirement, and management hasn't the foggiest notion what is going on in the department."

The gutting of the government employment roll has taken place to thunderous ovations on the part of all the Best People. The BP know that government is overblown, awkward, slow, cumbersome, mean, extravagant, silly, and permanently constipated; the bureaucrats have been battening on fat salaries and ballooning the national debt for years. The BP know these things because they have been told so by the media, by the think-tanks, and — to give them clout — by our American cousins, who always know better than we do how to view these matters.

Among the facts that we "know" about the Goddam Guvmint is that the bureaucracy is huge and growing grosser every day, that it receives stupendous salaries and bountiful benefits, and that it is, at one and the same time, bone lazy and far too busy. The workers lag on really important things like sending out a fishing licence on time, but seem to have endless energy to poke their noses into places where they are not wanted or needed. Filling out forms, creating red tape, and interfering with free enterprise — that's all the GG is good for.

This cynical view is relatively new to this country. In the years between 1956 and 1976, the welfare state, as we have seen, made its shy appearance in the nation. However we view those two decades, they marked a period of vigorous expansion and an almost chesty belief in ourselves and our worth. Part of that faith was centred on a conviction that our public service was one of the finest, if not the finest, in the world. Although we whined about them, as always, we had a sneaking admiration for our employees' fussy ways and we expected them to be both civil and servants, a notion that draws nothing but a wry smile today. In 1963, if a federal cabinet minister spent $298,000 to hire outsiders to write speeches and memos, as the *Globe and Mail* reported Defence Minister David Collenette did in 1995 and 1996,[4] the action would have brought as much derision as anger. The work was supposed to be done by the civil service, who were paid to do it. Not surprisingly, our brightest young people competed vigorously to join that service, not for the perks — which were few — but because that was where the action was. The teeming hordes who now file off applications to the Harvard School of Business, or, if all else fails, the Master of Business Administration course at the University of Western Ontario, then lined up for application forms to take the public service exams.

Ottawa was the place to be

David Ross, now the executive director of the Canadian Council on Social Development, remembers what it was like:

> When I first came to Ottawa in 1966, I worked in the Department of Labour for a couple of years. This town then was the most exciting place to be. I mean people were coming to Ottawa; almost everyone with an MA was coming to Ottawa. Nobody knew what the hell we were doing, but it was the age of social engineering. You identify a problem, you get the best minds to examine it, and you spend money and poof it's gone — well, we found it wasn't quite that easy. But it was an exciting place to be. Now, people have to apologize for working for the government, and I feel sorry for them. I have a lot of respect for the civil service, still, but I have to admit not many people share that view. I agree with John Ralston Saul that government is the only thing between us and the power elite, that government is the only thing we have and we've got to use it. We don't want it off our backs; frankly, I like it on my back.[5]

The federal civil service that Ross joined employed 199,000 people, out of a population of just over 18 million;[6] today, the number is 275,000, out of 30 million.[7] Despite the huge increase in public activity, the proportion of federal bureaucrats has gone down, from one federal civil servant per 90 Canadians to one per 109. (We will come to provincial and municipal bureaucrats later.) The proportion is still decreasing, both in numbers and spending. In 1998 the federal civil service will dispense approximately 12 per cent of the gross domestic product (the GDP, the sum of all the goods and services produced in Canada annually) — just about the same share it occupied in 1949, long before the huge expansion in government enterprise.[8]

Our contempt for the civil service has little to do with its numbers and everything to do with the notion we have been absorbing over the past decades that government is rotten, collective action oppressive, and the social safety net a trap from which there is but one escape — hack it down. As John Ralston Saul expressed it: "People become so obsessed by hating government that they forget that it is meant to be their government and is the only powerful public force they have purchase on."[9] If it seems weird for Canadians to hate the governments they alone have elected, it is even weirder to have the governments themselves devoted to the slash-and-burn tactics that have come into vogue in recent years. But we have been busy electing representatives who, in a majority of cases, don't really believe in government or politics and who think the whole process should be run on business lines. Within the civil service, at federal, provincial, and municipal levels, we have been promoting those whose dedication to the market system is loud and reliable, and downsizing those who still think there is a place for an active state. The *Globe and Mail* ran a profile of deputy finance minister Scott Clark in December 1997 in which he boasted that the finance department meant to make sure that the deficit was kept under control, "despite the mounting pressures to revive social spending and cut taxes."[10] This approach should have drawn at least a rebuke, but it went without comment. Top civil servants are expected to sound like Ayn Rand these days.

It is not surprising that we are developing a civil service that has no sense of worth or purpose. Its brightest members head for the door every time they are offered a golden handshake, and the less able remain behind. The bureaucracy is getting smaller, older, and dumber day by day; inevitably, the complaints about its inefficiency will become a self-fulfilling prophecy.

Behind this change in attitude lies the certainty that we are a much poorer nation than we were in the past, when we turned these spendthrifts loose in the 1980s. Even if we could afford the welfare state in better days, we cannot afford it now. But this impression is wrong. To see how "poor" we actually are, I have set out in table 1 of the appendix a series of calculations based on data collected by Statistics Canada. Measured in constant 1996 dollars, to get rid of the distortions of inflation, we were far better off, both as a nation and in per capita terms, in 1995 than we were in 1980. While the population increased by 23 per cent over this period, our gross domestic product went up by 29 per cent; our personal expenditures, by 36 per cent; and the revenues of all levels of government, by 26 per cent.

In short, we have been bamboozled into making decisions about our capacity to afford compassion by a series of falsehoods, many of which revolve around the Goddam Guvmint. To get at the current debate about the uselessness of governments in general, and the federal civil service in particular, it may be useful to consider three of the myths that becloud our vision.

Myth 1: Civil servants multiply like rabbits

The civil service has been steadily pruned, hammered, and slashed throughout all three levels of government for more than two decades. In table 2 I compare the growth of employees in public administration to Canada's population growth. Between 1976 and 1995, while our population expanded 29 per cent, the number of employees in public administration went up by about half that. Of course, there are slothful employees in government, just as there are in the private sector. But the claim that government payrolls have been swelling while the rest of the economy suffers is not true, and has not been true for decades.

What has grown is an attitude of distrust and dislike that has nothing to do with performance, but is driven, rather, by ideology. With the onset in the 1970s of the New Economy — a catchall phrase the academics use to sum up the advent of new technology (particularly information technology), massive changes in the social organization of work, and globalization — the view has grown that civil servants have become not merely an expensive adjunct of the state but a positive hindrance. They were slow to adapt to the new technology (which erased many of their jobs), they resisted changes in the organization of work (privatizing their jobs, or hiring outsiders on contract), and they were not sufficiently attuned to the glories of globalization (which often conflicted with the common weal, of which they were the defenders).

The New Economy chewed them up and spat them out by a process now familiar to us all. Almost every new budget, at every level of government, introduced "reforms" of the civil service, usually by an abrupt, across-the-board, percentage decrease in the money available to pay them. They were offloaded, often by offering them bonuses to quit, sometimes by firing them, but mostly by attrition — by not replacing those who left or retired. In the interests of fairness, very little attention was paid to the value of the work being performed by the individual bureaucrat or group. Once the budget came down, it was easier to hack clean across a department than to justify displacing, say, a food inspector while retaining a museum employee. By the end of 1995 the auditor general was complaining that cutbacks at Revenue Canada had led to a loss in revenue, since there were so few sheriffs on the job and so many outlaws.

Revenue Canada was one example of the operation of the Law of Unintended Consequences: you fire bureaucrats to save money, and it costs you several hundred millions of dollars. In another instance, employees were cut from the immigration service, with two unintended consequences. First, refugee applicants jammed Canadian entry posts, waiting for a hearing, but there was no one to process them. They got to remain in Canada while they waited — with an average of one year for a first hearing and up to five years for appeals. In November 1997 a *Toronto Star* investigation revealed that there were more than 38,000 applicants waiting in line. As a result of these delays, many refugees get in who do not meet the strict criteria for their class of immigrant, while thousands of others who have gone through all the proper channels are denied entry.

Second, hundreds of suspected war criminals, including

death-squad members from recent Latin American bloodbaths, entered Canada illegally, but no one is available to track them down and expel them. The immigration department had a unit to track suspects in cases of modern war crimes; it consisted of one manager and two members, tracking 450 suspects. Then the manager retired. When the department succeeds in obtaining a deportation order, there is no centralized system to make sure the villains leave when they are ordered out. A computerized tracking network was to have been purchased, but, after spending $1.7 million on its development, the federal government scrapped it, "due to reallocation of resources."[12]

Nobody said, Hey, let's make the refugee system really unfair, or let's welcome foreign killers to our shores. Rather, we cut the funding and applauded the savings. It is easier, cheaper, and less of a nuisance for Immigration Minister Lucien Robillard to say, "There is a strong commitment on the part of my government to act,"[13] than for the government to spend the money to realize on the rhetoric.

The slashing was not judgmental, or personal, or even sensible, it was just a fact of life. Because many of the workers belonged to unions, length of service, rather than value of service, became the main criterion for escaping the cuts. Because middle and senior managers made the decisions, most of the layers of fat that people complained about were retained, while the men and women who delivered services to the public were let go. By the same process, most of the "trouble-makers" vanished, leaving behind their stodgier fellows — the non-complainers and the brain-dead. In a development almost majestic in its wrong-headedness, we offer senior civil servants bonuses for getting rid of their staff and cutting costs. The argument is that they have more responsibility because they have off-loaded their colleagues; the lesson is that the public service is no place for anyone with brains.

Inevitably, we have paid out golden handshakes to transfer a huge amount of leadership, knowledge, and expertise to the private sector. In 1996 nine senior deputy ministers quit the federal civil service, out of a total of twenty-three.[14] Among them were Ian Clark, former head of the Treasury Board, who joined KPMG, the giant consulting firm; Pierre Gravelle, deputy minister of Revenue Canada, who became the chief operating officer of a banking subsidiary; Nick Mulder, deputy minister of transport, who joined the Stentor policy group, a telephone lobby; and Robert Giroux, deputy minister at Customs, Public Works, and the Public Service Commission, who joined a university lobby.

The federal government lost 55,000 people — more than one in every five of those on staff — between 1993 and 1997; whole departments were wiped out; and the average age of those who are left is forty-seven.[15] Within the remnants, seven out of ten of the bureaucrats described as "senior executives" are due for retirement before the year 2005, and, for the first time in history, there is no band of eager young recruits ready to take their place. According to an Angus Reid poll in mid-1997, only 6 per cent of Canadians between the ages of eighteen and thirty-five consider public service to be a "desirable profession."[16]

Clever kids. Who would want to go into a racket with such an uncertain future and such a noisesome reputation? We have a new organization, *La Relève* (the recovery), within the Public Service Commission, whose daunting task it is to try to breath life back into the corpse on the table and find new enthusiasts for the public service. But it has no power to improve wages or to offer a return to the creative policy-making exercises of an earlier era. The chance that our best and brightest youth will flock to the public standard once more is remote.

It is going to get worse. The cuts imposed by former budgets were all spread out over several years. Long after Finance Minister Paul Martin and his colleagues decided they had done enough damage, the cuts already in place in Ottawa and in other jurisdictions continue to exact their toll. The metaphor of the giant ocean liner trying to turn around in a hurry springs to mind; so does the looming iceberg.

Myth 2: They wallow in wealth

The average salary of a full-time, unionized, federal civil servant is about $24,000 a year;[17] it has been frozen at that level since 1991. The "poverty line"* was established at $16,318 for a single

---

*The poverty line is a catchall phrase for Statistics Canada's low-income cutoffs, or LICOs, a measure of how much of a family's income is spent on the basics: food, clothing, and shelter. If these costs eat up more than 54.7 per cent of family income, that family is below the low-income cutoff; we would call them poor.

person in a major metropolitan area in 1997; $22,117 for a couple; $28,115 for a family of three; and $32,372 for a family of four.[18] A bachelor or spinster is safely above the low-income line in a federal job, although a single-parent clerk is in trouble; a married worker barely breasts the low-income threshold; and a civil servant who has two children had better hope that the spouse can earn a paycheque. There are some well-paid civil servants, certainly — and they are the ones who can decide to give themselves raises, while freezing everyone else — but the widely held view that the bureaucracy is overpaid is simply not true.

In addition, more of the work is being "outsourced" — performed outside the service — for a cost that leaves the worker much worse off and the government coffers not much better. The rate from a temporary help agency for the work done by a $24,000-a-year civil servant is $36,000.[19] The agency keeps about $12,000 and the worker gets about $24,000 — the same as a unionized government employee. However, the "temp" receives no benefits and no pension. The federal government is now spending more than $5 billion a year contracting out work that could be done by its own staff.[20] In theory it saves money on salaries and benefits, but in fact the money goes to cover the overhead and profits of the outside firms.

The other new development in the bureaucracy is "telework," or electronic homework, where the bureaucrat either works full time at home or takes home a computer to work after hours. Telework is appealing to some workers — especially those with small children — but it is also advantageous to the government, for it yields more production for the same pay. A study of 6,000 federal workers conducted by Linda Duxbury of Carleton University showed that those who had access to technology in their own homes worked, on average, 2.5 hours more per day than office workers.[21] Most of this toil, according to another study, takes place after the children are put to bed;[22] it amounts to an extra workload of more than 30 per cent for those "fortunate" enough to have a computer at home.

Finally, there is the process known as Alternative Service Delivery, or ASD, by which the bureaucrats form themselves into little corporations either within or without the civil service and sell their goods to the department of which they used to be employees. "Instead of being program centred," gushes an Ontario paper on the subject, the team is becoming "customer centred."[23] The citizen is no longer a citizen but a business client; and the civil service is "shifting from rowing the boat to steering the boat." Think of medicare, say, as a kind of cruise ship that is being steered by one gaggle of experts on the public payroll, but propelled by private enterprise. Get the picture? The point is, apparently, that if you hive off a group of the workers into a separate unit and have them sell their services back to the same people they dealt with before, the process will, by the magic of private enterprise, become more efficient, even though the same people are doing the same work and charging another administration cost. The notion is that salaries will be lower, and benefits nonexistent; that's where the savings come. In fact, the client usually has to pay an administration fee to the outside firm that takes on the work, and that fee eats up most of the savings. However, because the fee appears under a different heading on the books, the department can claim a saving that does not exist. The whole process is buried in an avalanche of meaningless buzzwords that sound ever so keen and mean absolutely nothing: "We're rethinking our work, reinventing government, restructuring organizations, reskilling the public service and redesigning accountability."[24]

A federal food inspector described to me what ASD means in practice:

> There used to be three groups of food inspectors, one in Consumer and Corporate Affairs, one in Fisheries, and one in Agriculture. There were 4,500 of us in all, and our job was to see that the food Canadians put on the table is safe. Suddenly, there is going to be a new agency, shoving all three groups together, which is now proposing to set up on its own and sell the service to the government. But here's the catch; our jobs are guaranteed for two years, and after that, you can bet many of us will be out on the street, which means that the standard of inspection will be lower — it has to be.
>
> But from the government's point of view, it's wonderful. They get rid of the union; they get rid of pay equity; they get rid of having to train and promote people according to the old

rules, and pretty soon, they'll switch from food inspection to promoting the food industries, just you wait and see . . .

. . . We had a meeting with the president and proposed board of directors of this proposed new outfit not long ago, and the first thing I noticed was that there was not a single woman among them, and the next thing I noticed was that I was the youngest person in the room, and I'm 37.

What it is, really, is the triumph of the old farts.

But the numbers on the expense side of food inspection will show a sharp drop over the next few years, and if there is a parallel rise in food poisonings, well, too bad.

Another civil servant, in a middle management post in the defence department, told me that his group is looking at three ASD choices:

One way to go in the supply area where I work is to have the civil servants buy out the agency and operate it on their own, but within the civil service. Another is to form a separate outside agency, and charge for our work. The third is to keep the same structure, but go into competitive bidding for the work against other groups of civil servants and outside agencies. The purpose, every time, is to get a lower price, but in fact all you are doing is cost recovery. You charge for your work, even if you are doing it for your own department, and of course it takes money to work out the cost structure. There is no saving, there is just a paper-shuffling exercise.

To prove that ASD is the way to go, we have cheerleaders like David Zussman, one of Ottawa's most prominent get-government-out-of-government gurus, writing in the *Financial Post*:

The promise of the new approach is that there will be a marked improvement in service quality. We already have some history to judge by. Since it left the confines of a federal government department to become a Crown corporation in 1981, Canada Post's on-time delivery rate has improved from below 85 per cent to where it is now consistently in the 97 per cent range.[25]

Canada Post Corporation was established on October 16, 1981, as a Crown corporation, just like the CBC, VIA Rail, Atomic Energy of Canada Limited, or dozens of other companies. It remains as it was. The improvement in its on-time delivery rate, gained mostly through increasing automation, and almost entirely in the 1990s, proves that there is no need to de-Crown a government body to make it more efficient. Or, to put the argument another way, it proves exactly the opposite of the point Zussman makes. He does make one interesting observation, though, which is worth repeating in this context:

> But those who hope that improvement in service delivery will lead to tax cuts will probably be disappointed. Actual administrative costs are estimated at less than 20 per cent of total government expenditures, so even major efficiencies will have only a marginal effect.[26]

He might have reworded his argument to say, Hey, folks, there is very little fat left to cut in the federal civil service, so hacking away at it will not produce any savings. How this translates into a call to shift everything over to ASD, where a margin of profit has to be added to the bill, is one of the eternal mysteries.

It is not ASD, but the combination of increased efficiency available through computers, paper shuffling, and longer hours, that has allowed the federal civil service to get by with less. In one of the few studies that has looked at this phenomenon, Jan Borowy and Theresa Johnson note: "This work intensification is reflected in the fact that the federal public service is currently operating with the same numbers as in 1973, despite a 20 per cent increase in the Canadian population and programmes which are increasingly complex."[27] The bureaucracy may be operating with the same numbers, but few who have to deal with them imagine they are doing the same job. Every time you try to call a federal bureaucrat and get nothing but an answering machine, you are contributing your little mite to savings.

In short, the federal civil service is much smaller, leaner, and more productive than in the past, although we may be on the way to making it much less efficient by destroying its morale and purpose, and its formerly high level of energy and intelligence.

Myth 3: *The bureaucrats have spent us into poverty*

The debtload facing Canadians today is large. Collectively we owe about $650 billion, taking into account all the money payable at all three levels of government.[28] The federal debt alone at the end of 1996 was $469 billion, and is now over $500 billion, which is nearly 60 per cent of the annual gross domestic product. In 1940 it was 70 per cent of the GDP, so that need not spook us. Still, it is a huge amount of money and it has been growing too fast. If you keep on spending more than you take in, even if you are a government and not an individual, the long-term consequences are likely to be unpleasant. Mr. Micawber put it well in *David Copperfield* when he said: "Annual income, twenty pounds, annual expenditure, nineteen nineteen six, result happiness. Annual income twenty pounds, annual expenditure twenty pounds ought and six, result misery."[30] We have been spending more than our income for more than forty years. It has to hurt. However, before we decided that the solution was to slash government services, we might have asked ourselves one crucial question about our debtload: How did it get so big?

Obviously, if overspending on programs — pensions, medicare, family allowances, and all the panoply of state support — caused the difficulty, we had no recourse but to cut the spending. But what if the debt originated elsewhere? What if we were hacking away at the social safety net when it was not the origin of our troubles? Wasn't that pointless as well as cruel?

The simple answer to our question is that we appear to have dug ourselves into a pit simply by the magic of compound interest. To understand, we need to keep in mind the difference between the public debt and an annual deficit. A deficit is just that, a difference between the money taken in and spent every year. The public debt is the amount of money already owed, and on which interest must be paid. Because of the interest it must pay on its accumulated debt, the government can run its normal spending at a level well below its revenues and still wind up with a deficit. If Mr. Micawber had said, "annual expenditure, twenty pounds ought and six and, oh, yes, the interest on my Visa card," he would have described modern misery.

Table 3 of the appendix compares federal government revenues, program spending, and the growth of the debt from 1955 through 1997. Overall, program spending — which includes pensions, unemployment insurance, medicare, transfers to other governments, business subsidies, defence, and payments to Crown corporations — came to $1,925 billion during this period. Government revenues during the same forty-two years came to $1,983 billion, or $58 billion more. I have grouped the numbers by decades to highlight the fact that there was only one period, between 1975 and '84, when Ottawa was spending, year by year, more on programs than it was collecting in revenue (during this time, both Liberal and Conservative governments were in charge). For every other period, program spending was less than our federal income. Looked at another way, 85 per cent of our new debt had nothing whatever to do with providing Canadians with services; it was all due to the ever-rising interest charges.

But then we get the debt charges. In 1955 we already owed $16 billion, and the debt charges on that came to $7 billion over the next decade. Because we had spent $8 billion less than our revenues during that decade, we were able to cut $1 billion from the debtload — the last time that happened. In the next decade, we again spent about $9 billion less than we received, but the debt charges came to $19 billion — we were behind by another $10 billion. Then came the decade when we spent $20 billion more in operations than we took in, to say nothing of interest charges, and what had by now become a permanent obligation ballooned by $107 billion.

At the same time, when we had already accumulated a massive debt, it became and remained government policy to keep interest rates high to control inflation. John Hotson, an economist at the University of Waterloo, wrote: "Interest on Canada's public debts grew from 1947–1996 from $559 million to $75,990 million, or by 135.9 times. But the Bank of Canada has tried to stop inflation by raising interest!"[29] Yet the Bank of Canada took many years to accept the argument that when you increase interest rates, you also increase costs across the board, and therefore inflation. The central bank still keeps our interest rates substantially higher than those in the United States.

The effect of soaring interest rates — the bank rate hit 21.07 per cent in 1981, in the middle of the government spending spree — was to send the debt into the stratosphere. Even while we were cutting costs, the debt kept rising because of the huge load already accumulated. Once established, this burden continued to grow, and is still growing, even after the recent savage cuts to spending. A peek at the 1997 federal *Budget Plan* shows how it works. In 1994–95, program spending came to $119 billion; by 1996–97, it had been cut by $10 billion, to $109 billion; at the same time, federal government revenues went up from $123 billion to $125 billion. We were $12 billion ahead of the game but the interest cost on the public debt during this same period went from $42 billion in 1994–95 to $45.5 billion in 1996–97.[30] So we cut $10 billion, took in $2 billion more in revenue, and lost $3.5 billion of our savings on the basis of old debt charges that kept climbing because of earlier interest costs.

In 1995 the auditor general of Canada turned his mind to this problem and concluded that if real interest rates had remained the same between the mid-1970s and the mid-1990s, the result would have been a savings of $13 billion in the 1994–95 fiscal year alone, and a cut in the long-term debt of $159 billion. [31] Our present predicament, then, is the product of an insane interest-rate policy, not overspending.

A good many economists have been saying that if interest rates were lowered, the economy would expand. It turned out to be true and, according to current predictions, it seems that we will have a budgetary "fiscal dividend" of somewhere between $9 billion and $25 billion over the next few years. Our political masters are already fighting over it.[32] However, they are not being honest with us. Sure, the cuts in service helped to curb the expense side of the ledger, but the real action was on the income side, where revenues soared as the economy came to life again. Between 1994–95 and 1996–97, federal revenues leapt by $19.2 billion; almost every cent of this increase came from higher tax takes (nontax revenue remained almost exactly where it was). Program spending was cut in these two years by $9.7 billion. The interest on the public debt kept increasing, and was $8.4 billion higher during this period.[33] When we shake all this down, we see that increased income from renewed economic activity accounted for almost twice as much of the gain on our deficit as the spending cuts.

The bureaucracy did not create our debtload; compound

interest did. It follows that throwing Canadians off the welfare rolls on the grounds that this was regrettable, but necessary, marks a high point in hypocrisy and stupidity.

In Ontario, voters were told that spending cuts were necessary to balance the budget, and these cuts are now said to be paying off. Yet the Mike Harris government spent $56.6 billion in the 1996–97 fiscal year, a little *more* than was spent by Bob Rae's New Democratic government in its last year of office ($56.2 billion).[34] The provincial budget deficit was cut almost in half, but not because of the spending cuts that did so much damage to some sectors; as Ian Urquhart, the *Toronto Star*'s Queen's Park columnist noted, the improvement came "almost entirely as a result of increased revenues from a growing economy."[35]

At all levels of government, most of what we have been told about our debt is nonsense. The single parents who banged on the doors and assaulted the telephones of the Ontario Family Support Plan were the direct victims of the wrong-headed notion that the only way to escape the debt trap was to cut government services. What we are cutting is not the fat but the meat; we are making it impossible to deliver the services people — pardon me, the customers — require, and blaming the resulting chaos on the inefficiency of the civil service we have disembowelled.

When the Canadian Union of Public Employees conducted a survey of unionized social workers in Winnipeg, it found that 90 per cent of them do not feel that the current child-welfare system is able to meet the needs of families and children adequately. Nearly half of them believe that, because of the huge increase in caseloads dumped on them in recent years, a majority of the children in their charge are "currently at risk of neglect and/or physical, sexual or emotional abuse."[36]

Manitoba's family services minister, Bonnie Mitchelson, responded to this cry for help by suggesting that the solution might be to privatize the whole process: "What I'm saying is, are we spending the dollars the best way to deliver the service?"[37] She did not explain how privatization would lessen the average caseload per social worker from thirty-eight, where it is today, to fourteen, where the professionals believe it should be. The process is all about making sure the bureaucracy carries the can for the tragedies that result from the cuts.

We mustn't get too worked up about this situation. We are killing people, damaging people, harming our children by these senseless cuts, but look at it this way: the banks and other bond-holders feel much better about things these days, and isn't that worth a few hundred, or at most a few thousand, lives? Besides, aren't these regrettable incidents forced on us by those wicked years of overspending? In a word, no. We are abandoning the whole notion of an activist state, responsive to the needs of the majority of its citizens. Professor Harry Arthurs of York University has written an epitaph on the subject:

> Of course the state still has its uses. The state alone can sign international treaties (which oblige it to abstain from acting like a state). It will retain its functions as nightwatchman (pending further experimentation with security firms and privatized prisons). It will continue to provide education (or education vouchers), welfare (or workfare) and health care (of a minimal sort, for those who cannot afford to buy private insurance) . . .
>
> . . . If this is indeed to be the future of the Canadian state, who would wish — who would presume — to undertake its administration, and to what end?[38]

Aftershocks

**The success of the wealthy is important
for the maintenance of the unfortunate.**
— Michael Fraser of the Fraser Institute, 1987

*This part deals with a number of areas where, in the currently popular
phrase, "hard choices" had to be made. No one set out to devastate
medicare, education, justice, or the environment, but we could no
longer, it was argued, afford to maintain these artifacts of civilization
in the opulent style to which we had become accustomed.*

3

Medicare: The Sick System

**My feeling is that Canadians don't give themselves
enough credit — I really believe that. People
get taken care of in this country and I can't say
enough about a system, as a practising physician,
where that happens.**
— Dr. Carter Snead, formerly of Los Angeles, 1997

*This corridor of the Civic Hospital in Peterborough, Ontario, is, well,
a hospital corridor. It is clean, but it doesn't feel clean; the mingled
scents of antiseptics and that indefinable, sick smell found in any
hospital pervade the place. People are bustling to and fro; a nurse
scampers past, her arms full of folders; and half way along the hall
a doctor is listening carefully to a distressed elderly woman who
obviously wants to know the best, or the worst, about a loved one.
A number of gurneys line the sides of the corridor, each carrying a
patient waiting for treatment. It was here, not long ago, that an
eighty-two-year-old man was found, dead, by relatives, when they
arrived to visit him.[1] He had been there all night.*

*No one is to blame, certainly not the hospital. It has always had an
excellent reputation and now it is struggling to meet an ever-growing
workload with an ever-diminishing set of resources. Everything that
could be done was done — within budget, of course. Hospital officials
have explained that all is in order, except, of course, that an old man*

died, alone, unregarded, and that his family will live with that horror for the rest of their lives. Still, look at it this way: just as you cannot make an omelette without breaking eggs, you cannot cut health-care costs without some "sacrifices." The trick is to ensure that neither you nor any of your loved ones ends up this way. But we can give no guarantees of that.

Hey, if people keep getting born, and getting sick, and getting old, and the money to pay to look after them keeps getting less, something has got to give.

Medicare is the acid test. Can an advanced, wealthy nation afford to provide medical care to its people on a universal basis, with the major costs covered by the public, rather than the private, purse?

Tommy Douglas assumed that it could: universal health care was his measure of a civilized country. On April 1, 1954, discussing what was to become the nation's first universal medical insurance plan in the Saskatchewan legislature, he said: "I made a pledge with myself that someday, if I ever had anything to do with it, people would be able to get health services, just as they are able to get educational services, as an inalienable right of being a citizen of a Christian country." For a time, we believed him; we even, astonishingly, took pride in a system so demonstrably superior to anything the Americans had. And then we began to have doubts, so we took our dismantling axe to the medical system in the same way and for the same reasons that we attacked every other government service. We are substituting a two-tier system of health delivery because we believe we cannot afford to do better.

We regret, but accept, the heart-wringing stories that appear in our newspapers, on our radios, across our television screens:

- In Edmonton, Hazel Campbell, 71, died after she was left waiting in a holding ward for three days because there was no bed available for her. In the richest part of one of the richest nations on earth, two other patients died in emergency wards because there was no one available to perform their necessary surgeries.[2]

- In Northern Ontario, three heart patients died while waiting for surgery; they are among 250 patients caught in a backlog because of a shortage of facilities. In a fourth case, a man sold his house so he could buy an operation sooner in the United States. Dr. David Gould, who reported these incidents in a letter to Ontario's health minister, wrote: "This is exactly the sort of situation which our health-care system was supposed to prevent — patients being reduced to financial ruin by the cost of obtaining health care."[3]

- In Toronto, Dr. Carolyn Bennett told a forum on women's health that cutbacks have eroded services so badly that all hospital patients should have a family member standing by at the bedside to ensure they get proper care. "Don't ever dream of sending someone to the hospital on their own," she said. "The family should show up and do shifts. It's just safer."[4]

- In Vancouver, the visit of an elderly couple from Ontario to their daughter's home turned into a nightmare when the father, Harry Cunningham, fell ill from emphysema. After two weeks in hospital, he was released, but he couldn't enter a subsidized nursing-home because British Columbia had imposed a three-month residency requirement. Besides, there was a year-long waiting list. The daughter didn't want to split up her parents, in part because her mother was suffering from Alzheimer's disease. In the end, the elderly couple were put in a private nursing home, which cost $4,000 a month, none of which Ontario would pay. Harry Cunningham died there, and his widow was eventually found a place in Kelowna, 270 kilometres from her daughter's home.[5] Medicare, incidentally, is supposed to be portable from province to province.

- In Perth-Andover, New Brunswick, five of the fifty-three members of the Hotel Dieu's nursing contingent took leave because of stress due to overwork, leaving the staff, which had already lost five nurses in cuts, in even worse shape. Fifteen other nurses have left for jobs in the United States because of conditions here. One of the survivors told a reporter from Maclean's: "We don't have time to spend with our patients anymore. You just go into their rooms, throw their pills at them and then rush to the next room."[6]

• In Toronto a seventy-five-year-old man who was dying of bone cancer slipped and fell in hospital, breaking his arm. He was given some medication for pain, but had to wait sixteen hours to have the bone set. The hospital staff explained that it had "weekend problems."[7]

The only way to save medicare was to wreck it?

That's too bad, we say, as these stories and dozens like them roll across our consciousness. But we can't do anything about them because, the way things were going, the system was bound to crash. Salvation equals obliteration. Dr. Duncan Sinclair, head of Ontario's Health Services Restructuring Commission, said, as he announced the ordered closing of eleven of Toronto's forty-four hospitals over a three-year period: "We don't have a genuine health services system in Ontario. As good as our health system is today . . . we must change or risk losing what we cherish so deeply."[8]

Once again, we have been deceived. We could and can afford the costs of medicare, including both hospital insurance and medical care, although we would be better off if we could lower these costs. To accept the argument that, because costs rose too fast over the past few years, the answer is to close hospitals, withdraw ambulances, cut off preventive medicine, deny service, substitute minimum-wage workers for registered nurses, and send patients home when they are still too ill to manage for themselves, all to save money, is, literally, to wreck the system and call it reform.

To understand how we came to accept this argument, we need to know where we came from on this issue, where we have arrived, and where we appear to be going.

Hospital beginnings

The notion that the state should intervene in the health of its citizens is a recent invention. In New France, the hospitals were entirely church-run charities. The first was set up in Quebec City in 1639, a gift of the Duchess d'Aigullon. It was staffed by doctors imported from France on a fee-for-service basis; the poor went without professional medical treatment, which, considering the standards of the time, was probably just as well.

The General Hospital in Montreal was taken over by the Grey Sisters, an order founded by Marguerite d'Youville in 1755, only four years before the battle of the Plains of Abraham. The order was set up under the Suplicans to serve the poor, but the towns-people, unable to imagine why a group of women would want to live by themselves and associate with the riff-raff, assumed that their real purpose was to sell the brandy they made to the Indians.[9] People called them the "Soeurs grises" as an insult, but the nuns later embraced the term and began to wear the colour.

After the Conquest, when funding from the French Crown disappeared, the British were uncertain whether the nuns should be allowed to continue with their work. The new administrators were opposed to religious communities. A British judge, Hugh Finlay, proposed that no novice should be permitted to take the vows of a nun before the age of forty; convents did more harm than good, he said, "inasmuch as they bury before it is time many young women who might be useful in producing subjects to the king."[10] Still, there were all these poor and sick to be cared for, and no one else volunteered, so the nuns were left to get on with the job. To finance their activities, they turned their cells into workshops, where they produced purses, workboxes, artificial flowers, slippers, maple sugar, jam, peppermint, and biscuits, and sold them to the British merchants. They were candy-stripers, two centuries ahead of their time.

This religious charity was better than nothing, but the hard-working nuns could only begin to cope with the poverty, disease, filth, and unemployment that marked the life of the under-classes in Montreal, Quebec, and Trois Rivières. The help they got from the church itself was grudging, and was aimed more at keeping out the *anglais* than actually helping anyone. The Roman Catholic Church, as the bulwark of French-Canadian language and culture, rejected state interference in the social life of the colony, on the grounds that it would mean domination by the anglophone, Protestant, merchant minority. As late as 1938, a leading Catholic sociologist wrote:

The Church lays on the faithful the personal duty of charity even unto the gift of one's self . . . It is the bounden duty of each individual to provide, according to his means, for assistance to the destitute and unfortunate, and the state should intervene only when private initiative finds it impossible to supply existing needs.[11]

Only state funding could get the job done

Through most of the French-speaking province's history, private initiative found it impossible to supply existing needs. Because the shortfall was borne by the noncomplaining classes, however, their survival was deemed less important than the need to protect the church against the state.

As society became more complex, the shortcomings of church charity became more obvious and insupportable. Hospitals and education — which became a battleground among the churches — were two of the areas where it became obvious that only state funding could get the job done. Large capital costs required the infusion of government funds to supplement what could be raised by and through wealthy individuals. The first provincial operating grant for a hospital in Upper Canada was allotted in 1830 to York General, and grants-in-aid, operating grants, building grants, and all the large apparatus of state funding gradually assumed a major role in building and operating these institutions, long before there was such a thing as medicare. As Alvin Finkel notes in his account of this development:

> Public health measures were seen as essential to fight cholera and smallpox epidemics. In an urban environment families and charitable institutions were unable to provide sufficient funds and services. The state was called in to fill the gap. Since neither crime nor cholera could be contained within the ghettoes of the working poor, the wealthier classes supported a minimum of state measures.[12]

"Minimum" was the operative word; most of the task of looking after these matters was to be left to private individuals for two more centuries. The amount of succour offered depended on the whims of the well-to-do, until it became chic to be seen as a volunteer. In the twentieth century, serving on a hospital board became essential for politicians, provided they remembered, as one Ontario member of the Legislative Assembly put it, that "it was well known that establishments supported by voluntary contribution were invariably more efficient than those assisted by Government grants."[13] Since it was well known, there was no need to prove this purported truism, and nobody ever has.

Private sources could not provide even a minimum of care for the fast-expanding nation. J.S. Woodsworth, the Methodist preacher who became a social worker, visited the homes around his mission in North Winnipeg in the early years of the century and noted the appalling conditions in which many of the community lived. They remained untouched by any form of public or private assistance, and their children often died without ever receiving so much as an aspirin. Woodsworth was often asked to conduct the burial services of infants who had died of minor illnesses that might have been cured with a doctor's visit. He refused to use the words "The Lord giveth and the Lord taketh away" in such ceremonies because they appeared to him "blasphemy of the worst kind, an attempt to fasten on the Lord the responsibility for the criminal negligence of the citizens of Winnipeg."[14]

It was the failure of private charity to meet the medical and other needs of the poor that made Woodsworth into a politician and led to the formation of the Co-operative Commonwealth Federation (CCF) in 1933. One of the members of parliament sent to Ottawa from the West with him was Tommy Douglas, who returned to Saskatchewan to become premier in 1944. Douglas, who nearly lost a leg to osteomyelitis as a boy, was saved by the intervention of a Winnipeg doctor, who performed several operations free of charge. Douglas later recalled:

> I always felt a great debt of gratitude to him; but it left me with this feeling that if I hadn't been so fortunate as to have this doctor offer me his services gratis, I would probably have lost my leg . . . I felt that no boy should have to depend either for his leg or his life upon the ability of his parents to raise enough money to bring a first-class surgeon to his bedside. And I think it was out of this experience, not at the moment consciously, but through the years, I came to believe that health services ought not to have a price-tag on them, and that people should be able to get whatever health services they required irrespective of their individual capacity to pay.[15]

However, every attempt to launch a national health scheme was smothered by the opposition of business and organized medicine. In British Columbia in the mid-1930s, a health insurance proposal was supported by 59 per cent of the voters in a provincewide referendum, but the Liberal premier who put it forward, T. Dufferin Patullo, never introduced the necessary legislation. At the federal level, when Prime Minister R.B. Bennett's minister of health, D.M. Sutherland, was pressed to take some action in the House of Commons, he replied that the government was awaiting the development of a plan by the Canadian Medical Association. No such plan was ever put forward.[16]

Douglas was more driven and less patient. He had campaigned on a promise to provide hospital insurance as the initial step towards full health insurance. In 1947 he succeeded, with passage of North America's first comprehensive hospital insurance legislation. He was building on an already considerable foundation, laid down as much by his Liberal predecessors as by anyone in the CCF. In 1914 one Saskatchewan town, about to lose its only doctor, put him on salary and kept him. Two years later, the Union Hospitals Act allowed local municipalities to set up hospitals where townfolk could receive treatment paid for by the community; some towns financed the plan by land taxes. In 1939 this coverage was extended to permit a tax of not more than $50 per family to finance common care. Within a few years, 107 municipalities, 59 villages, and 14 towns were paying 180 doctors, some full-time, others part-time, to take care of their citizens.[17]

Hospital insurance had been established, in part, in Newfoundland in 1935 with passage of the Cottage Hospital and Medical Care Plan, but Newfoundland was not yet part of Canada, and no other eastern jurisdiction showed much interest in the subject. In Quebec, a commission on hospital services recommended such insurance in 1942, but the project was dropped. The nation was carpeted with provincial hospital associations, physicians' groups, and private insurance companies, all of which wanted no part of a state-run plan. They preferred prepaid plans of their own.

For its part, the federal government pursued a policy of benign neglect. A Department of health had been established in 1919, but it was concerned, mainly, with combatting the spread of venereal disease, and, later, with promoting physical fitness. Health appeared to have been dealt to the provinces by the British North American Act, and Ottawa was happy to leave it there. In 1943 the total health expenditures of all levels of government came to $11.2 million; of this, the federal government spent less than 10 per cent.

A breakthrough of sorts came in 1945, when a Reconstruction Conference of federal and provincial delegates was convened to establish ground rules for governmental relations in the postwar period. The federal delegation came up with a comprehensive health plan, based on similar plans in Europe and England, which would be implemented in two stages. The first included hospital insurance, general practitioner care, and visiting nurses. The second stage would cover specialist care, dental care, drugs, and laboratory services. When both stages were in place, in three years, the total cost of the plan was estimated to come to $250 million a year, of which the federal government would contribute two-thirds. Ottawa would also provide health grants to the provinces and help finance hospital construction through low-interest loans.[18] This proposal, which was set out with little detail in just five pages, was based mostly on guesswork and received little attention at the conference.

Saskatchewan made a detailed reply to Ottawa, suggesting that the entire nation should adopt the hospital insurance plan it was about to implement as the first stage of complete medical coverage. This response was the only serious proposal to come from the provinces. Ontario explained that its health facilities were already overburdened and would require expansion before any new duties could be taken on. In the meantime, poor folks who were not covered by private medical plans could expire in peace; the system was not yet ready for them.

Saskatchewan went ahead with its own plan. The Liberal government had already passed a Bill Respecting Health Insurance, but was defeated before the law received royal assent. The new Douglas government set up a Health Services Planning Commission, which recommended starting with hospital insurance. The plan came into force on January 1, 1947, and in return for a compulsory monthly premium, provided free hospital care at the standard ward level for all citizens in the province.

The plan was a resounding success from the start, not only in providing care for thousands who had had none before but in setting the pace for Canada. Every other province sent officials to Regina to see how the plan operated. British Columbia introduced a parallel act in 1948, although it bogged down for four years in arguments about how to collect the premiums; eventually they were replaced by an increase in the sales tax. Then Alberta set up its own plan, followed by Nova Scotia.

Ottawa was finally persuaded to act by the examples of Saskatchewan and Alberta; by an extensive inquiry in Ontario which recommended public health coverage; and by a Dominion Bureau of Statistics study, released in 1953, which underlined both the widespread incidence of illness in the nation and the uneven burden of health costs on its people.[19] The federal government reluctantly included the subject in a federal-provincial conference in 1955. Meetings of the federal and provincial health ministers followed in 1956, together with a long-drawn-out series of negotiations to decide who would pay for what. Ottawa eventually offered to pay each province an amount made up of two calculations based on population: 25 per cent of the average cost per capita of hospital services in Canada as a whole, and 25 per cent of the average per capita costs in the province itself. Together they equalled about half the cost.

The Hospital Insurance and Diagnostic Services Act was passed in April 1957, came into effect on January 1, 1958, and gradually covered the entire nation. Any province that was not signed up came under direct pressure from its taxpayers, who were helping to pay through their income taxes the federal share of a scheme from which they were excluded. Quebec was the last province to join, on January 1, 1961.

The troubled birth of medicare

Saskatchewan established a medical-care program for those on social welfare in 1945, followed it soon thereafter by expanding two of the municipal plans, and immediately ran into the two issues that still vex medicare: Who pays and how?

The choices were simple, and, thanks to the vigour — or stubborn selfishness — of the medical professsion, the nation as a whole settled on a process that was bound to balloon costs. The doctors could be paid in one of three ways — a fee for every service performed, a charge per capita of patients enrolled with the doctor, or a salary. Canada opted for the first, paying the price, in vain, to try to win the doctors over to support a national scheme. The Canadian Medical Association adopted a policy in 1949 to provide health insurance only through existing organizations — there would be no state plans.[20] Government-run medicine was communism at worst, socialism at best, it held, and would lead us all to ruin. Bureaucrats would tell physicians how to practise, and their freedom would vanish.

When Saskatchewan, after sixteen years of planning, discussion, argument, surveys, and commissions, implemented the nation's first comprehensive medical care plan on July 1, 1961, Saskatchewan's doctors instantly went on strike, with the overwhelming support of the Canadian medical profession as a whole. They stayed out for twenty-three days, delivering only essential services. There were marches and counter-marches, demonstrations and counter-demonstrations. Finally a mediator, brought in from England, worked out a twenty-nine-point compromise which, among other things, allowed doctors to practise outside the scheme if they chose. Very few chose, or choose; the doctors soon found that, for the first time, they were paid in full and on time, and they could order necessary treatments for their patients with the assurance that the treatment would be provided, even if the patient had no money. Dr. Efstathios Barootes, the Regina urologist who led the strike against "state medicine," became a staunch defender of the system. "I have changed my mind," he said.[21]

To pay for medicare, which allowed doctors 85 per cent of the schedule of fees approved by the Saskatchewan College of Physicians and Surgeons, Saskatchewan increased the retail sales tax from 3 to 5 per cent, jacked up corporate and personal income tax by 22 per cent, and charged an annual premium of $12 for individuals, or $24 for a family. The cost of the plan was about $25 million a year, out of a total provincial budget of about $125 million. This sum represented an increase in expenditures, and therefore of taxes, of one-fifth — a huge amount. However — and this is the part of the argument that seems to get lost — individual taxpayers were being relieved of much higher costs; they were financially ahead of the game.[22] And, for the first time in Canada, illness or accident were not the inevitable precursors of ruin for average citizens. The costs were shared.

The federal Liberal Party had had a medicare platform as far back as 1919,[23] but had done very little about it. Then, between 1957 and 1968, a series of minority governments put it in the position of having to depend on the New Democratic Party, successor in 1961 to the CCF, to remain in power. The NDP demanded action on medicare and finally got it. The process began with an initiative of the government of John Diefenbaker, who appointed a Royal Commission on Health Services in mid-1961 under the chairmanship of his old friend and former political pal Emmett Hall, then chief justice of Saskatchewan. The Canadian Medical Association backed the appointment of the commission, confident that the fix was in; Hall was bound to return a recommendation that any national medical scheme be based, not on government insurance, but on private, prepaid insurance plans.

When the commission report came down in mid-1964, however, it favoured universal medical care on a basis very similar to the Saskatchewan plan already in operation. Hall later told me that he had no fixed views on how such a plan should be run when he began his work, but the overwhelming evidence before the commission at its hearings, and in its own research, convinced him that a government plan was the only one that made economic, medical, and social sense. His report argued that medicare would not only be of great economic benefit to Canadians but would have other higher virtues as well:

> Economic growth is not the sole aim of our society and, given the growing wealth of Canada, economic considerations should not solely be used to deny to indviduals the health services needed to alleviate illness and disability and to extend life expectancy. Although we recognize that resources are limited, and individuals cannot expect to receive unlimited amounts of health care, the value of a human life must be decided without regard to whether the person is a producer or not. Health services must not be denied to certain individuals

simply because the latter make no contribution to the economic development of Canada or because he cannot pay for such services. Important as economics is we must also take into account the human and spiritual aspects involved.[24]

That paragraph was written more than one-third of a century ago and has not been surpassed as an argument for a universal medicare system. The report recommended that the government should "make the fruits of all the health sciences available to all our residents without hindrance of any kind."[25]

The Hall Report was the beginning, not the end, of the struggle at the federal level. When the Liberals won the 1965 election, again with a minority government, they had promised a universal plan, but splits within the cabinet, over both the idea itself and the cost, kept putting it off. The right-wing ministers, led by Mitchell Sharp and Robert Winters, said that Canada could not afford a universal plan, and even ministers who were in favour came up against the familiar Canadian conundrum: How could a universal plan, financed at least in part by the provinces, be imposed on them against their will? This problem was solved, as Tom Kent, Prime Minister Lester Pearson's policy adviser, makes clear in his memoirs, by Al Johnson, who had been deputy provincial secretary of Saskatchewan when medicare was introduced there and was now assistant deputy minister of finance:

> The federal government did not need to legislate the details of a shared-cost program. It needed only to define, clearly, the principles of what was meant by medicare. Then it would contribute to the costs of any provincial program that satisfied those principles.[26]

Ottawa would pay an amount equal to half the average national per capita costs of any provincial schemes that met the guidelines. This approach not only got around the constitutional hurdle of provincial control but attempted to control the eventual cost, since provinces that spent more than the national average would not get anything more than half that average out of Ottawa.

The guidelines the provincial regimes had to meet were strict and simple. There were four of them:

- all services provided by doctors must be covered (dental care and pharmacare were considered, but discarded as too costly);
- the plan must be universal, covering everyone in the province on the same terms and conditions (deterrent fees and extra billing were allowed, but minimum coverage on a universal basis was guaranteed);
- the plan had to be publicly administered; it did not have to be run by provincial bureaucrats, but the province had to have primary responsibility (every province set up a separate administration for this purpose); and
- benefits had to be transferrable between provinces.

Although the plan had to be universal, not all doctors in a province had to join. The Liberals ran on this version of medicare in the 1965 election and were returned with another minority government. They fiddled with the plan, delayed it — for financial reasons — and finally, with more prodding from the NDP, which still held the balance of power, implemented the necessary legislation on July 1, 1968. A number of the provinces were outraged. Johnson's clever manoeuvre had put them in the same whipsaw that had been applied with hospital insurance — their citizens would be required to pay, through taxes, for benefits they could not receive unless they accepted the federal plan. A number of provinces, led by British Columbia and Ontario, had developed versions of their own much more in line with the thinking of the Canadian Medical Association. The Ontario Medical Services Insurance Plan, for example, left medical care in the hands of private insurers and simply paid for insurance for most of those who were not already covered; a better version of the model now followed in the United States. It was not universal, it was not publicly administered, and it was not transferrable.

Still, Ottawa was imposing its will on the province. Even if the solution it offered to the nation's needs was much superior to the provincial one, it was resented, especially since the additional costs to the public purse would use up any tax money that might have gone to its own scheme. Ontario premier John Robarts fumed: "Medicare is a glowing example of a Machiavellian scheme that is in my humble opinion one of the greatest political frauds that has ever been perpetrated on this country."[27] Even so, Ontario, vowing it would never consent, signed on to medicare on October 1, 1969. In the end, every province and territory passed the necessary legislation, often after considerable wrangling. Quebec passed its own Health Insurance Act in March 1970, which conformed to the federal legislation but allowed "up to 3 per cent" of the province's doctors to opt out. This ceiling led to a confrontation with the doctors, especially the specialists, who wanted a plan whereby they could opt out but still collect from patients who would, in turn, collect at least part of the cost from the plan. There was a brief doctors' strike, followed by legislation to end the strike. The doctors were preparing to resist when the October Crisis flared and other priorities took over. The doctors went back to work, and medicare was established.

In 1981 Mr. Justice Hall produced a second report. It declared that extra billing, which had either begun or was contemplated in several provinces, should be banned.[28] This decision paved the way for passage of the Canada Health Act in 1984 to establish the rules under which federal aid to the provinces would be paid. Now there were five conditions to be met: the plan must cover all physicians' services, as defined; and it must be universal, portable, publicly administered, and free of either deterrent (user) fees or extra billing. Ottawa could hold back, dollar for dollar, an amount equal to extra-billing charges or user charges, such as the extra fees many hospitals had begun to levy.

Ontario doctors rebelled at the removal of extra-billing charges, which they had be levying at the rate of $50 million a year.[29] They staged a strike that lasted twenty-five days and earned them a reputation for pig-headedness and greed. The government stood firm and allowed no extra billing.

It was a plan without financial controls

Can we still afford universal medicare? The scheme we adopted was initially imposed on most of the provinces and the medical profession against their wishes. It was inspired by a small minority of left-wingers, who happened to be right. Because of all the backing and filling made necessary by its method of imposition, it had no effective financial controls. Whatever the hospitals spent or the doctors prescribed would be provided, and the costs passed along. Administrators could budget costs, but only by figuring out what was spent the previous year and guessing what would be needed the next.

Not surprisingly, public medical expenses soared. They rose for many reasons: costs that had once been private were now public; Canadians were getting a new, improved service — decent medical and hospital care for every person in the country; new treatments and devices always cost much more than the ones they replaced; and the population was aging, with much higher costs incurred by those over sixty-five. In 1994, the average per capita expenditures of children up to the age of fourteen was $513; for those over sixty-five, it was $6,943.[30] The amount of money required every year skyrocketed because medicare never had any effective budgetary control. The provincial medical groups, perhaps the most powerful unions in the nation, simply issued their demands and the provincial governments, after a lot of hemming and hawing, acceded to most of them, passing half the bill up the line to Ottawa. The drug firms doubled, trebled, or quadrupled their prices, and governments had no choice but to pay them, since they refused to face the drug companies head on. Table 4 of the appendix shows that the fastest-rising costs by far in medicare over the years have been doctors' fees and drug costs, which have multiplied more than ten fold. Hospital costs have increased at about half that rate.

There was some cheating, both by doctors and by patients, but it was not, and is not, a significant cost factor. There was and is some overuse of the programs by a small minority of people, but, again, this factor is not what has driven the costs so high. We handed the medical and pharmaceutical professions the national wallet, invited them to take what they wanted, and then expressed surprise when we got back only an envelope of limp leather.

In 1945 Canadians spent $250 million on health, of which governments spent $68 million, or just over 26 per cent.[31] Health care was costing 2.2 per cent of our gross national product, or GNP, the total sum of our spending, both within Canada and abroad. By 1962, after the introduction of hospital insurance, we were spending $2.56 billion on health, almost half of it through governments, and the total bill came to 5.9 per cent of our GNP. A decade later, health costs were nearly $8 billion; 70 per cent of it was government spending, and 7.3 per cent of the GNP was going to health. A decade after that, in 1982, we were spending $31 billion, with seven dollars out of every ten spent through government, and the health bill was 8.6 per cent of our GNP. We hit the ceiling in 1992, when health costs, at $70 billion (government share, $52 billion, or 74 per cent), ate up 10.2 per cent of the GNP.

It was not so much the absolute cost of medicare as the trend that set off alarm bells. Costs were escalating much faster than our population, cost of living, or gross national product. Economists produced charts with dark red lines to prove that, at this rate, there would soon be no money left in the country; it would all go down the health-care gullet. Then the brakes were fully applied, and the cost cuts, begun in 1993, took hold; by the end of 1996, while the current costs had gone up to $75 billion, health's share of the domestic product was down to 9.5 per cent and falling.

Two points ought to be made about these alarming figures. The first is that we were getting a constantly better result. Canadian life expectancy, general health, disease control, and child mortality — almost every standard measure of health — showed huge improvements during this time. We were not just throwing the money away. The second is that, compared with the Americans, who have kept fooling with various combinations to avoid any government-run plan, we did very well indeed. In 1975 our health costs consumed 7.1 per cent of the gross domestic product, while theirs consumed 8.2 per cent; at the end of 1996 our figure was 9.5 per cent, theirs 14.2 per cent. Our health system was costing us much less in administration costs, not only because medicare was run as a monopoly but because there was no profit to be paid at every step of the way. When you nail patients $15 for an aspirin, as many U.S. hospitals do, it adds up.

And the Americans still have 40 million citizens who have no coverage whatever, while their general health statistics sink lower and lower. In 1995 the Americans were paying more per capita for health-care spending than any other advanced nation, while infant mortality was higher and life expectancy lower.[32] The Americans had, in a vain attempt to save money, herded most of their people into health maintenance organizations, or HMOs, to negotiate group charges for panels of incorporated doctors hired by insurance companies. As a result, most U.S. citizens have little real choice of doctor, although it was the cry of "free choice" that led them to reject the Canadian system, where we do have free choice. And for millions of Americans, any serious illness spells financial ruin. No one knows how many Americans die needlessly because of their lousy health system, but it is probably between 10,000 and 100,000 deaths per annum.[33] But there is no question that Americans pay more and get less out of their system, which they persist in calling the "best in the world." So it is, but only for the richest in the world. For the nation at large, it is an expensive disaster.

Again, coming back to table 4, in the twenty-one years from 1975 to the end of 1995, health costs soared by $63 billion in Canada. However, you will also see that the major contributors to health costs are hospitals, drug costs, and physicians. Of all the elements contributing to rising costs, drug costs shot up faster than anything else, increasing by 984 per cent, while pay to doctors went up 586 per cent and hospital costs by 470 per cent. Hospital costs actually went up just slightly more than the increase in the gross domestic product, which rose 452 per cent during the period. Yet, of this trio, it was only the hospitals that got chopped. Why?

We get some inkling when we look at what happened to drug costs, which equalled about 20 per cent of hospital costs when the period began, and two-fifths of it ten years later. They are by far the fastest-rising element of the increase in medicare funding, and they are almost entirely uncontrolled. Drug costs are in the market sector of the economy, but this does not mean that they are competitively priced. Indeed, the whole process of drug pricing appears to be aimed at protecting the large pharmaceutical companies, nearly all of which are foreign owned, from having to compete. Costs have soared behind the protection of patent legislation, which the Conservatives passed in 1992 and which keeps Canadian generic drug manufacturers from producing cheaper versions of the products for as much as twenty years. In theory, this subsidy — for that is what it was — was granted to keep jobs in Canada and promote research here, but, in fact, no new jobs appear to have been created in Canada; rather, 2,300 jobs disappeared in Montreal and Toronto as the foreign firms closed and merged operations here. In the meantime, between 1989 and 1994, pharmaceutical imports from the United States grew by 200 per cent.

As for research, the only part performed in Canada is that required by law to get new drugs through the regulatory approval process; in 1995 only two of eighty-one new patented products were considered to be "breakthroughs," substantial improvements over existing therapies; the rest were mostly modifications of existing drugs. In all, Canadian pharmaceutical companies spend $1 billion annually on product promotion, and $89 million, after tax writeoffs, on basic research. Meanwhile, their average rate of return on equity between 1988 and 1995 was 29.6 per cent[34] — or, to put it another way, they do about twice as well as our banks.

When the Liberals were in opposition, they vowed to end the drug patent protection. Once in power, however, they extended and improved the protection. They discovered, belatedly, that Canada was powerless to act because of international trade deals they had signed early in their mandate.[35] Apparently the way it works is that we sign one of these treaties, then we read it.

A study produced by Queen's University in January 1997 concluded that Canadians would save between $6 billion and $9.4 billion over the next two decades if the patent protection period was shortened to seven years from the present twenty.[36] No one paid the slightest heed.

If it seems strange that we would be handing foreign drug firms up to $9.4 billion at a time when we are chopping health costs by firing nurses, we only need remember that the drug firms have an active and effective lobby in the old-boy network of Ottawa, while the nurses do not. The House of Commons Industry Committee prepared a report that recommended drastic changes in the patent protection legislation. By the time it reached the House for debate, it had been gutted, no one seems to know how or by whom. The Saint John *Telegraph Journal*, reporting the story, noted parenthetically that "patent drug companies, which in 1996 donated more than $100,000 to the Liberal Party of Canada, generally praised the committee's final report."[37]

In Germany, the government set firm targets for drug costs and proposed to take any amounts spent over the targets out of the money paid to doctors. The result was a drop of 20 per cent in claims for pharmaceuticals within the first six months of the new system.[38] In Canada, doctors earn more with every prescription they write.

We could hire back thousands of nurses for $9.4 billion, and if we are looking for ways to bring health costs down, we might begin by looking at where they went up. The most recent salary figures compiled by Statistics Canada, which cover the year 1992, showed that physicians' average net professional earnings were $129,036 that year, more than double their average take of $60,830 in 1980, while nurses earned anywhere from $29,700 to $59,300.[39]

We certainly needed to do more to bring costs under control, but there was no rational argument for the hacking and slashing that took place. Still less was there an argument to adopt the messy, expensive, unfair, and futile approach taken by the Americans.

The strange case of Dr. Klein

What we did to medicare had nothing to do with reason; it was driven by propaganda. Take the case of Alberta, where Premier Ralph Klein, who came to power in December 1992, announced that spending on all public services in the province, including health services, was "literally going through the roof."[40] To prevent chaos, it was necessary to make "reforms" — to slash costs, instantly. In fact, Alberta's fiscal troubles were real enough, but had nothing to do with overspending on health and social services, which had been severely and constantly cut by the previous Conservative government of Don Getty.

Spending on seniors had been falling since the mid-1980s, sometimes dramatically. Spending on housing had dropped 14 per cent and on social services, 31 per cent. On health care, where Klein insisted costs were "running away," they had changed very little; they had risen overall, but had dropped when measured per capita in the fast-expanding province. In constant dollars, health spending had declined per capita from $1,660 in 1986 to $1,518 in 1991.[41] The damage inflicted on Alberta finances in the 1980s was caused by two circumstances: a drop in oil prices and corporate handouts. When oil prices revived, Klein was rescued, proving once again that it is better for a politician to be lucky than smart. The corporate giveaways continued.

Kevin Taft, a research consultant hired by the provincial government to advise how services to seniors might be managed in the future, quit in disillusion when his report, which showed that costs had gone down, rather than up, was altered, suppressed, sanitized, and finally shredded in February 1993. Every copy was tracked down — they were all numbered — torn apart, and fed into a shredder. It took two weeks to destroy the entire supply, until, as Taft writes, "the store room was once again empty, and all evidence of the report was gone. Almost."[42]

Out of that "almost," Taft wrote a book, *Shredding the Public Interest*, which shows that the real problem was not government spending on health or other social costs but handouts to corporations. The total cost of corporate handouts between 1986–87 and 1992–93, the years in which the province went into debt, was $9.97 billion. During the same period, Alberta collected corporate taxes of $4.64 billion; the net drain on the Alberta taxpayer was $5.3 billion. Alberta gave itself the most heavily subsidized private sector in Canada, while, at the same time, its public services went from among the finest in the nation to the poorest.[43]

Klein's attack on the health sector created chaos, and stories of pain inflicted on Albertans began to blossom in the newspapers. A retired radiologist, who was also the brother of one of Klein's campaign workers, entered the lists against the premier in his own riding to emphasize his concerns about the crisis. And then, on the eve of the 1997 provincial election, the premier suddenly discovered that he had overdone it. He found another $145 million for health care, and another $15 million for seniors.[44]

Klein had slashed health budgets by $515 million over three years, put back less than one-third of that amount, and then was hailed as a nice guy who just happened not to know what he was doing. During a radio open-line show, he was asked precisely what he meant by "health-care reform," and he let it slip that he really had no idea. It was, "like, you know, reform." The ploy worked, and his government rolled back into office with another fat majority.

There is something particularly obscene in the performance of a government that slashes services to save money, on the argument that it has no choice, and then, when public outrage boils over or an election looms, puts a bit back and says, "There, feel better?" Alberta did it, Ontario did it, and Ottawa did it. It is as if, having scalped someone and noted that he is bleeding to death, we hand him back a tuft of hair and wonder why he is still complaining.

Alberta balanced its budget when oil revenues increased once more and interest rates dropped, making the cost of servicing its debt much lower. In 1996 the province produced a surplus of $2.2 billion, but the turnaround had little to do with budget slashing, despite the premier's repeated claims that "we had to get health-care costs under control." In health care, the area cited most often by the premier as "out of control," Alberta's costs, as a proportion of the provincial gross domestic product, were the lowest in the nation. Per capita, health costs had been falling steadily since 1987, when measured in constant dollars.[45] The exercise had to do with appearance, not reality. For example, the government set a target level of 2.4 hospital beds per thousand residents, but, in Edmonton, a study for the Capital Health Authority showed that bed levels were already below that level when the cutting began; provincewide, by late 1995, hospital beds were down to 1.47 per thousand, nearly 40 per cent below the target.[46] The problem was mythical, but the damage done to correct it was real, as, all across the province, hospital doors shut, nurses were fired, and patients were turned away. In all, 9,000 nurses lost their jobs to help pay subsidies to oil companies.

In the meantime, the shortages were shared equally among the customers, who got to wait in line for food-bank handouts or found themselves turned away from hospitals. In one case, a Calgary mother was forced to beg for food. A study of the 52,000 people expunged from welfare rolls showed that most of them had not, under this spur, been able to find jobs. There were no jobs. Welfare payments, such as the $394 a month allowed a single person, were the second lowest in the country after New Brunswick, and Alberta recorded the lowest minimum wage in the country.

But Klein won the propaganda war. He cancelled the fall session of the legislature in 1997, replacing it with a two-day policy rodeo where invited guests took the place of elected representatives. This PR show produced, instead of impolite questions from opposition members, a series of 234 recommendations, none of which had the power to produce action or even, if the premier didn't like them, to see the light of day.[47]

Ottawa gets spooked — and slashes

The same mythical forces that spooked Ralph Klein spooked the federal government as well. The rising numbers, not just in health but everywhere in social spending, provoked a reaction that was out of all proportion to the real danger of precipitating a crisis. Armed with the latest "studies" from the wealthiest think-tanks money could buy, the federal government — whether Conservative or Liberal — and the federal bureaucracy became convinced that only savage, across-the-board cuts imposed from above would bring the spending back under control. Since Ottawa was bound to pay half of whatever qualifying costs were incurred by the provinces, with no limit, the only way to impose a limit was to abrogate that deal. So that was done.

The process began when the federal government, in 1977, transferred 13.5 per cent of the income-tax points to the provinces, increasing their taxing power, and decreasing Ottawa's. At the same time, federal transfers to pay for all social services, including health, were divided into two elements: a direct cash payment to each province, plus the revenue that came from the tax points. Ottawa updated the value of the tax points it transferred in 1977 in line with the growth in population and other factors. However, there was no full correspondence with growth on the cash side of the equation. There, any growth in transfers was tied to growth in the gross national product, so that it would rise with increasing national income. But, beginning in 1986, the increase was limited to any gain in the GNP over 2 per cent annually.[48] If the national income increased by 3 per cent, for example, the cash part of the transfer would go up by 1 per cent.

It was a little more complicated than that, but the effect was to cut back the federal contribution to health and post-secondary education without appearing to do so. Every year, the cash portion of the transfer declined.

The federal support for provincial health care, which had covered 42 per cent of the costs in 1977, fell to 32 per cent in 1995. Because of the change in the cash funding, the drop was even more precipitous; by the end of 1995, Ottawa was covering only 16 per cent of provincial health expenditures. In effect, Ottawa was moving towards its balanced budget by cutting its help to other levels of government. Successive federal budgets claimed $14.4 billion in lower spending between 1993–94 and 1997–98; $6.8 billion of this total consisted in cuts to these transfers.[49]

The provinces complained, rightly, that they had been lured into federal programs with high costs. Once again, they had been abandoned.

Then came another savage blow; in 1995 the federal budget bundled all these transfers into a single block and reduced it. Instead of separate programs, each with its own budget and regulations, all transfers for health, post-secondary education, and social assistance were combined into one block grant, known as the Canada Health and Social Transfer, or CHST. The CHST is to be considerably lower in future than the combined grants.[50] The effect of these hammer blows was to justify the provincial governments in making similar cuts, which they did.

In Ontario, a Health Services Restructuring Commission, armed with extraordinary powers and no right of appeal, ordered the closure of twenty-five hospitals across the province, without public hearings, consultation, or, in many cases, even visiting the hospitals they ordered closed.[51] All hospital budgets were to be cut by 18 per cent over three years, at a saving of $1.3 billion. Thousands of nurses were discharged, often to be replaced by nursing assistants who cost less, knew less, and were less effective.

The process, which is known as "deskilling," consists of replacing nurses with less-qualified and cheaper staff. Housekeepers, cafeteria help, and janitors take courses as "patient care assistants" (PCAs) to bathe, feed, and transport patients. A nurse performing the same task may notice something amiss and take action, but we don't count that. What we do count is the fact that a PCA costs the hospital between $12 and $17 an hour, and a registered nurse may cost anywhere from $17 to $31. A number of studies in the United States have suggested that hiring cheap help costs more, in the end, because hospitals with lower ratios of nurses have much longer average bed-stays, as well as higher rates of reinfection and re-entry. They also have, on average, a higher mortality rate.[52] But they do have lower costs. In the United States, deskilling is killing patients, but we don't know whether this is happening in Canada. We can guess, though.

In Quebec, which argued with some justice that its annual deficits could be traced entirely to Ottawa's funding cuts, seven hospitals were ordered closed and another twelve were merged or turned into long-term geriatric care centres. More than 13,000 health-care jobs were wiped out (none of them doctors'). And hospitals were required to reduce stays and increase day surgery: send them home "quicker and sicker," in the vernacular. In the Atlantic region, acute-care hospitals were closed, hospital beds were slashed by about one-third, workers were fired, and people were admitted more reluctantly and released more quickly.

The same pattern was followed across the West and into the territories. In Saskatchewan, fifty-one rural hospitals were closed or converted into primary-care centres; acute-care beds were cut by about one-third, and the health-care budget by $33 million. Manitoba's cuts have been less painful than most, with no major hospital closings. Like most provinces, Manitoba is establishing regional health authorities to share services and avoid duplication.

In all, more than 50,000 hospital beds were closed in Canada between 1985 and 1995, but we were told not to worry because we had too many of them anyway. We had more beds per capita than any of our fellow members of the Organization for Economic Co-operation and Development. We are getting rid of hospital beds just as we move into an era when our ageing population will need them. As a Toronto physician told me:

From where I sit, the governments have no idea what they're doing. Two hospitals have been closed near us, so we will be getting anywhere from 40 to 60 per cent more emergency cases, for example, but you can't just wave a wand and expand emergency facilities. There are eighteen beds in this hospital for these people, and they are always full. So when you add to the burden, you simply push people out into the hall, you delay treatment, you create one gawdawful mess, and you do it without even thinking about it.

My age group, the end of the baby boomers, will soon be needing more health care and more hospital beds. We will have more heart attacks, more cancer, more long-term illnesses, and then you will see the demand for hospital beds shoot up. But we have closed them down, so we will be put to the expense of replacing them, almost certainly at higher cost. Where's the sense in that?

The cuts, usually made in haste against self-imposed deadlines, were always defended on the grounds that they were unavoidable, but that was simply not true. The choice that was made every time was to transfer the bleeding to those who could not defend themselves as well as other groups — to patients, hospital workers, and nurses rather than doctors and pharmaceutical companies.

In Ontario in 1997, at almost the same time that nurses were told that the freeze on their salaries that has been in place since 1993 would be continued,[53] a deal was struck with the Ontario Medical Association to pay the doctors 1.5 per cent more each year for the next three years, adding $594 million to their tab. This deal swallows more than all the projected savings claimed by the province for its hospital-closing program in Toronto — $430 million.[54] To look at it another way, Ontario cut $800 million out of the hospitals between 1995 and 1997, then gave $594 million to the doctors, who make more than twice as much as the nurses. The increase won by physicians may be justified; but if it is, why should the nurses, who make so much less, not get a boost as well? The answer is easy. The nurses can't, or won't, bring the whole system to a halt, and the doctors have already shown that they can and will. The decision has nothing to do with financial necessity; it is all about clout.

As the waiting lists grew for everything from cosmetic surgery to cardiac operations, we began to turn back to the private sector to provide the care that had been removed from the system. In 1996, when, for the fourth year in a row, real per capita health spending declined, private spending grew by just over 5 per cent; it has grown by more than 35 per cent since 1990, and now represents more than 30 per cent of all health spending.[55] In Calgary, a fancy new building has opened that looks more like a hotel than a hospital; private patients can pay extra here to get the kind of care we once all took for granted, but which is now disappearing.[56] This facility is the first of a projected chain of private hotel-hospitals across Canada.

In Toronto, the Blue Jays' third baseman, Ed Sprague, within hours of injuring himself in a baseball game, was given an expensive test on a diagnostic device called a Magnetic Resonance Imager to see what was wrong with him. Other patients had been waiting for months. It turned out that the Blue Jays have an insurance policy that pays extra for the service, and the hospital has to rent out its machine because it doesn't have the funds to operate it full time on behalf of the patients who need it.[57] This is two-tier medicine.

The $20 billion annually spent on private medicine is no longer money spent on nose-bobs, holistic medicine and other non-covered items. A lot of it represents money paid by those who can afford to jump the queue to get preferential treatment. Preventative medicine, where the best returns for money spent are to be found, is being abandoned. The costs are incalculable, but preventive medicine has no effective lobby.

Can we continue to afford a universal medicare system?

The answer to the question whether we can afford medicare is yes, of course we can. What the system needs is some prudent pruning and reworking, not wholesale slashing. Tom Kent, perhaps the nation's most fruitful policy mind, suggested that one way to control costs would be to add the imputed costs of medical services received "free" to the individual's taxable income:

> It would not prevent people with low incomes getting needed service, but it would have an important psychological effect through the whole medicare system. It would make the public

at large, and the providers of medical services in particular, far more conscious of the costs of treatments. With richer people in effect paying 30 or 40 per cent of the cost of personal treatments through their tax returns, the climate of opinion would be one in which there was far more incentive to avoid wasteful practices and to establish priorities in service.[58]

Kent imposed an important pre-condition — "a fair tax system," which we do not have. I still think his idea is worth exploring, perhaps with limits at either end. People at the lower end of the earnings scale would pay little or nothing, to make up for the fact that the tax system is not fair; and there would be a maximum to be charged against anyone in any single year, to prevent beggaring someone just because he or she started out well-to-do.

The attack on medicare has produced savings, but they have been borne almost entirely by those who could not afford them, led by the sick and dying. There have been improvements — in the consolidation of hospitals and the establishment of regional authorities. But the overall impact of the "reforms" has been to degrade a system which was once our national pride into one which satisfies almost no one, on the grounds of a financial crisis that never existed.

Much the same process occurred in the next area we will examine: education.

The New Three Rs: Retrenching, Retreating, and Retailing

> Achieving excellence in postsecondary education
> is essential to achieve the maximum possible benefits
> from the investment of time and money, both by the
> public and students, in postsecondary education;
> to help meet employer and workforce requirements
> for well-educated and well-trained graduates and
> high-quality research; and to help make Ontario
> competitive internationally in all fields of endeavour.
> — Province of Ontario, *Future Goals for Ontario Colleges and Universities*, July 1996

Bobby is a pain in the neck to his teacher, and his mother is even worse. She is the one who insisted that he be in class, although he is, in the euphemism of the day, "developmentally challenged." She is forever charging into Bobby's Vancouver school to complain that he isn't getting enough attention. Of course he isn't; nobody is in school these days. Doesn't she realize that? Doesn't she know that having a child like Bobby in the class means that the teacher can pay less attention to the other children? Bobby gets around in a wheelchair, as he has ever since a childhood disease left him physically and mentally handicapped. His speech is slurred, and his hearing is impaired.

He has to sit at the front of his grade 3 class, and his teacher, partly out of kindly concern and partly because she is terrified of his mother, tends to teach directly to him, ignoring his classmates.

Actually, having Bobby in the class should be a good thing all around. He needs to be in a regular school setting, not hived off in some special stream just because he looks a little strange and has trouble keeping up. Moreover, his presence in class should be educational. It should teach the other children a lot about compassion and sharing. Far more important, it should teach them that a child like Bobby is just a kid — about 90 per cent like them and only 10 per cent different.

To get this two-way benefit out of Bobby's tragedy, what is really needed is a trained assistant at the boy's side, all the time. But that costs money, and there is no money.

The teacher is ticked off. She has larger classes than she ever had to teach before, more claims on her time by all the bureaucrats who keep trying to squeeze more work out of her for less money, and more angry phone calls from parents who complain that their children are not getting a decent education. On top of all this, she has to deal with Bobby, and Bobby's mother. Sometimes she wonders why she ever gave up waitressing to get a teaching degree.

She doesn't know it, but Bobby's mother has a good deal of sympathy for the teacher's plight. "I know what it's like," she says, "I was a teacher myself for a while, and I know there is never enough time or enough money. But I didn't slash school funding, and neither did Bobby, and I'm going to fight like hell to get him the best schooling I can. If that upsets somebody else, well, too bad."

Education is no longer about teaching and learning. Education today is one long, noisy squabble about money.

The subject of education in a nation like Canada contains complexities far too exquisite for most of us. Education is a provincial responsibility, and religious and language rights in some of the ten provinces and soon-to-be three territories are jealously guarded. Still, the current crisis, in light of severe government cuts in funding, can be reduced to a simple question: Is education the task of creating intelligent, sagacious citizens who will be able to function well in society, or is it a training ground for the remorseless maws of corporate demand and international competitiveness? Are we preparing our children for the cosmos or for Coca Cola Corp.? Most of the upheaval now wracking our school systems from coast to coast can be understood in terms of this contest, which at present appears to be going in the direction of Coca Cola.

Actually, as we have seen with medicare, what we are doing is retreating to the methods, and even the language, of an earlier era. Early education in Canada followed patterns established in England during the Industrial Revolution. Decent education there had been purchased privately by the moneyed classes. The lower classes were given only enough education, mainly through charity schools, to supply a pool of tractable servants, apprentices, and domestics trained in the "habits of industry" to meet the needs of the upper classes. In pre-confederation Canada, too, schools were established more to produce good little Christians, adaptable to their station in life, than to educate in any broad sense. In Quebec, of course, "Christians" meant good little Catholics. When the United Empire Loyalists landed in Quebec after the American Revolutionary War, they discovered a system of schooling that was controlled entirely by priests, who weren't making much of a job of it. William Smith, appointed by the victorious English as the new chief justice of the province, pronounced it "the darkest corner of the Dominion,"[1] and declared that in most parishes "not half a dozen could read or write." So began Canada's history of state intervention in education.

Smith's proposed solution was a state-supported secular system, with an elementary school in each parish, to be supported partly by fees and partly through taxes; and, in each county, a secondary school, to teach mathematics, grammar, and languages, as well as such practical subjects as surveying, navigation, and bookkeeping. In Quebec City there would be a university, which would begin with four tutors "without prejudice" — that is, neither priests nor Anglican clergy — to teach mathematics, literature, philosophy, and science.[2]

Until this time, Quebec had been getting along well, in the opinion of the church, with only two classical colleges, one in Montreal and the other in Quebec City. The students, all teenage boys, spent six years translating from French into Latin and memorizing the Gospels.[3] The offspring of the rich, destined for the professions, usually crossed the Atlantic for the necessary higher learning, as had the sons of most wealthy Americans before the war.

Although girls in Lower Canada received some schooling in the monasteries, Bishop Jean-François Hubert felt there was little need to waste education on most of the boys "while there was still such an abundance of uncleared land."[4] Better to put them to work. He also suspected that the university tutors "without prejudice" that Smith proposed would turn out to be "enemies of morality and discipline" — in other words, non-Catholics.

This clash marked the beginning of a battle that continues to this day. (In 1997, Quebec finally rearranged its educational system along linguistic lines, but the religious authorities are in revolt against the change.) The Loyalists, who had been used to American parish schools, where at least some rudiments were taught, were impatient with the narrow rigidity of the Catholic regime in Lower Canada — as were an increasing number of their French-speaking co-citizens. The upshot in 1801 was the passage of a law establishing the Royal Institution for the Advancement of Learning, which gave control of primary and secondary schooling to the state — that is, to the governors.[5] And they were Protestants.

The Catholic clergy set up an uproar over this infringement of the church's well-established and exclusive right to control education. They suspected, quite correctly, that the arrangement was a dastardly plot to turn little Catholics into little Protestants. It took until 1824 to beat back the threat; that year, the Parish Schools Act returned control to the curés and the local parish wardens. The schools that had been established by the Royal Institution did not disappear but were overwhelmed, and it would be more than a century before state schools re-emerged to challenge the dominance of the church in Quebec education.

"British principles" would be subverted

In Upper Canada, the first lieutenant governor, John Graves Simcoe, did not think there was any need to worry about "people in the lower degrees of life." He asked the Crown for money for "the education of the superior classes of the country" to forestall the danger that they would drift back across the border, where the Americans were rapidly building a superior educational system. In this event, their "British principles . . . would be totally undermined and subverted."[6] He was told to wait a while. In 1797, the year after Simcoe returned to England, Loyalists petitioned the Crown for school support. They received a grant of half a million acres of land, the school lands, which could be sold to provide money for grammar schools and, eventually, a university.[7] The catch was that most of the land was poor, and land prices were low, so the new province got by as best it could with the private academies set up by men like Rev. John Strachan, the Anglican cleric and teacher, who educated many of the children of the "leading families."

Attempts to create public schools in 1804 and 1805 were defeated in the Legislative Assembly, but in 1807 a law was passed to establish a grammar school in each of the eight provincial districts, with the schoolmaster to be paid £100 a year out of provincial funds.[8] These district schools turned out to be of benefit only to children in the larger communities, where they were established, and to those whose parents could afford to pay boarding and tuition fees. In 1812 a petition was sent to the assembly complaining that the school in Kingston, "instead of aiding the middling and poorer classes . . . casts money into the lap of the rich, who are sufficiently able, without public assistance, to support a school in every respect equal to the one established by law."[9]

The assembly, firmly in the grip of the Right Sort, paid no attention whatever. Here and there, parents would band together to hire a teacher for their children, but often these teachers turned out to be wayfaring Americans who taught "American geography and even American arithmetic."[10] Again, Rev. Strachan came to the rescue and, by 1815, he had established three academies. He pointed out to the ruling Family Compact that if their children wanted to avoid the long trip across the Atlantic by getting their higher education in the United States, they would learn "nothing but anarchy in politics and infidelity in religion."[11] Upper Canada was repeating Lower Canada's problem, except that the home-grown ideal was Anglicanism, not Catholicism.

In 1816 Strachan pushed the legislature into providing £6,000 to support public schools, mainly by paying for teachers, and to establish the province's first boards of education. Four years later, however, it snatched back most of the money and reduced the state's annual support to £2,500. The reason? "A financial crisis."[12]

Strachan finally managed to get his university, but it took quite a time. In 1827 he went over to England and obtained a royal charter for an institute of higher learning. The new King's College would be devoted mainly to the training of Anglican clergy. But an "unholy" battle erupted in the colony over the college's close ties to the Anglican Church, and the opening of the new institution was delayed. The people were getting restless, working themselves up to the Rebellion of 1837, and no longer could the Family Compact dictate what got done. In the end, Strachan's precious charter was taken over by the godless University of Toronto in 1849. Strachan, in riposte, established Trinity College, which was steadfastly Anglican.

The province wouldn't finance the schools

The lower ranks of education remained in dismal condition, in large part because of a quarrel over exactly how they should be financed. The reformers in the assembly wanted money raised through the clergy reserves, school lands, and Crown lands in general. Education was something that should be financed by public funds, they argued, so that children in sparsely settled or poorer districts could obtain schooling. The conservatives argued that each local district should raise its own funds, and that the province should do no more than match what was raised locally to support education in each area. They won.[13]

In Quebec, or Canada East as it was called between 1841 and 1867, two state-aided school systems were established by the School Act of 1846, one Protestant and one Catholic. Although both remained firmly under the control of their respective religions, their financing was removed from the private to the public sector and was supported by property taxes. The province was on the long, winding road to public education.

Much the same scenario played out in Atlantic Canada. As the Loyalists poured into Nova Scotia and the newly created

province of New Brunswick, they noticed that the local populace, except for the very well-to-do, had little or no schooling,
while even the dullest Yankee in their old homeland had at least
some opportunity to learn to read and write. The provinces left
schooling to local initiatives and paid part of the cost. But the
overall effect "was to compel the poor to pay for the instruction
of more well-to-do families in well-populated areas."[14]

As in Upper Canada, there was a general feeling that the lads
would be better employed chopping down trees or planting
potatoes than wasting time in school. The first two generations
of Loyalist offspring grew up with the impression that education
was an unnecessary luxury.[15]

The only higher education available in the region was at
King's College, which had first been established in New York
under British rule. After the American War of Independence,
King's College moved itself, lock, stock and library, to Windsor,
Nova Scotia (and later to Halifax, where it is still). But to attend
King's, students had to sign on to the Thirty-Nine Articles of
Anglican faith. So for four out of five Maritimers, post-secondary
education was either non-existent or an ocean voyage away.

When Lord Dalhousie was appointed lieutenant-governor of
Nova Scotia in 1816, he introduced the notion that education,
or at least higher education, should be free and open to all on a
non-sectarian basis. He converted £11,000 in customs duties that
he had on hand into a fund for this purpose, and began the construction of Dalhousie University in 1820.[16] Such use of the royal
prerogative only roused the envy of the province's considerable
population of Presbyterians, who wanted their own university at
Pictou. Then the Baptists followed suit and founded a small college at Wolfville. The harassed Legislative Council finally decreed
that no more money could go to denominational universities.

In New Brunswick yet another King's College was set up in
1828 at Fredericton, again firmly in the grip of the Anglican
Church, although, after a tussle, the need for every student to
sign the Thirty-Nine Articles was withdrawn.

In Prince Edward Island, what little support there was for general education was not tied as closely to religion. A Catholic
cleric who applied in 1829 for a grant to support a clergyman in
a proposed grammar school was turned down, on the grounds

that "the legislature would make its policy without reference to the requirements of religious denominations."[17] When the Central Academy was opened at Charlottetown not long after, it was non-denominational and publicly supported.

Newfoundland had nothing but two sets of charity schools, one for Catholics and the other for Protestants, until the Newfoundland School Society, financed by the Colonial Office and managed by both religions, was established in 1823. The society's forty-three day schools were established to deal with a pressing social problem:

> The growth of population, especially by immigration, had created a large unskilled labour force, illiterate or semi-literate — a naval officer noted in 1818 that in St. John's, in the winter months, "numbers of the low Irishmen were nightly parading in the streets, in a state of intoxication" . . . It was of great consequence . . . that the children of this class should be "early trained to subordination and their moral habits generally improved."[18]

Teachers in these schools were required, as part of their extracurricular activities, to "counter or eradicate disobedience, pride, lying and blasphemy among children and to inculcate in adults the virtues of sobriety, regular work habits and observance of Sunday or a day of rest."[19]

Each side suspected villains on the other side

Confederation, when it came in 1867, enshrined in the British North America Act the rights of religious minorities — Protestants and Roman Catholics — to keep their own educational systems, free of interference from the majority. The provinces were given control of education, with a proviso that the federal government be empowered to correct any infringement of the rights of minorities.[20] The need to protect the rights of Protestants in Canada East and Catholics in Canada West, where each represented a sizeable minority, overrode every other consideration. Each side suspected, with some reason, that the villains on the other side would foist their own religion on the minority, given half a chance.

The result was that the battle which had been settled early in the United States, where the separation of church and state was clear, went the other way in this country. Those who argued that the fledgling provinces needed national, non-sectarian schools were elbowed aside by those who believed that schooling was intertwined with faith and morals, and that the church — *their* church — should have control of all three.

We spent a century working our way out of this conundrum. The lead came from Egerton Ryerson, the superintendent of education in Canada West from 1844 to 1876 — from before to after Confederation. Ryerson had made a study of foreign educational methods before designing a new system for his own province. He had discovered that it was normal in most countries for the state to provide the funds to support basic schooling for everyone, not just the well-to-do. As early as 1846 he proposed a property tax to finance free elementary education for all children.[21] The Right-Thinking element in the province were opposed, on the grounds that they didn't want to pay for educating the bratlings of the poor, and it took twenty-five years to get the tax in place. Eventually, however, the merits of an educated populace that could adapt to the challenges of rapid expansion became clear, and, except in Quebec and Newfoundland, there was a gradual evolution to non-sectarian, publicly funded schools.[22] As the cost of education increased, the emerging middle classes clamoured for schools for their children.

In Quebec, where religion retained the upper hand (albeit with public funding) technical and scientific learning lagged woefully until the Quiet Revolution in the 1960s. There was even pride in the fact that education emphasized *la survivance*, rather than crude materialism. As a prominent churchman put it in 1902: "Our mission is not so much to manipulate money as to wrestle with ideas; it consists less in lighting factory fires than in keeping alight the luminous hearth of religion and making it shine from afar."[23] That same mission was to keep the working classes from realizing that their lowly status and poor prospects were part of the package. They were being taught submission to the given order, while their Anglo neighbours were learning how to make things and do things. When the reaction came it was complete. Its symbol was the *Collèges d'ensignement général et professionel*, or CEGEPs, which sprang up all across the province after

1967 to help Quebeckers catch up. By 1997 the Quebec system had been turned completely on its head, as it was divided on lines of language, not religion. Newfoundland also moved to take control of education away from the churches and to eliminate religious instruction in the schools. As in Quebec, however, a political struggle is still under way on the subject.[24]

For the rest of the nation, the crisis had struck earlier, after the Second World War. We did not have a labour force with the skills or education necessary to meet the demands of the rapid postwar industrial development. In 1951 fewer than half the men in the labour force had more than an elementary education, and less than one-tenth had post-secondary degrees. As a result, most of the best-paying professional jobs went to immigrants. Between 1953 and 1963, the number of physicians and surgeons who entered the country was equal to 53 per cent of those who graduated from Canadian universities; for engineers, the figure was 73 per cent, and for architects, 141 per cent.[25]

We began a huge expansion in education, at all levels, which ultimately revealed the fundamental flaw in the system we had evolved so painfully. The federal government controlled the funds to finance the expansion, while the provinces, under the British North America Act, controlled the delivery. The municipalities, where decisions were made as to where schools would be built, were creatures of the provinces. Federal funding of education soared. The share of national income devoted to education rose from under 3 per cent in 1950 to 9 per cent in 1970, before declining slightly to about 7 per cent in the 1980s. As a share of federal government expenditures, education costs more than doubled, from 10 per cent to 22 per cent, between 1950 and 1970, and, again, declined slightly to about 12 per cent in the 1980s. Ottawa increasingly poured money into education, especially at the higher and more expensive post-secondary end. In 1950 the federal government covered just under 5 per cent of education costs; the provinces, 39 per cent; and the municipal governments, 45 per cent. By 1987, the federal government was covering about 10 per cent of the costs; the provinces, 66 per cent; and the municipalities, 17 per cent. There had been a large shift to federal financing, and a huge shift away from municipal funding to provincial funding.[26]

In Ontario and most western provinces, the costs of education were shifted mainly onto the property tax, while the eastern provinces have financed schooling out of income taxes and general revenue or some combination of property and other taxes. In British Columbia 95 per cent of the financing has come through provincial grants.

Education had become a huge business. In 1994–95 the total bill for education in Canada came to $56.5 billion, with the provinces covering $31.4 billion, local governments, $12.4 billion, and Ottawa, $6.7 billion. Another $6 billion came from non-governmental sources.[27] By this time, however, we had become convinced that a lot of the money was wasted, or misdirected, and that our schools were doing a lousy job. We were right back where we were after the Second World War, with the difference that, this time, we didn't think the solution was to pour new money into the system — it was to take it out.

The difficulty with education is that it is the one subject on which we all have strong opinions based on our own experiences, and almost entirely unimpeded by objective information. Measured against other nations, in terms of the percentage of our population who attend secondary and post-secondary institutions, literacy rates, pupil-teacher ratios, and "repeater rates," Canada stands close to the top of the community of nations.[28]

In some batteries of tests, however, children in other countries do better than our own. These results feed a national inferiority complex that we are missing the boat and throwing away billions of dollars. The Ontario government, for example, announced in 1997, that, according to one set of tests of grade 8 students, Canada ranked behind students from Singapore, Japan, South Korea, Hong Kong, Belgium, the Czech Republic, and Slovenia. And, within Canada, Ontario ranked behind British Columbia, Alberta, Newfoundland, and New Brunswick. The tests were highly suspect, in that many who did well had been prepared ahead of time, while others, especially in Canada, had not. Still, it was a weird performance, with a province boasting about how stupid its students were, and how useless its teachers. It was all part of the process of demolishing the old system to replace it by one aimed at "Good Jobs, Solid Careers."[29] Canadians forget that similar observations about the dimness of the younger generation have been made since Plato. We allow ourselves to be convinced that the supposed failure of education is due to the fact that most of our education spending goes on school buses, vast edifices for boards of education, and the long vacations that teachers enjoy.

Why we think that cutting the funds will get the job done better is one of those unexplainable mysteries. Thus, there was very little protest when Ottawa began to cut its share of funding for education and switched to block funding, leaving the provinces to do what they could with the smaller amounts now transferred, and when, in turn, the provinces cut spending to the municipalities. In Alberta, for example, the Klein government cut the education budget by 20 per cent over three years, setting off an advertising campaign in defence of public education but not much more.[30] Four out of every five dollars cut from education budgets come from salaries of teachers and other education workers, most of them organized into strong unions that have done very well for their members in recent years. When they got cut, many Canadians responded, "And about time, too."

In Ontario, however, there was a huge battle, as the province reformed the entire system in two complex pieces of legislation, Bill 104, the Fewer School Boards Act, and Bill 160, the Education Quality Improvement Act. These bills, which led to a noisy, but finally futile and illegal, ten-day provincewide work stoppage, cut the number of school boards from 129 to 72; they trimmed school trustees from 1,900 to 700 and capped their pay at $5,000 a year (some had been collecting eleven times that much). There was more to come: the province removed half of the costs of funding education from the property tax, and gave the provincial cabinet, through regulation, the power to set budgets, hire and fire teachers and principals, control the amount of paid time teachers are allowed to prepare lessons, and determine class sizes.[31]

This was not so much a battle about money as about power. Ontario spending on education at the undergraduate level was nearly the same, in current dollars, in 1997 as it was in 1987. The province produced figures to show that spending had jumped by 61 per cent in that decade, but left out the increase in the population and the decrease in the value of the dollar.[32] Bill

160, in particular, became the battleground between the teachers' unions and the government. Not surprisingly, the government won, and many Ontarians thought it ought to win. What got missed in the exchange of broadsides in Ontario, Alberta, and British Columbia, where similar battles took place, was the fact that the new "reforms" came on top of cuts in transfer payments that have been going on for years. They took education finance back to where it was in the 1970s, whereas its tasks had been enormously increased, both in terms of population and in the complexity of the job it was required to do.

To take the simplest matter: schools are now spending huge amounts on computers, which are considered as necessary to a modern classroom as chalk was to an earlier one. But computers cost a good deal more than chalk and require a good deal more upkeep. In Victoria, the small Ontario county where I live, "computer services" came to $594,000 in 1996, more than the cost of general administration ($531,000). Then there are the school buses, laid on because we believe people ought to be able to live where they want to, even if it entails a lot of extra costs to get their kids to school. In Victoria County, school buses accounted for $5.8 million out of the 1996 budget of $69.7 million.[33] The money has to come from somewhere, no matter what the province does to funding. Teachers' salaries ($56,163 on average in 1997) are not easy to attack, given the protection of the unions,[34] so the additional cuts were often made by dropping such "extras" as music, art, and the support required to allow disadvantaged children like Bobby to attend class. More often, they were achieved by expanding class size, in the teeth of all the studies that show that smaller classes produce better results.

Canadian schools in major cities face the daunting challenge of coping with a large influx of students whose first language is not English. At the same time, they must cope with the new generation of children whose parents both work, and for whom school has become much more than a place to take classes — it is a social centre, baby-sitter, and, sometimes, the only place where children can get a decent meal. We have called on the schools to do far more, given them less money to do it with, and then complained because they are not doing it as well as we think they should.

Looking ahead, it is hard to see how any improvement will be possible given the two new trends that dominate education today — the increasing commercialization and privatization of the process, and the determination to make learning simply another useful adjunct to the corporate sector. John Snobelen, the high-school dropout who began the "reform" of education for the Harris government in Ontario but was moved to another portfolio when the teachers hit the picket lines, described the Ministry of Education as a "service organization," students as "clients," parents as "customers," and teachers as "front-line service providers."[35] The whole education process, as he saw it, was based on the kind of language that presupposes that "education" and "training" are synonyms, and that the role of schools, at all levels, is to deliver the kind of workforce that will allow us to hook rugs, flip hamburgers, and program computers better than our competitors in other nations.

In *Class Warfare: The Assault on Canada's Schools*, Maude Barlow and Heather-jane Robertson point out that no one, including the teachers, was really surprised when the Toronto Board of Education made a three-year deal with Pepsi Cola Corporation, at a million dollars a year, giving it exclusive control over all soft-drink and juice-vending machines in Toronto schools. The pop maker agreed to throw in "student-of-the-month plaques, prizes, Pepsi T-shirts and hats."[36]

Privatizing the education system

We caught something of the flavour of the new retailing approach to schools when Mike Harris, the premier of Ontario, remarked that students who graduate from universities in the humanities, geography, and sociology "have little hope of contributing to society in any meaningful way."[37] In its first budget, the Harris government cut funding to post-secondary education by 16 per cent and launched a Research and Development Challenge Fund that will pour money into research projects, but only if they meet private-sector, not public, needs.

Ontario already had the lowest per capita operating grants of any province for colleges and universities and had cut the share of the provincial budget in this area from 8.1 per cent in 1977–78 to 4.9 per cent in 1996–97.[38] Now the province froze funding,

despite the report of the Advisory Panel on Future Directions for
Post-Secondary Education, a panel appointed by the Harris government, which warned:

> Public financial support for postsecondary education in
> Ontario is seriously inadequate — indeed it has become so
> low that the sector's competitive position in North America is
> dangerously at risk. Much time, effort and resources have
> been devoted to building the structure of colleges and univer-
> sities that Ontario needs. It would be extraordinarily
> short-sighted to let it crumble now.[39]

Walking in the well-worn footsteps of Ralph Klein, premier of
Alberta, Harris appeared to be doing two things at once: making
post-secondary education the exclusive preserve of a small sector
of the population, and privatizing the system by selling it off,
piece by piece, to corporations that put up the cash — provided
the right things are taught and the right emphasis is struck at
our institutions of higher learning.

Tuition fees, which do not and cannot cover the cost of providing university or college educations, are the ultimate in
deterrent fees. The general population pays most of the freight
to provide a system that can only be afforded by the well-heeled.
Even with huge jumps, student fees covered only 24.3 per cent
of operating revenues at Canadian universities in 1995, up from
16.2 per cent in 1975.[40] The taxpayer was covering three-quarters
of the cost of an education that could be afforded only by those
who could come up with fees that range as high as $5,100 a year
at Dalhousie's Law School, or $6,000 a year in medicine.[41] Across
the nation, tuition fees have increased 140 per cent over the past
decade. At the University of Toronto, our largest university,
undergraduate fees in an arts course run $3,234, and the costs of
one year at university, including residence, athletic fees, and
health services, range from $8,300 to $11,000.[42]

There is no way to measure the number of students who have
decided not to go to university because they couldn't afford to,
or they feared the huge debt a university education now entails.
Statistics Canada calculates the average student debt for someone
graduating in 1998 at $25,000.[43] Not the rich students: they

don't face this problem, although most of the money required to educate them comes from their poorer neighbours. We are right back to the lament of the outraged burghers of Kingston in 1812; we are casting money into the laps of the rich, after extracting it from the purses of all.

Giving this process a really nasty twist, the government of Quebec imposed a "failure tax" on college students in 1997, fining them up to $700 if they flunk more than one course. They cannot register to take other studies until the fines are paid.[44] If your parents are rich, you can keep on flunking until you get it right; otherwise, you get a lesson in Social Darwinism right on campus.

Selling off bits of the ivory tower

Another side of this same approach is the increasing commercialization of education to compensate for the cuts. Computer manufacturers are allowed to put their product in schools in return for a gentle plug; courses in universities are sold to corporations. As part of the triumphant march of the market system, our institutions of higher learning are being thrust out into the harsh, cruel world of the hard sell. Our academics, so long sheltered from the need to make a buck or even to make ends meet, are hustling for customers, trying to carve bits off the ivory tower to flog to "partners."

Not long ago, a letter went out to potential corporate sponsors from top executives at Atkinson College, part of Toronto's York University. It informed them that "for a gift of $10,000, you or your corporation can become the official sponsor for the development and design of one of our new multi-media, high-tech courses, which will bear your name or company logo."[45] These same executives want us to know that the college is not being turned over to crass commercialism. "We're selling recognition, not course design," is the way a spokesperson for York put it to the press. In short, the university is not sacrificing academic independence, merely renting it out.

The situation reminds me of the story about George Bernard Shaw asking a famous actor if she would sleep with him for one million pounds. "Of course," she said. "How about five pounds?" Shaw asked. "Certainly not," the actor replied. "What do you think I am?" "We've already established that," the playwright said, "now we're haggling over price."

At our universities, the price has been set: $10,000 or more. The University of Toronto's Faculty of Management accepted a $15 million donation that gave the donor the power to claw back the money if he didn't like the way the university was spending it.[46]

There is nothing new about universities handing out degrees, naming buildings, even naming courses after members of society who donate the cash. But we do seem to have moved to a new level of prostitution when we declare that the aim of the whole process is to produce computer-pushers for the corporations. John Ralston Saul has pointed to the double difficulty this practice raises: the more money that goes to fund the specialists required to satisfy the corporate agenda, the less is available for the rest. And, as the general quality of education comes under fire, more and more parents opt out:

> There is no shortage of funds for those areas of higher education which attract the corporatist elites. Indeed, as money is siphoned off from the public-school level to the favoured areas of higher education, so the quality of public education drops and more parents opt for private schools. In removing these children they also remove any real commitment to the system.[47]

Charter schools: public funds, private access

The same thought process lies behind the drive to establish more charter schools at the elementary and secondary school level. These institutions, already popular in the United States, New Zealand, and Alberta, are not private schools, in that their funding comes from the public purse. They are, instead, publicly funded private schools that cater to special groups. In Alberta, where Canada's first charter schools were established in 1995, they have been clearly described:

> A charter is an agreement between a school board or the Minister of Education and an individual group regarding the establishment and administration of a school. Essentially the

charter describes the unique educational service the school will provide, how the school will operate, and the student outcomes it intends to achieve. If they are prepared to establish the charter school within their jurisdiction, the local schoolboards will recommend that the Minister approve the agreement.[48]

The idea is fine: if some groups of people don't like what is being served at the main table — it isn't religious enough, or technical enough, or brainy enough, or they want a school that emphasizes music, or computer learning — they can set up their own schools, as our ancestors did when ten families got together and hired a teacher.

The problem is that charter schools, like two-tier medicine, take funds that are raised from the general population and apply them to a small, usually elite, sector of society. The more charter schools there are, the fewer funds, teachers, and facilities are available for the general public. The end result is bound to be another decline in general education, spurring more charter schools, in a never-ending vicious circle.

Charter schools are given the same amount per capita from the tax system as other schools, but they in fact receive more cash per pupil since they receive the money directly and are not assessed the usual large administrative costs of the mainstream system. Charter schools don't have to pay part of the freight for the rest. In addition, they raise extra funds through private donations, to sweeten the pot.

Alice McQuade, president of the British Columbia Teachers' Federation, told the *Vancouver Sun*: "Canadians have a choice between maintaining a public education system committed to meeting the needs of all students regardless of wealth, geography or special needs — or a two-tiered education system; one for the rich and another for everyone else."[49] Charter schools are part of the same trend that inspired the education voucher system. It allows parents to collect a per capita sum directly, in the form of a piece of paper that can be taken to the school of the student's, or the parent's, choice. Vouchers, like charters, are a handy way for those who can afford it to leave behind many of the problems of a general education system, while still receiving state support for schooling.

Even without funding a whole new set of schools, public education is being hurt by the constant cuts. The loss of teachers, principals, and other professional and non-professional workers has had a devastating impact on teacher workloads, on all extracurricular activities, and, perhaps most cruelly, on those who need special assistance in the schools. When the money dried up, a bitter battle was set off between parents who wanted their special-needs children integrated in the school setting and those who resented the extra money and care this took.

As in so many areas of life, we are headed back down into the same pit out of which we clambered a few decades ago. To those who know nothing of our history, this may not appear to be a problem, but it is. Canada moved to state education, painfully, gradually, because trial and error taught us that it was the only efficient — to say nothing of fair — way to produce the scientists, technicians, and managers called for in the general economy as well as the scholars, planners, and thinkers we must have. Now we seem intent on trading in all these advances for a system like the one established for young miners during the Industrial Revolution in England, designed chiefly to make "idle, profligate and filthy boys [and girls, too] more orderly, tractable and attentive to business."[50]

This is not reform, but retreat.

5

How Much Justice Can We Afford?

**The effect of funding cuts has been terrible in terms
of criminal law, but it has been horrendous in terms
of family law — and that's women and children.**
— Harriet Sachs, president, Ontario Advocates' Society,
August 1997

*Courtroom 2 in the Provincial Building on Jarvis Street in downtown
Toronto is a small, square, windowless pit where, every day, driblets of
drama are played out that rival the soaps. The setting makes a stab
at legal dignity: on the back wall the flags of Canada and Ontario
flank the judge's chair, and over her head the lion and the unicorn of
our coat of arms glower down in dignified disapproval. There is
a clerk's desk; a witness box; the court stenographer's cubicle, where a
young woman mumbles into something than looks like a gas-mask;
and a long table for legal counsel, with five chairs ranged along it.
There are another twelve chairs for onlookers, six on each side of the
centre aisle; they are armchairs, quite comfortable, softened with a
green material that matches the rug on the floor and the pale, institutional tone of the walls. Overhead, banks of fluorescent lights line
the ceiling. The general effect is that the Holiday Inn has been called
in to refurbish the bottom of a mine shaft: tidy, but airless; liveable,
but locked in.*

Here, every day, battalions of the anguished troop in to seek relief, revenge, money, forgiveness, custody of their children, or merely a chance to speak out about the pain that wracks the heart in so many ruptured lives. It is one of society's safety valves, and it works, wearily, its wonders to perform. It creaks along in spite of the savagery of cuts that have left everyone connected with the process in some degree of distress. The clerks and stenographers are overworked; the lawyers, scrambling; the social workers, frantic; and the litigants, anguished, terrified, frustrated, and enraged by turn. Downstairs, on the doors of empty offices are signs telling those who look for aid in the complex cruelties of family law to conform or try again another day ("No baseballs caps beyond this point"; "Office Closed"). A young man who has driven in from Orangeville to inquire about the custody case he is bringing against the mother of his children slams his fist against a locked door and swears, before stomping off in a rage.

Upstairs, back in Courtroom 2, we are in a more serene setting. This is Her Honour Judge Lynn King's domain, and she rules it with patience, care, and scrupulousness, though in private conversation the day before the word "hopeless" kept cropping up. Many of her cases are hopeless. They would be difficult even if the court system had the money to provide the resources to help people as they need to be helped. But they have become much more difficult as a result of recent cuts not only to the court system but to the welfare system to which the family courts are closely joined.

We are dealing here mainly with people who are on family benefits. If they have a lot of money, they don't usually wind up here. When the government cut welfare across the board, the provincial people who give welfare to the kids said to the mothers, "Well, you've got to get the money from your husband." So women on welfare are asking their husbands for money, and the men haven't got it, or won't pay it, and the case winds up here.

It is as if you were privatizing the welfare system itself, and it leads to a lot of hopeless cases. The mother has no money, the father has no money, but when the case gets to court he hits back the only way he knows how — he brings an application for custody of the children. He doesn't want custody, usually; he just wants leverage. They had been going along just fine, but now, suddenly, we have a legal battle, and it ends up here.

In the thirty cases that cross the court blotter this morning, six parties are represented by lawyers. Half the rest are covered by duty counsel, who are paid $57 an hour to represent all comers. In the remaining cases, the combatting parties represent themselves.

It is a monumentally inefficient process. Family law is not simple; it is a jungle path, lined with snares for the unwary. It deals with some of the most explosive, intimate, and important details of our lives. The decisions made here can tear families apart, put people in jail, and, in a few moments, determine the rest of the lives of infants and small children.

The duty counsel can spare perhaps ten minutes to interview a young woman whose children's custody is in the hands of the court. Another duty counsel, in another tiny, crammed office, talks to the other partner. The three duty counsel assigned here today — usually there are only two — describe the process as "crazy," "absurd," and "hopelessly overworked." They are like deck stewards on the Titanic, doing their damnedest to provide aid and comfort in the teeth of overwhelming calamity. But no one would call them cheery.

At one point, the court has to be adjourned for about half an hour because there are so many clients lined up to talk to duty counsel; they cannot be in court and interviewing the parties at the same time. Part of the delay is caused by one woman, clearly distraught and in need of time in a hospital, who screams over and over that she is not going to give up her daughter to "that bastard." Not after what he did. Not again. But she can't tell the lawyer trying to help her what that was; she can only weep.

At least when the lawyers who take on this work are involved, the system proceeds better than when the combatants represent themselves. The litigants don't know the legislation or the court rules; they arrive with the wrong documents, the wrong witnesses, and the wrong idea of what is required; they have no notion how to perform the ghastly gavotte the law requires; and Judge King can only lead them through the process slowly, gradually, with many adjournments and much advice. First the state denies them counsel, to save money; then money is thrown away because they have no legal counsel.

Now we have a young man, working his own brief, leaning forward across the counsel table to demand that his wife, simmering 2 feet to his left, take a blood test. He has decided that their three-year-old girl probably isn't his, after all. He knows his wife was fooling around.

Even the court clerk is startled as this grenade, which somehow hasn't appeared anywhere in the months this case has been dragging along, lands on his desk. He hastily thrashes through his papers, in case he missed something. No.

"I see," says Judge King, without even raising her eyebrows. "But who is going to pay for it? A blood test costs $800 or so, I believe."

"I'll pay for it," says the young man, firmly.

"But you have no income," the judge points out.

"I'll pay for it," he says again. "Somehow."

His former wife will see his blood test and secure him a straight-jacket. She has an affidavit accusing him of mental instability; he is not fit to have charge of the girl.

The judge decides to put the case over, again, to allow both parties to think things through and to see what the social worker, who is waiting in court for another case, can do. This case is obviously going to end up in a mess, in part because the entire justice system is breaking down for lack of funds. These people need the help of social workers, psychiatrists, marriage counsellors, and lawyers. But there is no money.

The law deals with many questions, but the only one that counts these days is the one raised by Judge King: Who is going to pay for it?

The downsizing of government in the last few years has hit the administration of justice in four key areas: the courts, both criminal and civil; legal aid; the jails and penitentiaries; and policing.

Before we examine each of these areas in turn, we should note the curiously uneven impact of the changes. We have no money to aid the victims of the process, and we are rapidly running out of cash to supply an adequate stream of court clerks, defence attorneys, Crown counsel, psychiatrists, interpreters, stenographers, social workers, even messengers. We can no longer afford a standard of decency in these areas, and we have raised every fee we can think of, from the cost of copying documents to the charges for filing writs, effectively barring most Canadians from the relief of the law. A classic moment in jurisprudence came when Rosalie Abella, then a lawyer and now a judge, asked an auditorium full of lawyers how many of them, if the bills were not being paid by a client, could afford on their own to bring a case to court. No hands went up.[1] We have constructed a system to underpin society which most Canadians cannot possibly afford.

But what can we afford? Punishment.

The same strong voices that call for more cuts in legal aid call, as well, for longer prison terms, more cops, and bigger and stronger and more automated jails. There is no problem in finding cash to build prisons or hire police. It is only the mechanisms that keep people out of the hands of the police, and out of the jails, that are starved for support. A society that cannot afford justice can afford punishment. Seems odd.

Courting disaster

Not long ago I needed to examine certain parts of the legal file in a major civil lawsuit, so I went to the offices of the Ontario Court, General Division, in Toronto to find it. I had done this many times before in the past and there was nothing to it. You walked in, asked a clerk for help, received a file, asked the clerk to copy some pages for you, paid 15 cents a page, and left a few minutes later with your bundle of information. Not this time. I walked in off Queen Street, turned right at the sign pointing to Information, and found myself in a mob — a mob of lawyers. The collective noun is an "escheat of lawyers." This was one of the more extensive escheats, and included lawyers, law clerks, legal secretaries, and runners; it bulged out of the doors of the general office and extended half way down the hall. It was a pushing, heaving mass. I worked my way to the front of the line, after about half an hour, and was confronted by a harried clerk who said: "Well?"

It's hard to know what to reply to a "well" shot across the counter like that. I mentioned the case I needed by name. She told me I had to have the court docket number. I went away. The next day I performed the same dance and provided the number, which I had obtained in an entirely different office on University Avenue in a process that took up the entire morning and most of the afternoon. The clerk pointed to a computer sitting on the counter. Seven people were lined up to use it, but when my turn came, I hadn't any notion what to do. So, quite loudly, I called out "Help!" That got attention, and another clerk, equally harried, bustled over and told me what to tap into the computer. Then she looked at the clock and told me to come back the next day. It was too late to take any action now.

On the third day, I went through the same routine, got to the computer, hit all the right keys, punched "Enter," and went out to the hall to wait until I was called. About two hours later, my name soared over the hubbub. I went in and was told that everything I wanted was in Cooksville. There is not enough storage space for the courts in Toronto, so they have a huge warehouse in Cooksville. Everything anybody needs in Toronto seems to be in Cooksville. Probably everything anybody in Cooksville needs is in Toronto.

I filled out a form and was told that the material would be ordered from Cooksville. It should be here within a week or so. I paid a fee to bring it in.

Three weeks later, on what was now my sixth trip — and I live about 165 kilometres from Toronto — I struck lucky. My documents, I was told, had made the 50-kilometre trip from Cooksville. I went to another counter, in another room, and was given a number. A bare hour or so later the number was called, and when I moved up to the front, a young man hoisted four heavy boxes of legal files onto the counter. I had asked for three specific files, not four boxes. This made me nervous. I had been told by a lawyer that most of the material in the case I was examining was not public information and I was not entitled to see it. If I did see it, he warned, he would take action. He didn't specify the action he would take, and I didn't want to know. I tried to explain this predicament to the young man, whose knowledge of English was sketchy and whose interest in what I received was non-existent. He just shrugged and pushed across the boxes. I took the four of them off the counter, one by one, and piled them at my feet. I asked the young man if there was some place where I could go to look through them.

"Okay," he said, and gestured behind me. Back there was another escheat of lawyers, working off the arms of chairs, across a crowded room. I got a chair, piled my boxes around me, and started to work.

It took me four days in all to sort out what I needed, and every time I wanted to copy something I waited in line for any-where from 10 minutes to an hour to get at one of the four copying machines available. They cost $1.00 per page. A lawyer, watching me feed loonies into the slot, told me to go to Accounting and buy a plastic card that would work the machine for only 50 cents a page. It took an hour to do this, but it saved me a lot of money.

While waiting in line to use the copier on my fourth day, I tried to work out how much it must cost the court system to starve itself of the ability to retrieve information readily. I gave up. Most of the people cursing around me were either juniors or legal secretaries, but some were full-blown lawyers pulling in, let us say conservatively, $75 an hour to line up at a copying machine. The attorney general claims he cannot afford more copying machines, but, at these rates, they must make him a mint.

I also wondered how anyone could get information, public information, information to which he or she is entitled, without investing a lot of money: I spent about $200, not counting my time, to verify a handful of facts.

I talked to perhaps fifty people during my four days of research and they all said it was a darn shame. Some of them noted that it used to be worse. One legal secretary told me that, a few months earlier, her law firm had booked her into a hotel nearby every night for a week so she could get in line first thing in the morning to go through this torture chamber.

Thirty years ago, when I checked legal cases quite a lot, it was cheap and simple. Anyone who wanted to could obtain a lot of official information in a few minutes with the help of the court experts. Now, with the help of the computer, we have created an expensive zoo, and we call it progress. We have withdrawn a good deal of the public funding for this process, privatized as much of it as possible, made it easily available only to the well-heeled, and wound up with a system that is expensive in ways we never count. Anyone who receives a daily newspaper can make his or her own catalogue of recent court catastrophes:

- In Edmonton, Paul Moreau, president of the Alberta Crown Attorney's Association, warns that criminals may go free because spending cuts and work pressures are driving the best prosecutors out of the business. The workload is up, the number and quality of prosecutions is going down and morale is hitting rock bottom: "There was a time when people were fighting mad. Now it's more like despair. People are quitting, just getting out."[2]

- In Ontario, the degenerative process is already well advanced, primed by the trimming of $223 million from the attorney general's department between 1993–94 and 1996–97.[3] Chief Justice Patrick LeSage of the general division, in a memo to authorities, reminded them that seven years ago, an estimated 50,000 charges were thrown out of court because of unreasonable delays in bringing them to trial.[4]

- A memo from Madam Justice Susan Lang to LeSage which was leaked to the press showed that civil courts are on the brink of chaos, with missing exhibits, delays in getting orders signed, files gone astray, and case after case delayed, postponed, or adjourned — with attendant costs — simply because the paper work had been lost or misfiled, or was not ready on time. The layoff of clerks, she wrote, "declared surplus in an effort to cut costs," has led to "major" delays in trials. Court exhibits "are not only often missing, they are also frequently lost"; "profound" problems with the overloaded computer systems have resulted in court notices going to the wrong lawyers — creating more delays, along with the collection and circulation of inaccurate and unreliable statistics. One report purported to prove that nobody charged with a crime in Toronto ever pleads guilty.[5]

- In Kitchener, a man charged with sexual interference with a fourteen-year-old girl on February 15, 1994, was discharged on January 10, 1997, by Mr. Justice Roger Salhany, not on the basis of any evidence relating to the assault but because of a string of disasters and delays. First, the case was adjourned seven times while trial coordinators attempted to get a suitable court date for a preliminary hearing. When the hearing was finally completed, after more delays, on June 15, 1995, a trial date was set for January 4, 1996. Then the accused's lawyer filed a complaint because he had never been paid by the provincial Legal Aid Plan, which was trying to cut its spending by $153 million, and he had no assurance that he would ever be paid. The rest of that year was spent trying to straighten out that mess. Then the legal aid authorities wrote to say that the bills had been misfiled, but would be paid, sometime, somehow. Finally a trial date was set, but the judge threw the case out of court, noting that the courts were in a "no win" situation because "whatever steps they take to deliver speedy justice are undercut by a shortage of resources."[6]

- In Peel, west of Toronto, three men were freed on major theft charges in late 1996 because it took more than three years to get them to trial. Peel Region has a population of 900,000, 25 per cent more than it had in 1990 when the Supreme Court of Canada called the local courts the worst jurisdiction for trial delays "north of the Rio Grande."[7]
- In the same court, eleven months later, a man charged with drug offences was freed on the same grounds.
- In Newmarket, Ontario, Mr. Justice Peter Howden threw out a charge of breaking, entering, and theft against a local man because it took more than two years to get him into court. The judge noted that this case was all too typical of both criminal and civil trials in the York Region of Ontario, where a population of "close to 650,000" were served by, "at best . . . four judges and courtrooms."[8]
- In Whitby, Ontario, a man accused of sexual assault was acquitted not because of evidence but because of unreasonable delays in bringing the case to trial.[9]

Every time another of these cases hits the headlines, we hear the same refrain from our political masters: it is all most regrettable, but there is no money to keep up the courts. And there certainly is no money to mollycoddle the criminal classes by providing them with huge legal aid budgets.

The legal aid Band-Aid

All over the country, legal aid is in a mess, but taking an axe to it may not prove to be an effective solution. The idea behind it is simplicity itself: unless people who don't have much money get help with their legal problems, the two-tier system of justice, one for the rich and one for the rest, will never be eradicated.

And since we like to kid ourselves that justice should be a level playing field, the provincial authorities began, in 1950s, to fund a separate system. Clayton C. Ruby, an ornament to the profession, put it this way: "A Conservative government and the Law Society of Upper Canada created the legal aid partnership because it was anathema that the rich should have justice while the poor accept injustice as their natural lot."[10]

The average citizen might have thought that the way to finance such a system would be to dole out a budgeted, limited, but reasonable amount of money to the training, hiring, and establishment of stables of lawyers who would work, on salary, on behalf of those who needed help. People who fell afoul of the law, or who needed help with an immigration, family, or civil law problem, would go to one of these salaried lawyers in a government clinic and the bill would be paid out of public funds. But no. That system does not allow the client the full freedom to choose any lawyer he or she wants, which is a large item down at the Law Society. More important, it doesn't allow the lawyers' unions, aka provincial bar associations, to lever up the costs. Lawyers work in the same way as auto mechanics. The mechanic has a book that tells him that the rate for changing a tire is half an hour, at $70 an hour, and the fact that it takes only four minutes doesn't come into it. Thus with lawyers; everything they do, from answering the phone ("To, attending to telephonic communication, $18.75") to pleading before the Supreme Court of Canada (more than $18.75) has a fixed rate attached to it. Clayton Ruby doesn't accept this argument. He opposes the use of salaried lawyers in clinics because, he argues, clinics do not provide legal services more cheaply; they only provide second-class service.[11]

Under the present system, the client proves that he is poor enough to qualify, and, after surviving the lineups and filling out of forms, gets a legal aid certificate that specifies how much money the state is willing to disgorge on his behalf for every piece that comes up in this action — unless, of course, more is needed for unforeseen contingencies. Then the client takes the certificate around to one of the high-profile lawyers whose name has featured in some recent newspaper article — and is ushered out the back door with many a merry laugh.

The legal aid fees do not, after all, quite come up to the rates a good lawyer needs to pay for the office, the stationery, the art-work, and all the necessary accoutrements of the profession. So the client winds up with one of three groups of lawyers: neo-phytes, who can't get any other work; old hacks, who find it less challenging than other law; and a considerable body of able counsel who do the work at lower than their usual rates because they are citizens or because it is good public relations. Most legal firms perform a fixed quota of legal aid work. In Ontario, about one-third of the lawyers take on legal aid cases; or, to put it another way, two out of three Ontario lawyers would not touch them. We are right back where we started: the client does not have anything like full freedom of choice in legal counsel, but the legal counsel are getting much more than they would under our salaried proposal. In Ontario, up until 1986, the lawyers col-lected their standard fee for any particular service under the plan, and then returned 25 per cent of it to help finance the plan. They were working for three-quarters of the tariff. They didn't like it much, and the kickback was reduced to 5 per cent; at the same time, all lawyers were assessed $175 each annually to finance the plan.[12] Now they were working for 95 per cent of the tariff, minus a little bit.

Again, when the legal aid system began, there were a number of clinics where lawyers were on salary, and about 40 per cent of legal aid spending was paid in ways other than direct certificates to lawyers. Over the years, however, as the law associations tight-ened their grip in most provinces, this mixture of certificates, clinics, and salaried counsel was almost completely replaced by a certificate system.[13] We call it "judicare," which is faintly remi-niscent of "medicare" and carries the same open-wallet approach for the practitioner.

The unsurprising result of a system where demand alone sets the limits was that legal aid expenditure went off the charts. Legal aid costs across the country rose from $283 million in 1984 to $651 million in 1994, measured in constant dollars.[14] This increase was not due to a higher crime rate, or a larger popula-tion; it was simply that the legal profession was sucking more and more out of the system. In Ontario, in the decade beginning in 1984, the population grew by 1.7 per cent per year, the crime rate by the same amount, and legal aid spending by 15 per cent.

Lawyers' fees, which made up most of the spending, grew by 16.1 per cent every year. Legal aid was in crisis.

At this point, the government stepped in. Legal aid in Ontario was, and still is, for the time being, administered by the Law Society of Upper Canada, which has the same effect as putting auto repair rates in the hands of your mechanic — but he can't pass the bills on to government. Ontario could not shovel funds into the system as fast as the lawyers sucked it out again, with the result that, by the end of 1994, the plan faced a huge deficit.

Well, thank God, we know how to deal with deficits by now. Take an axe to the costs; for 1995–96, they were to be trimmed from $263 million to $230 million, and so on down to $159 million in 1998–99. This reduction would be worked in the main by cutting the number of certificates issued — eschewing the unthinkable alternative of cutting fees by the same amount, 40 per cent, that was being withdrawn from the funding. And the result? Deprive the poor and lower middle classes of legal aid in all but a handful of court cases.

In late 1994 the Law Society and the government drew up a memorandum of understanding to implement the four-year reduction plan. It had no effect whatever; the costs in the next year refused to budge. So they drew up another memorandum, to run until early 1999, with three major features: the first was a one-third reduction in the number of legal aid certificates; the second, "prioritizing remaining certificates" according to the seriousness of the case; and the third, the establishment of a new tariff system that would impose a set limit on the amount lawyers could receive from legal aid funds. The rates did not come down, just the money available. We were to have less justice, not cheaper justice.

In 1991–92 the Law Society issued 230,000 legal aid certificates. In 1996, 100,000. There had not been a corresponding drop of about 60 per cent in legal costs, population, or court activity. Just justice. Owen Lippert, a student of these matters, put it delicately: "Because the Ontario Legal Aid Plan now lives within its means, there have been some reductions in services."[15]

To put it clearly, legal aid was withdrawn from thousands of people, particularly the most vulnerable members of society, with brutal abruptness. The people floundering around in family

court are the direct inheritors of the way the cuts were implemented. A study by the York University Policy Centre in 1997
noted that the legal aid plan had been brought into fiscal order
only by gutting the very services it was created to provide: "In
our view, the social costs of this method of cost control have been
very high . . . Low-income Ontarians' access to justice has been
severely restricted, resulting in a sharp increase in unrepresented
litigants in the province's courtrooms."[16]

The reason family courts, which ought to be the best-funded,
most equitable courts in the land, bore so much of the burden is
that much of the other parts of legal aid funding are beyond
control. Immigration cases, for example, just happen, and keep
on happening, as Canada struggles to deal with an immigration
system that makes very little sense, but which contains generous
provisions for legal appeals. These cases are the responsibility
of the federal government, but the costs are borne by the
provinces. When the cuts came, immigration lawyers found they
had much less pre-hearing time in which to prepare a case, but
the money still continued to flow. The number of refugees
Canada receives and the way Ottawa administers its policy, not
provincial restraints, determine the caseload.

Again, criminal cases — which absorb anywhere from 35 per
cent of direct legal aid costs in Quebec to 92 per cent in the
Northwest Territories — cannot really be capped. If a poor client
is charged with a serious offence, a certificate must be issued.
Lawyers complain that these certificates are now too meagre to
allow them to do a proper job, but at least they are still coming.

But for civil cases, and family court cases, the effect has been
heartbreaking. Harriet Sachs, president of the Advocates' Society,
which focuses on the administration of justice in Ontario, notes:

> In the General Division, we now have 30 per cent of the people
> appearing without representation, and in family court, it is
> about 70 per cent, and growing . . .
>
> . . . You have the majority of people going into family court
> without legal assistance. They're there trying to figure out how
> to get support for their kids, how to straighten out custody for
> their kids, how to make sure their kids are safe, and they find
> that the chances of getting a certificate are very slim and even

if you can get a certificate, they will pay the lawyers who will take legal aid so little that it's very difficult to find a lawyer who will take your case.[17]

In September 1997 the Ontario Legal Aid Review, a government-commissioned report, suggested that the whole business should be turned over to a new superagency, the Legal Services Corporation of Ontario, and taken away entirely from the Law Society. It noted, among other things, the point made above: "Choice of counsel is often illusory."[18] The new corporation would be given multi-year funding, and seven of the eleven directors would be government appointees. The Benchers hate it because it puts the direction of the system in the hands of the attorney general.

The government adopted some, but not all, of the recommendations of the Ontario Legal Aid Review, which set up a new system to come into effect when the current memorandum of understanding expires in April 1999. The Law Society will have no control over the plan, although the Benchers hope to gain most of the seats on the new corporation's board, an issue that remains very much up in the air. John McCamus, the York University professor who wrote the original report, proposed a wide-based board with members from the legal profession, government, and the general public; at this writing, it appears more likely that the business community and legal bureaucrats will dominate. A little more money will be put into the plan and the rules will be relaxed slightly, so that more certificates will be issued. In 1997 the plan actually ran a surplus of $30 million because certificates were made so difficult to obtain. Finally, duty counsel will see their hourly rate raised from $57 to $70, and the 5 per cent clawback charged for administration will be dropped. The lawyers will get a little more, the clients will get a little more, and the government's grip on the system will get a little tighter. The government calls it "reform," although it amounts mainly to tinkering with a plan whose inadequacies are to be made a little less obvious.

Sachs wonders whether the damage now being done can be justified, considering "the small percentage of the Ontario budget that is represented by legal aid." She has a point. The attorney general of Ontario's budget for 1996–97 was $753 million, and the cost of legal aid was $230.3 million, just about $26 per Ontarian; it came to a little less than half of one per cent of the provincial budget. That year, Ontarians spent about $488 million on dry cleaning, or a little over twice as much as they spent on legal aid.[19] Nationally, as we have already seen, the legal aid bill came to $652 million, or a little more than it will cost for the fifteen new helicopters being ordered by the Department of National Defence.[20]

The difference between the costs of legal aid in Ontario in 1994–95 — $263.4 million, the figure that caused the crisis — and 1995–95 — $230.3 million, the figure that caused chaos in the courts — is $33.1 million. This is about $3 per provincial resident per annum — the cost of a fast food meal. Does this make any sense? Of course not. But the cuts aren't supposed to make sense, they're just cuts.

Iron bars do not a prison make; money does

Out along Highway 36 in Ops Township, just outside Lindsay, Ontario, the construction gangs are preparing for, and the locals are salivating over, the new "Super-Jail" that will be opened in 1999 at a cost of $75 million. It will replace five other institutions, in Lindsay, Cobourg, Peterborough, Whitby, and Milbrook, and house up to 1,200 inmates. It will cover 10 acres. Together with five other similar institutions around the province, it is expected to save a lot of money: "Economies of scale achieved by efficient building designs and greater use of technology will permit annual savings in the order of $75 million a year."[21]

Sometimes these government-projected savings tend to vanish, but if they do come about, they will be achieved by using machinery — automatic gates, surveillance cameras, and other toys — instead of custodians. The prisoners will get less human care and more computer care. If there is one thing criminologists agree upon, it is that prisoners who are looked after by buildings and computers are more likely to offend again than those in small institutions with a large element of personal contact. The super-jails will average 1,200 prisoners each; they will move prisoners from five or six other locations and dump them into one; they will require the families of prisoners to shift to places close to the super-jail and drop all the increased welfare costs created in this way on the local community. A puff pamphlet pushing the super-jail in Lindsay offers this comfort: "Family migration is unlikely to be much of a factor."[22]

We are already putting more people in jail than any other advanced nation in the world except the United States, which happens to be the most violent industrialized democracy on earth.[23] On any given day, 33,800 Canadians are behind bars, 5,000 of them between the ages of twelve and seventeen. There are already more young offenders than adults in prison on a per capita basis, and the numbers are rising sharply.[24] According to the Task Force Report on the Young Offenders Act presented to the House of Commons justice committee: "In Canada as a whole . . . the number of young offenders on probation and in custody has increased sharply since 1986, and the increase is well out of proportion to the increase in the youth population during the same period."[25]

Part of the reason, the MPs were told, is that we are getting much tougher on the young, calling in the cops for schoolyard fights, and cutting off the funds to support alternatives to custody. We spend about 3 cents on crime prevention for every $100 we spend on police, prisons, and courts.[26]

About the same time, and in the same area that the Peel regional courts were turning drug suspects loose, the province announced that it was cutting the $1.6 million a year that kept the Ontario Correctional Institute going in Brampton. The institute emphasizes rehabilitation and responsibility, and the prisoners are called "residents." They have a much lower rate of repeated offences than inmates in other jails; for example, 35 per cent of released prisoners among sex offenders committed new crimes, compared with 80 per cent from other jails who had no treatment. This difference alone saves $1.2 million for every one hundred prisoners treated more humanely, according to a study done by the institution's research department. Forget that. The place is to be closed and the inmates shifted to one of the six new super-jails.

In another trend, we are putting larger numbers of Canadians behind bars each year simply because they cannot pay fines levied against them by the courts. One in four of those in provincial jails in 1995–96 was there because of non-payment of fines.

It costs a lot of money to keep someone in jail — in Canada, the average figure is $42,000 per annum[27] — but we have the satisfaction of knowing that at least the buggers are suffering for the one unforgivable crime in this country — the inability to pay.

We are also putting more and more people behind bars because they are a danger to themselves or others. They belong in psychiatric institutions, but we have closed many of these facilities, so we have no place to secure them but in jail.

We are led by those of our fellow citizens who think the way to deal with social problems is to whack a lot of people behind bars, as a deterrent. It doesn't work, and never did — pickpockets circulated on Tyburn Hill in the seventeenth century, lifting the wallets of those who had come to see someone else hanged for theft — but it is popular.

In the United States today there are 1.5 million in prison and another 3.5 million under penal control outside prison. Nearly 5 per cent of all adult American males are under penal control; the figures have tripled since 1980. Nils Christie, a Scandinavian expert, told the *New Internationalist*, "It's not crime control, but a kind of war situation."

While Americans have been slashing the budgets for social work, education, and every other ameliorating influence, they have been happily pouring out cash for punishment — and demanding more. The Rand Corporation, a U.S. think-tank, estimated that a jail sentence of five years for a $300 theft cost the state US $125,000, and that California's "three-strikes-and-you're out law," by which anyone convicted of a third felony receives an automatic life prison sentence, will add about $5.5 billion to that state's annual prison costs. Lobbyists for the law included the prison guards association, which contributed $100,000 to the campaign that led to its enactment.[28]

It is astounding that the hard-headed accountants who harry us into spending cuts have yet to work out that cuts on the social side translate into expenditures on the prison side. Advocates of prison reform, who once argued about the senseless cruelty of the system, have to sound like accountants to get their point across. When the National Crime Prevention Council presented the federal government with a detailed program to cut crime by training schemes to help abused children and abusive parents, substance abuse counselling, and alternatives to incarceration for teens, Johanne Vallée, vice-chair of the council, struck the acceptable note: "We must focus on results. What outcomes do our prisons generate? What kind of return are we getting? We think there are better ways to invest some of the tax dollars."[29]

Legal enforcement authorities dismissed even this cash-on-the-barrel-head approach out of hand. "There is nothing new in here," commented Police Chief Julian Fantino, of London, Ontario. He was right. The futility of jail terms was made manifest when John Barlow Martin wrote *Tear Down the Walls* half a century ago.

We have twice as many private cops as public ones

While chucking more of our co-citizens behind bars, we are privatizing the police system itself. We're returning to the days when our thirteenth-century ancestors used to hire thugs with clubs to keep them safe from footpads.

The Statute of Winchester in 1285 decreed that males over the age of fifteen were responsible for enforcing laws in their community. The men were organized into "watch and ward" bands whose task it was to arrest strangers and guard the town. The wiser and richer citizens paid others to serve their terms and then, because many of the watch and ward types were turning into snatch and grab types, took to hiring their own gangs. The first recognizable public police force was the one created by Robert Peel (hence, "Bobbies") in 1829. Private cops, it appeared, didn't work very well.

There was a steady evolution of police forces from that day until a decade or so ago, when, according to the Canadian Centre for Justice Statistics, two things happened:

> Because of the increasing scarcity of public resources, and because some security needs do not fall within their primary mandate, public police forces have not been able to dedicate resources at sufficiently high levels to satisfy the need for security of private agencies. Thus private policing emerged to satisfy this need.[30]

But there are a couple of other factors the experts were too polite to mention: first, the increasing emergence of industrial espionage and counter-espionage; second, for a large corporation, it is cheaper to pay a security agency minimum wages for bodies-in-uniforms than to pay the taxes to support a decently paid, unionized police force.

Between 1971 and 1991 the number of Canadian police officers increased by 41 per cent, a good deal faster than the increase in population (26 per cent). In the same period, private security employees increased by 146 per cent. By 1991 "private security employees outnumbered police by slightly more than two to one." The bean-counters picked up only two groups of employees in their survey; private investigators, of whom there were 5,925 when the survey was done, and security guards, of whom there were 115,570. The numbers significantly underrepresent the private police because, as the study notes, "there are a large number of other persons who work in the private security industry."[31]

An increasing number of the private flatties will be found in the guardhouses of "gated" communities, making sure the riff-raff don't soil the sidewalks or disturb the rest of those who dwell within the walls. There is nothing surprising in this, either. If the public loses its confidence in a civil society, those who can afford to retreat to a place of walled safety.

I can see the next big surge in home architecture — the draw-bridge, portcullis, and moat.

Does anybody find it creepy that we now have more than twice as many private cops as public ones in this country? These private operatives are all written off on the taxes of the corporations who hire them. They may get lousy pay, but about half of it comes from the public purse. So we are paying through the tax system for cops who do not work for us, but for private individuals, because we can't afford to hire enough real police.

Now we are hiring public cops privately. I refer not only to the common sight of uniformed flatties directing the traffic at supermarkets on their day off for hourly pay but public cops on outside payrolls as well. In Winnipeg the city airport authority agreed to pay for sixteen police officers to replace the RCMP, who no longer provide policing at airports. Not long after, Autopac, the Manitoba Public Insurance corporation, agreed in mid-1997 to add $500,000 per year to the Winnipeg Police Service Budget to hire six more officers to the auto-theft squad.

City council, far from being alarmed, hoped to encourage "other businesses to make similar deals."[32]

Well, why not? I presume, although I can't prove it, that an anti-auto-theft cop who came across a citizen garroting another in an alleyway would ask him to stop, though it was not part of his regular duties. I can also see whole new vistas opening up in which public cops for private hire would specialize in insurance fraud, stock scams, and making sure the rich get through traffic first — for a fee, of course.

Paul Palango has drawn attention to the fact that cutbacks in public policing have created a new international reputation for us: "Canada is now known as a global leader in commercial, or white-collar, crime. And, increasingly, it is becoming the land where the Mounties do *not* get their man."[33] Squeezed by budget cuts, the men in red are giving up on commercial fraud — which is often complex, and expensive to prove, so the fraud artists are swarming in to take advantage. Palango, who puts the annual loss from white-collar crime at $12 billion in this country, notes that "Canada now has a two-tier system in which corporations are expected to defend themselves against fraud." He adds, "Canada is seen as a safe haven."

If his estimate is even close to the mark — $12 billion up in smoke annually — you would think it might be worthwhile to invest some public funds to get it back, and thus into the public, taxable sector, but Palango got the last word on this aspect from Philip Murray, commissioner of the RCMP: "The general public is simply not willing to spend more, to invest more in taxes."

Perhaps the strangest of these episodes, where cutbacks have cost money, surfaced when the *Ottawa Citizen* claimed on June 13, 1998, that the RCMP had helped to put drugs on the street by financing a sting operation. The cops would dole out seed money to the bad guys and then catch them when they used the cash to set up drug runs. However, because there was not enough money to follow up the cases thus produced, the net effect was that the Mounties were financing the smuggling operation, by providing seed money. They paid out $141 million to get various operations going, and lost $125 million of that; nobody seems to know exactly where it went. The *Citizen* estimated that the flatties probably put $2 billion worth of illegal drugs into circulation, while "very few arrests" resulted. The fallout from this one continues; Ottawa is embarrassed and annoyed, although not, apparently, much wiser.

And so, as with medicare, we have created two tiers, one well-heeled system for the well-off, and one down-at-the-heels model for the rest of us. They are both financed in the end from the public purse, either directly or through tax writeoffs, but the benefits flow increasingly to a smaller and smaller group of richer and richer people. All in the name of justice, fairness, equity — and economy.

6

Defanging the Watchdogs

It is inconceivable to think of "lessening the
regulatory burden," as some put it, at a time
when private industry has the power to alter our
genes, invade our privacy, and destroy our
environment . . . Only the government has the
power to create and enforce the social regulations
that protect citizens from the awesome consequences
of technology run amok.
— Susan and Martin Tolchin, *Dismantling America*, 1983

*The Food and Drug Administration in Washington began to receive
information that a new intra-uterine contraceptive device called the
Dalkon Shield was causing pain, discomfort, infection, and perhaps
worse soon after it went on the market in 1971. However, agency
lawyers determined that it was a "device" and not a food or drug, so
they could take no regulatory action until there was evidence that it
was doing real harm — "sufficient cause," was the wording. Thirteen
years later, the manufacturer was persuaded to remove the device
from the market after 4.5 million of the devices were distributed in
eighty countries, including Canada; fifteen women had died; and
there were at least 66,000 miscarriages, not to mention uncounted
numbers of septic spontaneous abortions, premature stillbirths, and
grave congenital defects, such as blindness, cerebral palsy, and mental*

retardation.[1] By this time an avalanche of lawsuits had pushed the company into bankruptcy protection, so its majority shareowners, the Robins family of Richmond, Virginia, split the firm in two, closed down the part that was responsible for the Dalkon Shield, and sold the remainder to another drug manufacturer for US$700 million.[2]

The Dalkon Shield was distributed in Canada for eleven years. Our authorities took the view that if it was good enough for the American regulators, it was good enough for us. In 1981 — ten years after it came on the market — the Health Protection Branch of the National Department of Health issued an advisory telling Canadians to stop using the Dalkon Shield. It washed its hands of any responsibility in the matter.[3]

Since that time, the FDA has been under almost constant threat as a bureaucratic barrier to the free operation of the market system. Its budget has been cut, its personnel reduced and demoralized, and its mission attacked. In the same period, the Health Protection Branch has been lined up for a 60 per cent cut in its budget.

Apparently, we think we have been overregulated.

At Cabot Head, on the Bruce Peninsula in Ontario, the light-house has been turned into an interesting museum of local ecological history. One of the displays features logging artifacts — old saws, photos of giant pines, memorabilia. However, there are no giant pines left anywhere along the 100 kilometres of this Lake Huron peninsula. The explanation is here: in a period of less than ten years towards the end of the last century, private lumber companies clear-cut the entire area. They hacked down the trees, hauled them away, and left behind the slash. In 1906 fire started in the mess of rotting vegetation and wiped every-thing out, including the buildings that housed the logging operations. The entire forest was destroyed. An ecology that had worked successfully for centuries was plundered and despoiled in a couple of decades simply because there was no one to say no. There is no way ever to replace it.

We seem to be heading back down that same path in every aspect of society. The apostles of deregulation say they are getting rid of "red tape," but the rest of us call it "protection." What is officious government interference to some is, to the nation at large, merely the cop on the beat. But the cop not only has been taken off the beat but has been given a sandwich board to plug the products made by the miscreants he used to prosecute. The Health Canada Web site was, until recently, found to be using most of its space to promote sales of products made by Canadian health industries abroad.[4]

No segment of society has escaped this process, from health to the environment, from mining regulations to food protection, from child care to highway safety. In some cases the rules are being shredded because politicians and senior bureaucrats believe that regulations impede progress. And so they do, from time to time. The trouble is that these officious regulators are often the only defence we have against public disaster.

Take the case of thalidomide. This tranquillizer, prescribed to pregnant women, caused horrendous birth defects. It was kept off the market in the United States by one courageous bureaucrat in the Food and Drug Administration, Frances Kelsey, who refused to accept the argument that it had already been approved by authorities in West Germany.[5] She held firm, although the company made more than fifty approaches to the FDA. In Canada, the drug was accepted here because it had been accepted elsewhere, but it was only on the market for a short time before reports began to flood in of deformed children being born all over the world. In all, 115 babies were born in Canada with thalidomide defects. The drug was withdrawn in March 1962, but the federal government did not compensate the victims until 1991. It paid out $8.5 million, which might have been better invested in reaffirming regulation than in dismantling it.

Or take the case of the Westray coal mine at Stellarton, Nova Scotia, where the regulations were not enforced and where, on May 9, 1992, a predictable and avoidable gas explosion killed twenty-six miners. Justice Peter Richards, in a four-volume report on the disaster, noted:

> It is a story of incompetence, of mismanagement, of bureaucratic bungling, of deceit, of ruthlessness, of coverup, of expediency and of cynical indifference . . .

. . . Management failed, the inspectorate failed, and the mine blew up.

The mine management "clearly rejected industry standards, provincial regulations, codes of safe practice and common sense," and, at the same time, "the Department of Labour was ill-prepared for the task of regulating Westray."[6]

In other cases, the damage results from cuts to government funding. There is no money to do the job, so we get deregulation by neglect. Or strangulation. Consider what happened when Mad Cow disease struck in Britain. Maggie Thatcher's hatchet job on her nation's public regulators left them ill-equipped to respond to the first reports of the disease. In Canada, at the first hint of trouble in the mid-1980s, health officials ordered the destruction of all the cattle that had the potential to carry it, despite the vigorous protests of the cattle industry. A decade later, the British beef industry lay in ruins. The cost of deregulation, it turned out, was a good deal higher than the cost of regulation, but that has not spared our health department, as we will see.

In quite a few cases, ideology and economy support each other, and the cop on the beat turns his nightstick over to the private sector on both counts. We call it "self-regulation," an oxymoron that translates: Anything goes. To get a small taste of what is going on, consider several representative items culled from recent history.

Is regulation a drug on the market?

In Ottawa, senior officials in Health Canada are proceeding with a plan to cut research laboratories and contract out the testing of products, including medical devices, to non-government laboratories. The Health Protection Branch of the department is responsible, on paper, for preserving the public interest in four key areas: the blood system, new drugs, food safety, and medical devices. As part of the across-the-board cuts, it was deemed necessary to scoop $12 million out of the branch's budget, and to eliminate 123 jobs. When the news became public, it was not well received.

Canadians had been reading a lot about the way the blood system was run and they didn't like it much. In effect, the blood system had been contracted out to the Red Cross, which had screwed up, and the country was now coping with the fallout from the infamous tainted blood scandal of the 1980s. In mid-1997 the government announced that it was taking away the blood business from the Red Cross and its funding authority, the Canadian Blood Agency, as soon as possible. A new National Blood Agency was scheduled to take over in late 1998.[7] But the damage had been done: thousands of grieving families blamed the old agency for the fact that loved ones had contracted HIV or hepatitis C, and a huge number of lawsuits could be expected. The law still made the government the caretaker and regulator of the system. The government simply passed the job on and then declined to take the blame for its neglect.*

Now we were going to apply the same loving care to food, drugs, and medical instruments — and many Canadians complained. Accordingly, Allan Rock, the minister of health, announced that the projected cuts would be put on hold for at least six months. He declared a moratorium, and said he would bring in a new group of experts to see what should be done.[8]

Back at the department, however, the beat went on. "There is

---

*Later, the federal government agreed to pay $1.2 billion to 1,068 HIV victims, and further funding was to be forthcoming from the provinces. Once that was in train, thousands of Canadians who had contracted potentially fatal hepatitis C from blood transfusions pressed for compensation, and the result was a dubious arrangement indeed. In April 1998 federal and provincial health ministers, meeting together, agreed to pay $1.1 billion to 22,000 victims of hepatitis C, but refused compensation to another 20,000. The guideline was "fault." Canadians who contracted the disease between January 1986 and July 1990 were eligible for compensation because health authorities knew at the beginning of this time that a test was available to screen for hepatitis C, but did not take any action until 1990. Thus, victims from that period alone deserved help. This notion was specifically rejected by Mr. Justice Krever, who said that compensation should be based on "need," not fault. Health minister Allan Rock's reasoning was that this approach would "open a floodgate" to claims, according to a report by Rosemary Spiers in the *Toronto Star*, April 25, 1998. Rock asked, "Can we sustain public medicare if we make cash payments to all who are harmed through the medical system regardless of fault?" That was precisely what was done in the case of thalidomide, but Rock ignored the precedent. If the government could not be shown to be at fault, let the victims bear the burden alone. They weren't at fault, either, but they're the ones who are sick.

no moratorium," one health bureaucrat told the *Toronto Star*. "Perhaps the minister is unaware." Then came the clincher: "The entire objections within the department are that the entire focus is on saving money."[9] The only way to keep going with the cuts already made, never mind the new batch, was to contract out some of the work. An internal memo prepared by the Laboratory Science Review, a departmental committee, explained that transferring the testing of medical devices to outside laboratories would save $500,000 a year.[10] If saving money is the only rationale, it will be done, and the minister can explain it to the public at some future date.

I spoke to a man who used to work for the department in this very area and who now runs an independent company doing much the same work he did before:

Our favourite client, Health Canada, began to go outside in the first place because they didn't have the staff to do the job, and they couldn't hire anybody. The drug companies, in particular, were complaining that they were hampered by this backlog of new drug submissions and they basically decided that one way to speed it up was for the government to have some of the work done outside.

There is a core staff at Health Canada, but most of it is now done by consultants, by ex-employees of drug companies, by professors of pharmacology. So you have a new pesticide coming on the market and Health Canada is supposed to make sure that it does what it is supposed to do, and at the same time, it is not harming the public at large. You give the task of assessing it to an outside agency, and you fund it by collecting fees from the manufacturer, and the problem I have with this is, who are they actually working for?

In the United States, where they went this way some time ago, it was discovered that if you pushed your product through one particular laboratory, your results would be accepted, and you would get the piece of paper you needed. That backfired when approval was given to new pesticides on very dubious grounds. The problem was that it was found that some of these pesticides turned out to be more hazardous to humans than the data submitted by the so-called independent labs showed.

The books were cooked, in at least one case; instead of doing the required tests on animals, which takes two years and costs quite a lot of money, they simply wrote up the results that were called for in the guidelines issued by the department for that particular substance, and got approval.

Government can send out the work, but not the responsibility. If it shirks the responsibility, it cannot complain when things go wrong. The Laboratory Science Review memo suggested that, once the work was contracted out, the health department should eliminate any potential conflicts of interest "through such avenues as using accredited laboratories."

A *Globe and Mail* investigation revealed that "Some managers at Health Canada have repeatedly bypassed or ignored their drug reviewers' questions about possibly dangerous side effects of human and animal drugs, and approved them anyway." One of the parliamentary reporters, Laura Eggerton, turned up a memo in which a senior bureaucrat appeared to be promising to clear the way for a drug company's next submission for approval because a previous submission had been given a "rough time." The department, clearly, felt that its "client" was the pharmaceutical industry, not the public.[11] The cop is carting the sandwich-board.

In January 1996 Dr. Michele Brill-Edwards, one of the Health Protection Branch's most experienced regulators, resigned and left behind a memo in which she charged that there were "continuing deficiencies in the health protection program" which made it incapable of rendering "reliable, informed decisions in the public interest." She charged that the branch was putting the "interests of the pharmaceutical manufacturers ahead of the protection of public safety,"[12] a problem that can only get worse as the protectors move into the new mode of "cost recovery" — collecting fees from the manufacturer for the work required to approve their products. The Canadian Health Coalition warns: "While this may appear to be a tidy way to reduce public spending, it will also make the regulator dependent upon the companies it regulates for operating funds.[13]

The memo had no effect whatever and the policy remained in place. While work on promoting "strategic partnerships" with industry continued, research into key areas of health protection was cancelled for lack of funds. Among the projects discontinued were probes into the efficacy of vitamins and herbal food; the presence of "extraneous" matter in food, such as rat hair and insect dung; the impact of antibiotics and fungicides used in fish farms on the health of Canadians; the possible presence of cyanide in flaxseed, vegetables, and fruit; the problems posed by Toxaphene, a substance used in American pesticides, which may interfere with human reproduction and which is wind-borne into Canada; and the possibility that anti-oxidants in tea and fruits might counteract the carcinogens in barbecued meat.[14]

The fuss over the cuts to the Health Protection Branch provoked some outrage, and it may even provoke the minister into taking action. But it was only a small part of the damage being inflicted in the crucial area of health. Between the 1995–96 and 1996–97 budgets, $58,504,000 was cut out of four key areas: food safety, quality and nutrition; drug safety, quality and effectiveness; environmental quality and hazards; and national health surveillance.[15] This $58.5 million slash represented 26 per cent of the budget for this work. It tells us, in so many words, that we can no longer afford to maintain safeguards to our health at a level that seemed reasonable and essential two years ago.

The mining industry strikes paydirt

In the province of Ontario, 87 per cent of the total land surface consists of public lands. In November 1996 the Ministry of Natural Resources gutted the regulations covering mineral exploration over this vast area, through amendments to the Public Lands Act which were included in Bill 26, the massive omnibus legislation embodying the Harris Common Sense Revolution. The changes removed most of the rules from land clearing, mechanical stripping, bulk sampling, drilling and blasting, moving heavy equipment, drilling rigs, and building trails.[16] They included the repeal of most fire, travel, and work permit provisions and were intended to reduce paperwork by 80 per cent, saving the industry $1 million annually.

At the same time, amendments to the Mining Act effectively transferred the costs of restoring abandoned mine sites from the private to the public purse; the Ministry of Northern Development and Mines calculated that there are upwards of 5,000 abandoned mines in the province, and the cost of "remediation" will come in at anywhere from $300 million to $3 billion. What is involved, often, is the presence of huge amounts of mine tailings that can destroy whole river systems and cost vast sums to clean up. In the past, mining companies were specifically charged with restoring their sites when they finished work. Some of them got around this requirement by having a subsidiary do the mining and then go bankrupt. In response, the law was changed in 1989, requiring companies to post financial securities to cover the cost of cleanup before they could stick a pickaxe in the ground. These provisions have now been wiped out. The mines are still supposed to do the cleanup, but they no longer have to deliver annual reports on what they have done — it is taken on faith. Alternatively, mining companies can, under the new act, surrender mining lands to the government when they have extracted the ore and escape "any future environmental liabilities even if they arise as a result of the proponent's actions."[17]

The mine owners have not merely escaped regulation, but have been handed the keys to the mint.

Clearly, these changes have nothing to do with saving the government money, for they could cost up to $3 billion. The retrenching part of the equation was accomplished elsewhere by laying off twelve of the fourteen mine-closure inspectors and cutting the budget of the Ministry of Northern Development and Mines by 22 per cent. The government maintained the Ontario Prospector's Assistance Program, a $2-million-a-year subsidy to prospectors.

Ontario deregulated mining not to save money for the public purse but for the mine owners. Dr. Mark Winfield, research director of the Canadian Institute for Environmental Law and Policy, told me:

> It is not a question of saving money, but where you choose to spend it. They have fired virtually all the people who did the inspections. They have gutted the mine closure provisions of the mining act, saying, "Well, we don't have the staff to be able to enforce the old system any more, so we have to have a self-monitoring regime." At the same time, the minister is

trumpeting the fact that he has maintained a $2-million sub-sidy program to help prospectors buy tools.

You could have maintained the mine closure inspectors, in fact, you could have hired more for the same $2 million. So there was a very distinct choice made there.[18]

A mines inspector who has managed to escape the axe told me that it is not only the environment that is at stake in the cut-backs but human lives:

We used to make regular calls on all these sites, just to look around, just to make sure everything was safe, just to let the mine owners know that we were keeping an eye on how care-fully the rules were being followed, and how well maintained the equipment was. It was preventative. But, with the cut-backs, there is no time for this sort of thing; all your time is spent investigating sites where the accident has already hap-pened. Prevention has gone out the window; we're just the cleanup gang, now.

Unleashing the banks

Perhaps no sector of the economy has been unshackled with the same raw enthusiasm as the banking sector, with results that were predicted a couple of decades ago when the process began.

Remember the Savings and Loan debacle in the United States? In 1980, during the last throes of the Carter administration, lob-byists for the Savings and Loan institutions, which were mainly small-town banks aimed at providing house mortgages, per-suaded Congress to pass the Depository Institutions Deregulation and Monetary Control Act of 1980, also known as Diddymac. It wiped out most of the controls, including limits on the interest S&Ls could charge on loans and what they could pay to attract deposits. Next, the amount of a deposit that would be repaid by government-backed insurance was raised from $40,000 to $100,000. Finally, Diddymac tumbled all deposit-taking institu-tions into one grand lump; instead of having separate regulatory regimes for S&Ls, commercial banks, and credit unions, there was to be a single regulatory regime.

And along came Ronald Reagan. With the glad cry "Deregulate!"

the new president swept into Washington in early 1981 and began to throw all the rules out of the window. In 1982 the law was amended to allow the deposit-taking institutions into almost every form of investment. At the same time, regulations that governed how much an institution could lend on any given asset were wiped out. If the boys chose to lend $50 million on a building assessed at $5 million, where was the harm? This deregulation was "probably the single most damaging provision in the law," says Martin Mayer in *The Greatest Ever Bank Robbery*.[19] A property was worth whatever the lender said it was worth; the S&L could put up as much as a developer wanted on it; and, under new rules that relaxed conflict-of-interest regulations, there was nothing to prevent the lender from being the developer. The only hurdle that remained was that some official trying to protect the value of the federal deposit insurance might make a fuss, but that problem was taken care of by the complete attitudinal change in Washington under Reagan. There, no one wanted bureaucrats or inspectors to interfere. Regulation was out.

Reagan named Edwin J. Gray, who had been one of his campaign organizers as well as a former S&L employee, as chairman of the Bank Board, the overseer of the federal interest in the S&Ls. The industry purred its satisfaction. However, once Gray got into the job and began to see the sorts of loans the S&Ls were making, he turned out not to be the team player they expected. Rather, he kept warning Washington that trouble was brewing and called for a crackdown. Suddenly his staff was cut, his budget reduced, and his views ignored.

The rest is history. The S&Ls, backed with $100,000-per-account deposit insurance and freed of any effective regulation, plunged into an orgy of dumb and sometimes crooked investments. In the most notorious case, one involving Charles Keating, a real estate developer and S&L owner, it was shown that he had contributed substantial amounts to the campaigns of five U.S. senators, who then went to bat for him when regulators accused him of "unsafe and unsound" banking practices. The regulators were called off and, when Keating eventually went broke, the deposit insurance payoff cost the taxpayer $2.5 billion.[20] From his jail cell, Keating blamed government interference.

In the end, thousands of S&Ls came crashing down. The cost

to the American taxpayer is still being reckoned, but James Ring, author *The Big Fix*, estimates it "could well exceed $1.5 trillion."[21] In the meantime, of course, the U.S. government had saved on the salaries of a couple of thousand bank inspectors who were fired along the way.

The lesson the world drew from this disaster was that the banking sector is overregulated.

Accordingly, the wraps came off all over the world, and continue to come off, despite such occasional slipups as the failure of Barings Bank PLC, which was catapulted into insolvency by Nick Leeson, a young derivatives trader who operated out of Singapore. In the book he wrote about his short but lively career from Tanah Merah Prison, where he is serving a sentence of six and a half years for deceiving the auditors of Barings and cheating the Singapore Exchange, Leeson makes two points well worth considering.

First, although there were supposed to be dozens of checks on the operation he ran, including a daily meeting of the risk management group in the bank's London office and constant contact with his superior in Singapore, bank management did nothing as long as he appeared to be making profits. Second, the British regulatory authorities were singularly uninterested in having Leeson, who was arrested in Frankfurt, Germany, put on trial in England, although his most serious offences took place in London, not Singapore. Leeson suggests that no one in authority in Britain wanted to have the risks of derivatives trading presented to the courts, so he was allowed to plead guilty in Singapore, with very little said.[22] The Bank of England, the official regulator, got a slap on the wrist in a report to the British Parliament, and Barings management were raked over the coals, but there were no recommendations to change either the derivatives gambling or the way in which the central bank supervises the commercial banks.[23] Deregulation promotes commerce, not crime, was already the established dogma, and no one in authority wanted any evidence to the contrary.

In Canada, the deregulation mania began in 1987, when the rules separating the "four pillars" of the financial sector were collapsed overnight. Up until that time it had been illegal for any of the four sectors — the banks, insurance companies, stock brokers, or trust companies — to control any corporation in the other sectors. When those provisions disappeared, the banks gobbled up the trust companies and securities firms and set up insurance subsidiaries. Now they bestride the financial sector like a Colossus and make colossal profits, while Canadians pay more and more in service charges to keep them happy.

At the other end of the business, where government oversees the operations of the system, similar changes were being made. Canadians persist in the belief that our banking industry is run by paragons of care and honesty. This faith was put to the test most recently by a series of collapses that ought to have sounded an alarm, but never did.

First came the demise of the Canadian Commercial Bank (CCB) of Edmonton, followed soon after by the Northland Bank of Calgary. In both cases, the failure of regulation caused the failure of the banks.

The CCB was launched as a chartered bank in Edmonton in 1976, in the midst of a real estate and energy boom, and quickly made some bad financial moves. One of these was the purchase of a minority interest in a California bank called Westlands.[24] Then the CCB got itself entangled in "the Trust Company Affair," a series of real estate flips by three trust companies in Toronto at ever-rising prices, with the risk being assumed by the depositors and the profits by the three men who controlled the trusts. The incident ended with the heads of all three companies becoming numbered guests of Her Majesty the Queen for periods of up to five years, with time off for good behaviour.[25] The CCB had advanced $7 million to Leonard Rosenberg, one of the trio, the chubby charmer who had initiated the scheme. Then it turned out that Rosenberg and his partners owned or controlled nearly one-third of the CCB, although the law says that no single share-holder or group in Canada can hold more than 10 per cent of a chartered bank with assets of more than $5 million. The $7 million went up in smoke when the Ontario government, which had legal jurisdiction over the trusts, became alarmed at its mounting losses and seized the assets.

Mr. Justice Willard Z. Estey, who wrote the inevitable government report on this fiasco, noted that the impact of the vanished $7 million on the CCB, already in financial difficulty, was "a loss of confidence and a run on deposits, driving the bank to the Bank of Canada for liquidity support."[26]

To keep going, CCB indulged in some interesting accounting practices, such as accruing interest on loans when the payments had not been met. A borrower might owe $1 million in interest on a debt on January 1, for example, but when January 1 came along, no interest was paid. The bank then said, Never mind, I know you're good for the money, and rolled the loan over, with interest chargeable on the whole new amount. Whether the interest would ever be paid was a matter of conjecture, but it showed up on the CCB balance sheet as income. The bank's auditors approved the books without a murmur, and the inspector general of banks, the industry regulator, said, in effect, that if it was good enough for the auditors, it was good enough for him. At the time, the inspector general had a total of eight inspectors to scrutinize the activities of fourteen Canadian and more than fifty foreign banks, but instead of clamouring for more staff, he tended to rely on the banks' auditors, in line with the latest notions of self-regulation.

The CCB then moved into a twilight zone, a period when everyone, especially the government spokesmen, pretended it was not moribund but, at the same time, prepared for its demise. Even Gerald Bouey, the governor of the Bank of Canada, telephoned the *Globe and Mail* to insist that the CCB was a "solvent and profitable bank."[27] Presumably this information came to him via tea leaves or the Ouija board. The *Globe* duly ran this item, though with raised eyebrows. Every few days an opposition member would ask a rude question in the House of Commons and be reassured that all was fine. Still, a general sense of unease led to the withdrawal, over the next few months, of $1.3 billion in deposits from the CCB.[28]

On March 25, 1985, a government press release set out to prove that everything was under control because the six largest chartered banks, the governments of Canada and Alberta, and the Canada Deposit Insurance Corporation (CDIC), collectively referred to as "the Support Group," had weighed in with a rescue plan. The banks, collectively, and the two governments put up $60 million each, for a total of $180 million. For its part, the CDIC put up $75 million. This infusion of $255 million would look after the soft loans, and William Kennett, the inspector general, gave the banks a letter to assure them that, with their help, the CCB "will . . . be solvent."[29] It left one to doubt what type of inspection had been done to determine whether the assets against which the CCB had issued loans were still worth the figures shown on the books.

The banks wanted their own look at the loan portfolio and their examination showed what the deregulators had missed — many of the loans were floated on worthless assets. The CCB was already insolvent. In an attempt to breathe life back into the corpse, the Bank of Canada advanced $1.3 billion to the CCB, pumping in cash at one end while it leaked out at the other. Finally it became obvious to all that the bank could not survive, and it was put out of its misery on September 1, 1985.

At the same time that the CCB was spiralling into the ground, so was another western bank, Northland, which was centred in Calgary. Like the CCB, it was born in the energy and real estate boom in western Canada, put out hundreds of millions of dollars in real estate loans backed by shaky assets, and then, when these loans became non-performing, indulged in some very dodgy number-crunching. Estey described the accounting methods used in the CCB and Northland cases as "imaginative," "energetic," "bizarre," and "risky" at various places in his report. The weak loans were placed in a "workout" category, and the figures were made to look better by calculating "the projected success of the workouts and anticipated improved economic conditions generally." That is the description of Mr. Justice Estey; I would call it financial faith healing. The auditors and the inspector general choose to believe the projections, and Northland staggered on. In fact, it extended more loans, in hopes of getting some good ones to cover the bad ones. As Estey noted: "The financial statements became gold fillings covering cavities in the assets and in the earnings of the bank."[30]

By 1983 Northland was insolvent, but it survived so long as the inspector general was otherwise occupied. The collapse of the CCB in March 1985, however, led to a rapid withdrawal of deposits. Again, the Bank of Canada stepped in, with a total of $517.5 million in advances. The Inspector General's Office approved a new issue of debentures by the bank amounting to a new loan from the general public of $16 million. The investment firm that had undertaken to float the debentures onto the market was told that "the OIGB [Office of the Inspector General of Banks] was aware of nothing which would make it imprudent to proceed with the issue."[31] What is more, Bouey rejected a proposal from the Bank of Canada to reflect in its financial statements the writeoff of a large segment of its loans portfolio on the grounds that it would never be paid. This step would certainly have spooked the market by more accurately reflecting what had happened, but the calamity was averted.

Finally, the OIGB bestirred itself enough to examine Northland's bizarre banking practices and, reeling, tried to get the National Bank to merge with Northland. But the National's inspectors took one look at Northland's loan portfolio and backed away. A curator was appointed in September 1985, and the bank was liquidated in early 1986.

The eventual price tag picked up by the federal government for the two banks was more than $1 billion.[32]

What could be more natural, when the nation discovered that its regulatory system was not up to the job, than to deregulate? So that was done. The lines between banks, trust companies, investment firms and insurance corporations were blurred, and, in 1987, the Office of the Inspector General of Banks was rolled into the new Office of the Superintendent of Financial Institutions. The OSFI is now required to "regulate and supervise" not only the 6 large and 55 small Canadian banks but 19 loan companies, 52 trust and loan companies, 7 cooperative credit associations, 19 investment companies, 33 fraternal benefit societies, and 135 federally registered life insurance companies.[33] In addition, the office hires itself out to the Canada Pension Plan to help oversee its finances.

The next series of failures reflected exactly the same problem: a shortage of regulation. The Bank of Credit and Commerce International, or BCCI, also known as the "Bank of Crooks and Creeps International," represented the kind of international financial giant that our own banks would like to become. It was founded in 1972 by a Pakistani named Agha Hasan Adebi, who turned it into a personal piggy bank for a number of people whom the police of various nations were anxious to have assist them with their inquiries. Adebi managed to connect his bank with respected international financial houses, including the Bank of America, which bought a small quantity of the shares.

Although the bank began in the oil-rich sheikdom of Abu Dhabi — which was why the Bank of America invested, for the entrée to the oil lands — Adebi decided to incorporate it in Luxembourg, as BCCI Holdings, SA. The secrecy laws are strict in the duchy, while other regulations are evanescent and taxes are negligible. Later, another corporate headquarters was established in Georgetown, Grand Cayman, and a third in Gibraltar, giving the shareholders three places to play where the constituted authorities are singularly incurious about what goes on in the vaults.

By the mid-1970s BCCI was off and running. Pakistan was the second major centre of expansion, after Abu Dhabi, but soon the bank was popping up all over the Middle East, the Far East, Africa, and Europe — before it was done, there were 400 branches in seventy-three countries,[34] all lending vast sums of money. It became involved in a lot of noisesome operations, floated out loans based on dubious collateral, and indulged in some unusual giveaways to the customers — sessions with prostitutes as an incentive to do business, for example. A bank that is willing to pass money over the counter with only a cursory glance at the collateral does not have any trouble finding customers, and BCCI mushroomed.

As the years passed, a noxious stink was beginning to emanate from BCCI. It laundered drug money for Manuel Noriega, the Panama dictator; sold arms into South America out of an office in Boca Raton, Florida; bankrolled the sale of helicopters to Guatemala, and provided loans to finance an abortive attempt to ship prohibited materials from the United States to Pakistan, to help with its nuclear weapons program.[35]

The CIA, which actually used BCCI to pay off operatives, had submitted a report on the bank in 1986, pointing to money-laundering and other illegal activities, but no action resulted. By 1987, BCCI had managed to turn itself into a truly global bank, with 16,000 employees, branches all over the world, and assets listed at more than US$20 billion. Four of these branches were in Canada. The money was poured in through the Middle East, the bank's main operation centre was in England, but its corporate headquarters continued to be split among the three tax havens. No national regulator was willing, or able, to take responsibility for the bank's actions.

But BCCI was failing, as more and more of its large loans began to go sour, some because the assets against which they were borrowed, such as real estate, had lost much of their value; others because the loans were fraudulent from the beginning.[36] The bank was kept afloat by sucking in new money at high interest rates to cover the bills as they came due, thus piling up more debts.

In March 1990 the Bank of England was handed an audit report prepared by Price Waterhouse. It showed that BCCI was in such severe financial trouble that it would require $1.78 billion in new funding to stay afloat.[37] Absolutely nothing was done. The bank was kept going and the extent of the damage was concealed for fear of causing a run on deposits. The governor of the Bank of England, Robin Leigh-Pemberton, would later justify this course of action in a quote that should be stitched in needlepoint on the pillow of every institutional investor: "If we closed down a bank every time we had a fraud, we would have rather fewer banks than we have."[38]

Two new audits into the bank's operations, one by the bank itself, another by and for the Bank of England, turned up enough evidence to spur criminal investigations in both Britain and the United States. They showed that BCCI was in debt to the tune of at least US$5 billion, and perhaps two or three times that amount, and revealed that, while the bank's annual reports showed robust earnings until the late 1980s, it had possibly never earned a profit in its entire history.[39]

On July 5, 1991, bank regulators in eighteen countries seized the assets of BCCI in a coordinated shutdown, and bank branches were restricted in forty-four other lands. The accounts of 1.25 million depositors were frozen, businesses were paralysed all over the globe, ships were stranded in ports, factories shut their doors, and thousands of paycheques turned into useless slips of paper in the hands of people who had never had anything to do with BCCI except work for a company that kept its accounts there. In a score of cities, customers massed in front of the closed bank branches, demanding their money, but in vain.

In Canada, rumours that BCCI was running amok had been circulating for years. They were ignored,[40] and BCCI continued to operate here until mid-1991, long after it was out of money. Only when the Bank of England and the U.S. Federal Reserve System hauled out the handcuffs did the OSFI step in and close the doors of the four Canadian branches. In the end, creditors worldwide were paid just under 25 per cent of their claims. US$10 billion — about $14 billion in Canadian funds — went up in smoke.[41]

In the same way, two trust companies supposedly under the eagle eye of the OSFI — Standard Trust and Royal Trust — got into financial difficulties through accounting practices that were unusual, but nobody seemed to catch on until it was too late. Standard went into bankruptcy protection, and Royal Trust was gathered to the bosom of the Royal Bank. The Canadian taxpayer picked up the tab, through deposit insurance, for Standard. In the case of Royal, the bank took over these liabilities, so the real sufferers were the investors, who had bought shares on the basis of financial reports that showed non-existent strength, and the 2,000 employees, who were downsized to help pay the tab.

In the late 1980s the public was increasingly angry with the Ottawa authorities as case after case of insolvency, defalcation, deceit, or default came to light. From 1989 to the end of 1994, we lost fifteen banks, seventeen trust and loan companies, thirty-three life insurance firms, and seventy-four property and casualty insurance firms.[42]

Clearly, we needed reform. What we got, in June 1996, was An Act to amend, enact and repeal certain laws relating to financial institutions, which contained two key provisions. The first was a series of regulations allowing the OSFI to step into a wayward institution earlier in the proceedings, although it would not have the power to remove the chief executive officer of a wayward firm or any of the directors. The other provision was to change the system of deposit insurance; financial institutions with clean books will pay less into the general pot that finances failures than firms whose books are not so clean. But the public is not to be told when a bank gets into trouble. It may be headed for disaster, and the bank shares we hold may be increasingly worthless, but no matter. Most of us hold some bank shares, indirectly, since almost every pension plan in the nation includes them as part of its portfolio.

The essential problem in every one of the bank cases cited is that the regulator did not have enough staff, or enough knowledge, to remove the current leadership of the wavering institution before it was too late. This problem has simply been ignored in the new legislation. The OSFI is given some new powers to intervene, but no new personnel to do thorough inspections. Apparently we cannot afford the staff we need to keep on top of things. We can only afford a billion or so for the bailouts, when they come.

Given an impossible mandate, John Palmer, the current superintendent of the OSFI, has come up with a new approach to regulating the financial institutions of this country — tough love:

> The fate of the financial institution is the responsibility of the management and the board of directors . . .
>
> Our primary objective is to minimize losses. If we can do it by encouraging the institution to steer itself out of trouble, terrific. But if we have to put it down to minimize losses, we'll do that.[43]

To put it another way, since we cannot micromanage the financial sector, sometimes these institutions go bankrupt and then we have to step in to pay off the insurance. That's deregulation with a vengeance.

Then the banks all decided to merge, in a proposal that is still before Parliament as I write. First, the Bank of Montreal and the Royal Bank announced early in 1998 that they were going to join. Then the Canadian Imperial Bank of Commerce and the Toronto-Dominion Bank announced that they would also merge, as soon as the regulations barring such unions were removed. The banks said these mergers were necessary so they could compete abroad, and so, according to their newspaper ads, they could use the economies of scale to create savings for the customer. These were heavy stones to roll uphill. In the first place, if all five of Canada's largest banks were lumped into one, it would still be smaller than Citibank, the foreign competitor most often cited, so what was the point? In the second, the Laurentian Bank, with assets of about $10 billion, offers almost all its services to Canadians at prices that are exactly the same as the Royal, which is twenty-five times its size. How large would a bank have to be before customers would benefit from the economies of scale? Fifty times the size of any rival?

What the banks were doing was asking for — nay, demanding — the dismantling of any effective regulatory authority over them, on the grounds that other banks in other lands are roaming free, so why shouldn't they? When I was a kid and wanted to justify something on the grounds that Johnny down the street was allowed to do it, I was not well received. The banks, however, will probably get away with it, on the grounds that it is all part of globalization — which, in a way, it is. Globalization is the technique by which effective state action is blocked, or evaded, until the balloon goes up. Then the state is called in to clean up the mess.

When you read in your daily newspaper about the collapse of the financial sector in Indonesia, Japan, South Korea, or Mexico, or all of them at the same time, you are reading about the failure of regulation. You are also paying for that failure, since, in our global economy, these mammoth losses travel around the world faster than you can say "mutual funds." On the heels of the meltdown of Asian markets in late 1997, Canadian economists rejigged their forecasts for 1998 to show lower growth than had previously been predicted, and tied this drop directly to the mess in the Far East.[44] We will shell out a few billions in slower economic activity because we refuse to pay for regulation.

And so it goes, in our defanged world

- The auditor general notes that Parks Canada is failing to protect the ecology of our national parks — the money for that is gone.[45]
- The airlines, whose ownership, routes, and fares were all under rigorous control, are turned loose. The result is sharply lower fares for some Canadians, much worse service and higher fares for others, and a huge loss of money for the competing airlines. As Peter Newman notes in *The Canadian Revolution*: "Between 1990 and 1992, the world's airlines lost $15.7

billion — more than the total profit earned by the aviation industry since the Wright brothers first sputtered into the air at Kitty Hawk, North Carolina, in 1903."[46] By the time this new, deregulated competition sorts itself out, the world will be down to a handful of huge airlines, operating as an oligopoly, setting their own prices, and walking away from the responsibility to deliver adequate service to all but the most crowded, and therefore profitable, airports. In the meantime, despite what you see in the fancy ads for discount fares, average air fares have increased, in constant dollars, since deregulation in 1988.[47]

So far, only one air crash can be directly attributed to deregulation. An Air Florida jet flown by a crew that had never operated in winter conditions hit a bridge and crashed in the Potomac River outside Washington, killing seventy-eight people, including most of the passengers, all members of the crew, and four people who were on the bridge at the time. The aircrew were not familiar with de-icing systems, and, as it turned out, an ice buildup on the wings appeared to be the main cause of the crash.[48]

- Ontario passes the Safety and Consumer Standards Administration Act, 1996, to reduce "red tape that hinders economic growth." The act creates a new safety organization called the Technical Standards and Safety Authority, or TSSA, a private corporation to oversee the regulation of boilers and pressure vessels, elevators and amusement devices, hydrocarbon fuels, and "upholstered and stuffed articles." This change is being made because: "The Ontario government believes that some services can be delivered more effectively, efficiently, and appropriately by the private sector than the public sector."[49]
- The TSSA will also be friendlier. As the Canadian Institute for Environmental Law and Policy notes: "The overwhelming majority of the directors are to be elected by the members, who are to be the regulated parties under the various statutes."[50] The board, which sets policy, has fifteen members under the legislation; ten of them come from the industries it has been set up to regulate. Or not.

"This," Dr. Mark Winfield of the institute comments, "is putting Dracula in charge of the blood bank."[51] The board has no duty to protect the health and safety interests of the public, merely to promote "a fair, safe and informed marketplace that supports a competitive economy." No one has the responsibility to ensure that the new body acts in an appropriate way and avoids conflicts of interest, nor is the TSSA subject to the provincial auditor, ombudsman, freedom of information and privacy commissioner or the environmental commissioner. It has even been given the power to handle all prosecutions, although the members of the board represent the companies that are the likely defendants in any action.[52]

As of May 5, 1997, a private organization, run by the people who have the most to gain by deregulation, has become responsible for administering the statutes which ensure that our Ferris wheels and roller-coasters are safe, that our elevators don't fall down, and that propane tanks or underground gasoline storage tanks do not leak or explode.

- All across the country, we're experiencing a rash of flying truck wheels on the highways; the wheels come off, fly through the air, smash into a car, and kill somebody. A crackdown on truckers follows and shows, in case after case, that a majority of the trucks on the road do not meet the safety standards. Only then do we hire more inspectors.
- The withdrawal of inspectors and other regulators from the workplace has led to a sharp increase in injuries, and the damage is inflicted disproportionately on women. A recent report on this subject by the Canadian Labour Congress states:

The rate of injury to women is at more than twice the pace of women entering the workforce. In 1984, women represented 43.1 per cent of the workforce; by 1992, the percentage had grown to 46.6 per cent. But the percentage of women workers who were injured on the job increased from 19.1 per cent in 1984 to 26.0 per cent in 1992. In contrast, the number of male workers has increased over the past eight years by 5.8 per cent but the rate of workplace injuries sustained by male workers has declined by 18 per cent.[53]

There has been no measurable increase in injuries in the executive suite.

I began this chapter by quoting Susan Tolchin and her husband, Martin, who looked at the impact of deregulation in the United States fifteen years ago and foresaw many of the problems that resulted from the withdrawal of government protections in both our countries. It seems appropriate to end with another quotation from the same book:

> As technological and scientific advances lead us into unknown worlds with unimaginable dangers, society needs more protection, not less. This means more government regulation, intelligently crafted, skillfully managed and sensitively enforced. It means a new appreciation of government's role, born of a new sophistication in public attitudes. Finally, it means a shift in our national values to assure the public's protection in an increasingly hazardous world, and a realization that the power and resources to achieve that goal can be provided only by government.[54]

Let the Environment
Look After Itself

**There's not just a financial deficit to worry about
when you're talking about public policy. People talk
about the environmental deficit. We run down our
natural capital, we run down the stock of our natural
resources, we are as irresponsible with respect to
the future as we are if we build up a large financial
deficit, if not more so.**
— Dr. Peter Victor, York University, September 1997

*The place looks like a prisoner-of-war camp after the belligerents have
pulled down the barbed wire and left. There is a guardhouse, complete with a barrier gate, but the guardhouse is empty and the barrier
bar points futilely skywards; its work is done. Inside, three rows
of long, narrow, single-storey huts slumber beneath the summer
sun, two of them in parallel lines, the third across the bottom of the
other two, in the form of a large U. Beyond these huts looms the
splendour of the administration building, almost, but not quite,
empty, with a two-storey storage shed beside it. Farther back, an array
of meteorological equipment hums to itself behind an impressively
high wire fence. It would not be surprising to see Colonel Klink
striding about the place, slapping his boots with his quirt and barking*

orders to the assembled hordes — except that there are no assembled hordes.

This is the Dorset Research Centre, just outside the town of Dorset, Ontario, near the eastern entrance to Algonquin Park. It used to be called the Dorset Acid Rain Research Centre, one of the key environmental research stations in Canada, if not the world. Now it is a drowsy, drooping, dismal place of hollowed hopes and wasted dreams.

My guide is Peter Dillon, manager of the centre, a bustling, friendly scientist with an impressive record in environmental research and practical administration. As we walk from building to building, he explains that no one is here right now, but we can see the labs and the computers clucking to themselves. I think of that wonderful poem by Walter de la Mere which begins, "Is there anybody there? said the traveller."

There is nobody there. We open doors, but we meet nothing except the echo of our striding feet. The daycare centre and the luncheon hut are closed, but so, too, are the toxicity and the biochemistry buildings, and at least eight others — we don't go through every building on the premises, it is too depressing. When we finally come upon a scientist, in one of the biology labs, she is delighted to see us, to have someone to talk to. She is classifying invertebrates from nearby waterways and listening to Handel on the radio. "Who else but the CBC would play The Messiah *in August?" she asks.*

Dillon is very careful with me, as a public servant must be in a department where the downsizing begins with those who talk too much. But as we trudge from building to building, he cannot entirely conceal a nostalgia for the good old days, a few years ago, when the gate was guarded, the parking lot jammed, and these buildings bustled and brimmed with activity. When he first arrived here, in 1975, the bright young bearer of a PhD and an enthusiasm for environmental research, the place was just beginning. There was little equipment, a tiny staff, and a minuscule budget. But the centre grew and established itself, and did work that was recognized all over the world. Now it is sinking back to where it began, except that several million dollars worth of equipment clutters the place and there is no one to use it. Where eighty people once worked (some of them university visitors, part-timers, and students), there is now a permanent staff of seventeen. There are fewer workers than buildings. The research budget in 1997 was about one-quarter of what it was at its height. This year, although we are three months into the fiscal calendar, there is no set budget at all. The money, about $400,000, will be spent, and everyone hopes it will be okayed at some future date.

It was here that the first key work was done that showed the horrendous damage to our water systems of phosphates in detergents and that led to their banning from the weekly wash. Here, too, crucial work was done on acid rain, in conjunction with other research taking place in the experimental lakes area to the north, around Kenora, research that is also now severely curtailed. Recently, the scientists here were able to show, based on vast quantities of data collected over long periods of time, that mercury discovered in the ecosystem is, in the main, deposited by human activity, not nature.

In one building we come across a chart that covers half a wall, marked with lines that squiggle and soar from dot to dot. They represent the results of acid rain studies over the past two decades, but, in recent years, the results grow slimmer and slimmer and now may not mean much at all. "Does that tell us that acid rain is no longer a problem?" I ask. Dillon looks startled, then rueful. "No, it tells us that the politicians and the public look on it as a problem solved. They think that simply by saying you're going to do something, it has gone away."

The acid rain is still there, still poisoning the lakes and killing the trees. From the data, it is clear that we are broaching new problems that may present even more of a challenge than acid rain. But how will we tell what the new poisons are, or how extensive the damage, when we close down our probing posts?

The cries of scientific alarm that caused us to commit to control acid rain are dying down, not because industrial man has ceased to assault the world around him but because he no longer wants to pay to find out how much harm he has caused. Dillon tells me that Canada today has fewer centres for detecting acid rain than Croatia. We don't know whether our continental partners in the United States are meeting their targets for acid rain control or not, because we no longer have enough reliable measures to determine accurately where and when and how the damage is being done, or how much of it there is.

We are stumbling blindly into the future, shedding the scientists who might point out the pitfalls and hoping for the best. What Dorset will go on telling us, until the last scientist turns out the lights, is that what we are likely to get is the worst.

Let it not be said that, in the rush to hammer government budgets, we are letting the important work slide. A series of studies pinpointed 139 areas in national parks and heritage properties across Canada, from southern British Columbia to north of the Arctic Circle, that are regarded as "contaminated" and in need of remedial action before they get worse. The Department of Canadian Heritage is devoting the equivalent of one-half of one person's time per annum to get them all cleaned up.[1] Any time this employee has left over will be devoted, I presume, to writing press releases explaining that everything is well in hand. The auditor general raised a concern about these sites, which range from a landfill site in Jasper National Park next to the Athabaska River in Alberta, through a former coal mine at Banff that has left a legacy of highly dangerous coal tar, to the heavily contaminated Lachine Canal in Quebec, taken over by Parks Canada in 1977.

In 1993 Ottawa was promising to get after all these matters, and work was begun on a number of sites. However, as cash starvation set in, they were simply dropped. The auditor general demanded in his 1996 report to know what was going to be done to clear away what he referred to as "potential environmental liabilities." He wanted the government to find out how much damage had been done and was being done, and how much it was going to cost to fix things up.[2] As the 1997 federal budget put the matter: "This is a very complex area. The government is in the process of developing policies with regard to accounting for environmental liabilities."[3] What a comfort. In the meantime, there is this half-a-person, working away on the 139 sites.

Ottawa abandons the environment

The environment is one of those areas where the peculiar genius of Canadians to screw things up by dividing responsibilities between federal and provincial governments, on perfectly logical grounds, can be seen in operation. The British North America

Act didn't mention the word "environment," but it gave control of natural resources to the provinces. By logic, this would make them the protectors of these resources and, by extension, of the environment in general. However, it is the federal government that deals with other nations — especially the United States, with which we share the Great Lakes. The funds to finance such a major aspect of existence fell to the federal government when it established the temporary income tax in 1917.

Thus, when environmental concerns became a sexy political item, we had to have a federal department to look after things. Environment Canada was created in 1971 with overall responsibility to monitor and curb pollution and to share responsibility for managing Canada's resources.[4] More generally, Ottawa would work through External Affairs (as it then was) to deal with transborder issues, and with intergovernmental bodies such as the Canadian Council of Ministers of the Environment to ensure that standards were adopted across the country. It would also provide financing for research and for environmental protection. Then, when downsizing and deregulation became the order of the day, Ottawa abruptly withdrew much of the funding and left the provinces and territories on their own.

In 1984–85 the federal department had a budget of $819 million; a decade later, it was $715 million, and heading down. In all, Environment Canada has lost 30 per cent of its budget and 60 per cent of its staff. When Lucien Bouchard was the minister, there were 10,000 employees in the department; now, there are just over 4,000. Subtracting so much money and clout from an area where the problems were rapidly getting worse, not better, abandoned a number of international undertakings and left the provinces to deal, or not, with the mess left behind. We still have bold speeches about environmental protection, but very little action. To keep this betrayal from upsetting Canadians too much, the nation's only annual overview of the state of the environment was killed, for a savings of $1 million per annum.[5]

The 1993 Red Book, produced as the centrepiece of the Liberal election platform, promised one of the most ambitious environmental agendas in history. The followup, however, simply continued in the well-worn path of the Mulroney Conservatives, who decided early on to let the environment shift for itself.

Although there were some minor improvements, such as changes to the bankruptcy law to make it harder for corporations to walk away from the damage they had wreaked on the countryside, and tax changes to improve the treatment of alternative energy sources, the two major promised initiatives — a renewed Canadian Environmental Protection Act and the Canada Endangered Species Act — joined the dodo, the great auk, and other vanished natural creatures.

Other priorities, as we say down at the Treasury Board, won out. We decided that we could afford almost anything that would aid industrial development, but nothing that would control its noxious effects. Federal environmental laws, particularly those applied to the natural extraction industries — mining and petroleum — were gutted, or abandoned by non-enforcement. Our negotiators made it clear that Canada would block any future international agreements that could hurt the economic interests of these industries.[6]

As a result, our forests face a very real danger that they will be exploited, as many of our fish stocks have already been exploited, to the point of no return. A large number of species of animals and plants are threatened with extinction. Our cities are in danger of becoming unliveable in — after years of steady improvement. And now we are destroying the implements, such as the Dorset Research Centre, that can let us know what is going on. We are marching backwards into the darkness, and, to make the trip more interesting, we have decided we can no longer afford the batteries for our flashlight, which used to let us know where we were. We have gone, in a few short years, from being one of the most responsible nations on earth in environmental terms to one of the worst. The Commission for Environmental Co-operation, a Montreal-based group set up to monitor the continental ecosystem under the North American Free Trade Agreement, reported in mid-1997:

- the average Canadian factory spews twice as many pollutants into the air as the average American factory, and dumps more toxic chemicals into the water;
- Ontario produces more pollution than California, New York, or Michigan;

- five of the continent's top fifty polluters are Canadian companies; and
- Canadian air quality standards are lower than the American (though not quite so invisible as Mexico's).[7]

Scientists are usually not excitable types, so when they begin to shriek, we should pay attention. In May 1997 some of our top environmental scientists met at York University in Toronto and reported:

> Canada holds stewardship over almost one-seventh of the world's terrestrial and aquatic resources, yet over the last ten years our capacity to do long-term monitoring and assessment has declined at such a precipitous rate that we are almost completely incapable of making rational, informed decisions about sustainable management. Informed data-based decision making has been replaced with policies based on "best practices" or "expert opinion." In Canada, the dereliction of environmental duty is shameful![8]

Cooling off on global warming

One of the subjects that most upset the participants at the York conference was the way we have abandoned our commitment to come to grips with global warming. For a time, Canada was among the world leaders on global warming, the phenomenon that drew waves of scientists and lots of money into environmental research during the early 1980s. A debate on this topic has been going on for decades in scientific circles, but it did not get much attention until 1972, when the Club of Rome report, *The Limits to Growth,* raised the question of whether mankind could continue to exist on the globe.[9] This very solemn but essentially daffy report said that we were using up resources far too fast, wrecking the atmosphere, and poisoning the globe. We were looking at the collapse of world order, so we had to stop expansion, now. Or, to put it another way, we in the First World told everyone in the Third World to stay in their huts and stop making babies, because we had already used up all the available materials for growth, including population growth.

Still, the point was made: something had to be done about

environmental destruction. What came out of the argument, gradually, was a UN-sponsored study, the World Commission on Environment and Development, whose chair was Norwegian prime minister Gro Harlem Brundtland and whose secretary general was Saskatchewan-born Jim MacNeill, the main author of the Brundtland Commission's epochal report, *Our Common Future*,[10] in 1987. This report initiated the concept of "sustainable development," by which is meant, simply, matching economic change to what the environment can sustain without long-term deterioration. If the world continued to draw on environmental resources at current rates, we were looking at collapse. But we could do much more with what we have than we are doing now: we could both sustain growth and protect the planet. For example, if we continued to use the same sources of energy, the developing nations, to reach anything like the state of the industrialized world, would require a five-fold increase in consumption, even with no increase in population. But if we used the present resources more effectively and developed such new technologies as hydrogen-powered automobiles and turbines, the growth could take place without destroying the environment.[11]

This argument ran head on into global warming. There are two edges to this phenomenon. The first concerns the release of chlorofluorocarbons (CFCs) and other gases, caused mostly by human activity. These gases consume the protective ozone layer, which prevents most of the sun's harmful ultraviolet rays from reaching the surface of the earth. Second, the CFCs are also one of the "greenhouse gases" — the other main culprits being carbon dioxide, methane, and nitrous oxide — which accumulate high in the atmosphere and trap warmth escaping from the surface. Thus, global warming.

Greenhouse gases come from natural as well as human sources, but it is the additional increase due to human activity that created the problem. Carbon dioxide is produced when fossil fuels, such as oil, coal, and natural gas, are consumed; CFCs are produced by refrigerants, aerosols, solvents, and foams released into the atmosphere; nitrous oxide comes from deforestation, fertilizers and, again, from burning fossil fuels; and methane is relased from wetlands, rice paddies, and livestock.

The atmosphere had been able to cope with the natural emissions for eons, but now, the scientists said, unless action was taken, global mean temperatures would rise between 2.6 degrees Celsius and 5.8 degrees Celsius over the next century. This rise is more than the planet has warmed since the last ice age, 22,000 years ago, and it would lead to massive climate change, a rise in sea levels of up to 1 metre, the virtual disappearance of a number of South Pacific island states, flooding in some areas and drought in others, and the onset of ever more severe storms worldwide.

Global warming, if the scientists were right, was already with us. We could not sustain development unless we had an immediate and drastic reduction in carbon, carbon dioxide, and CFC emissions. But the industrialists and automobile makers responded: Prove it. Why should we put scrubbers on our chimneys, redesign our auto plants, and stop burning fossil fuels, just because of a few bumps in a chart?

It was the same reasoning that kept governments from taking action against tobacco manufacturers, when scientists could not prove a direct link between increased smoking and the increase in cancers. Gradually, however, such a massive accumulation of evidence piled up that action against global warming took on political sex appeal.[12] We might not be able to prove a direct causal link between that belching chimney and Hurricane Andrew, but it seemed prudent to take action, just in case. Accordingly, we all signed up to treaties to curb global warming, both by reducing the production of CFCs and by rolling back the production of other greenhouse gases. The first part proved simple: substitutes were found for CFCs, which were then legislated out of refrigerants, coolants, and sprays. Within a few years, their release was back below the level produced in 1965.[13] It could be done.

Canada, proud of its record in the past as a global good guy, signed on to sustainable development with the Conservative government's *Blueprint for a Green Economy*. As it turned out, the blueprint contributed to global warming mainly by releasing a lot of hot air. A National Task Force on the Environment and the Economy made forty specific recommendations on the implementation of sustainable development, and then the government cut nearly all the money to implement them. For example, expenditures on energy conservation and alternative energy programs were cut by 90 per cent between 1980 and 1991.[14]

When the Liberals came to power, they produced the same hot air. At Rio de Janeiro in June 1992, a UN-convened Earth Summit set targets for all the participating nations to reduce emissions of carbon dioxide, the chief suspect in global warming. The heads of 120 nations met for two weeks to rescue the world from the depredations and greed of its inhabitants. They passed many motherhood resolutions, as usual, and then they came up with some specific targets, the most important of which reduced greenhouse gas emissions to the levels they were at in 1990.[15] At the end of the summit, 166 nations ratified the convention, but the United States led, and Canada followed, a proposal to make the targets voluntary.

Still there seemed hope: the Liberal election campaign Red Book of 1993 promised adherence to the Rio targets. Once elected, Prime Minister Jean Chrétien pronounced that "an immediate priority will be to design a plan to achieve this target." Then he appointed a natural resources minister from Edmonton, Anne McClellan, who made it her mission to block any legislation that would upset the coal or oil industries, or what David Crane of the *Toronto Star* calls, "their captive, the Alberta government."[16] When the Business Council on National Issues was concerned that Chrétien appeared to be ready to clamp down on offending industries, he went out to Edmonton to promise that everything was to be done on a voluntary basis. The Red Book disappeared, like the CFCs, in a vague mist.

In the 1997 election the Liberals delivered the same green promises they had neglected so studiously after 1993: "The costs of inaction on climate change are too high for us not to take thoughtful and effective action now. We must contribute our fair share to international efforts, first by making progress at the domestic level."[17]

Action: Cut environmental funding

Canada did take action, almost as soon as the Liberals had won again. Not only was the Environment Canada budget slashed but the federal government shifted primary responsibility for environmental protection back to the provinces. Then it announced that we would not be able to meet the Rio goals after all. As a federal official explained: "It is clear that for us, achieving the goals set at Rio would have enormous economic effects."[18] He even made it sound as if Germany and Britain, two of the industrialized nations that will meet the targets, were cheating. They were, it appears, taking advantage of "unique circumstances" to meet their goals. After the reunion of East and West Germany, a lot of beaten-up factories in East Germany were closed down, causing an immediate drop in carbon emissions. Britain, too, had gone through a major overhaul of its manufacturing sector.

The environment was suddenly Canada's jilted suitor. There were two factors at play. One was the reluctance of the Americans, whose industrial lobby donates generously to both political parties there, to invest in new and cleaner technology. When President Bill Clinton announced in October 1997 that the United States was dumping the Rio targets and, instead, aiming to reach the reduction in emissions sometime between 2008 and 2012 — still on a voluntary basis — Canada again followed suit. We would be content, official government spokespersons said in Ottawa briefings, to do better than the Americans on controlling emissions.[19]

The second factor was the need to outflank the Reform Party. Rosemary Speirs, a long-time observer of parliament and politics, put it bluntly:

> The truth is that the Liberals are spooked by the Calgary oil patch. In the House of Commons, the Reform party keeps hammering away at how much a binding program to reduce greenhouse emissions would supposedly cost Canadians. Reform critic Bill Gilmour raises the spectre of a carbon tax (despite the fact the Liberals have ruled such a measure out), and says it could cost consumers up to 30 cents more a litre for gasoline.[20]

Real action on global warming will cost money. To offset some of the damage, a carbon tax, a straight levy on all emission-producing energy sources, strikes me as an eminently sensible idea. But in the face of intense lobbying by industry, Canadians are called upon to make sacrifices to bring down government spending and lower taxes, but never for something so impractical as preserving a liveable planet.

The Canadian oil lobby advanced the same argument as the American, producing full-page newspaper ads that sounded as if the industry was on the side of controlling emissions, while avoiding any enforceable rules. "Scientists are divided about climate change and whether man-made emissions are a major cause," the ads claimed, in a haunting echo of the tobacco-company ads of a decade earlier. There certainly are some scientists, possibly even some not on the payroll of the industry, who take this view, but they are few in number. Still, the industry said, we ought to be taking some action, as a form of insurance. "Two things are needed: better global rules and solid local action." But all this verbiage is either horribly vague or handily voluntary. Canada should push for a "smarter measurement system which recognizes that each country can help in different ways"; more Canadian companies should join the "national climate change registry program"; and, the key point, "we don't need more rules, just more effort."[21]

Some sneaky assumptions are hidden in this approach, along with the overt claim that, despite the evidence accumulated since 1972, all that is needed is a little dash of goodwill and the polluters will come on side. These assumptions are contained in the phrase that "each country can help in different ways." What is really behind this phrase is the claim that Canada ought not to be bound by the same degree of rigour as other nations. We are, after all, a northern nation and we have to keep warm. The global targets we dumped were straightforward; they said that each signing nation agreed to get its own emissions down to the 1990 level. What Canada wanted to do was to jack up our 1990 count or be allowed to slow down our target date. When these bizarre arguments were dismissed, we simply announced that we quit.

Another assumption, that nations have a legal right to pollute, was first aired in the United States in the 1970s. In this scenario, if a nation, or corporation, found it difficult to meet a common standard of control, it would be able, in effect, to buy a pollution licence. A pulp mill, for example, not only has the right but the duty, to pollute: "Paper mill owners choose to pollute because it is in their corporate interest to do so. And, it is their legal right to do so. They inherit, along with everyone else, the right to use such resources as rivers, streams and the air."[22] This argument is not satire; it was advanced by a prominent American economist, Robert Thomas, in a symposium convened by the Law and Economics Center of the University of Miami. If you and I and that billion-dollar pulp mill down the river have the same right to build a smokestack and dump a few hundred million tons of pollutants into the atmosphere, and the pulp mill doesn't do so, it is cheating the shareholders. Inevitably, some other pulp mill will pollute, reducing its costs and raising its return on investment.

When this argument met with resistance, its proponants gave it a neat twist: the right to pollute could be sold. By all means, they said, set firm targets to control pollution or greenhouse gases. Then, if company A, which has a new facility, can exceed the target, but company B, stuck with old equipment, cannot, company A can sell company B its unused pollution rights for a lot less money than it would cost company B to clean up. This is not from a skit on *Saturday Night Live*. It is an argument seriously advanced by academics, politicians, and corporate executives.[23]

In the months leading up to the Kyoto Summit in December 1997, Canada and the United States added a new wrinkle to this argument. As Chrétien put it: "When we export a product or service that reduces greenhouse gas emissions in another country, we should get credit."[24] Thus, when we flog a CANDU reactor to Turkey, we should be able to pollute more. Turkey, too, should be able to pollute more, because using a CANDU to produce energy results in lower carbon emissions than burning coal or oil.

Canada is behind its Rio commitment by 13 per cent; that is, we will be at least that far above our target when the year 2000 rolls around. Instead of lowering emissions, we have actually permitted an increase of 9 per cent since we made our pledge to reform. We are, per capita, the worst offender in greenhouse emissions in the world, save our glorious leader, the United States. Our position became even less defensible when, at the Kyoto Summit in December 1997, we proposed to cut emissions to 3 per cent below the 1990 levels — in the year 2010. That proposal was rejected, so we retreated to a previously prepared position and bound ourselves to a level 6 per cent below 1990 by 2010.[25] Even the Americans promised more — a 7 per cent cut. Other developed nations came up with other targets, ranging from 8 per cent cuts by most European positions to an 8 per cent increase in Australia. There are no sanctions, enforcement provisions, or even proposals as to how any of these targets are to be met.

Even this feeble attempt proved too much for Canada's federal and provincial environment ministers. On April 24, 1998, they met in Toronto to review the Kyoto agreement and decided to spend another two years studying the potential impact before taking any action. Federal environment minister Christine Stewart told a news conference, "We will not do anything that would jeopardize our economy." Or, to put it another way, the international undertakings we signed in Japan meant nothing; what counts is what they say in Calgary and other voter-sensitive environs. Jim Fulton, executive director of the David Suzuki Foundation, an environmental group, fumed: "This meeting reeked of political cowardice." What it reeked of was business as usual. Cleaning up the planet is bound to have an economic cost — to Canada, and every other nation. Of course, the cost of *not* cleaning it up is incalculable.

Jim MacNeill summarized the economic argument in *Policy Options* magazine in 1990 where he noted that the cost of reversing the damage was already high:

> Some preliminary estimates suggest that international funding of $20 to $30 billion per year would be needed, assuming the lowest-cost measures available are used. Other estimates run to $50 or $100 billion.
>
> That's a lot or a little, depending on how you look at it. Thirty billion is about one-fifth of one per cent of Gross World Product. It's also about half of the annual subsidies to the fossil fuel industry in the United States and Canada alone. When I hear governments arguing that we can't afford the costs involved, I am reminded of the man who refused to pump water into his burning house because his water bills were already too high.[26]

The late Great Lakes

The federal government has also withdrawn from environmental control over the Great Lakes. In 1978, after increasing evidence that the Great Lakes basin, the home of 35 million people along 1,600 kilometres of U.S.–Canada border, was in serious trouble, Canada signed the Great Lakes Water Quality Agreement. It pledged both nations, working with the International Joint Commission, to ameliorate the effects of three centuries of settlement, development, expansion, and exploitation. During that period, we dumped, dammed, shot, filled, and burned; we cut the trees, blocked the rivers, dried out the wetlands, slaughtered the animals, paved over the meadows, and turned the vast basin of connected lakes — not only the Great Five but many of the 80,000 other lakes within the region — into a giant contaminated cesspool. We kept increasing the chemicals we threw into the water, strewed on the lands, and blew into the air. Then we noted with astonishment that something was wrong: fish were dying, and the water was not as clear as it once was or the air as fresh. The environment could not, after all, absorb every pot of poison we poured into it.

Between 1978 and 1988, Canada and the United States spent more than US$10 billion building and improving municipal sewage treatment plants, curbing noxious emissions, and monitoring and cutting back pollution from toxic metals and organic contaminants.[27] The result was a marked and measurable improvement in conditions across the region. In particular, there was a general recovery of Great Lakes water quality, although serious problems remained. Then the money stopped, with predictable results.

In 1989 a report prepared jointly by the Conservation Foundation of America and the Institute for Research on Public Policy in Canada was presented to the International Joint Commission. It noted: "The swift progress in reducing toxic contaminants which took place in the late 1970s and early 1980s has since appeared to have slowed or stopped." Once again the area was "a sick environment," with the following symptoms, among others:

- Male herring gull embryos in the region tend to develop ovaries; fish-eating birds and mammals at the top of the food chain, where high levels of toxins concentrate, suffer from reproductive problems.

- Bald eagles cannot reproduce throughout much of the region.
- Many species of fish can no longer survive in the lakes, and many of the survivors can no longer reproduce naturally.
- Two-thirds of the most productive natural systems in the region, the wetlands, have been filled, drained or bulldozed out of existence.
- By the process called "biomagnification," which passes along toxic substances in higher and higher concentrations up the food chain, contaminants which are almost undetectable in clear water may be magnified millions of times within the flesh of fish taken from the Great Lakes. It may be safe to drink the water, but not eat the fish that swim in that same water. The same process ensures that we are constantly accumulating toxic debris in our own bodies, with results that are far from clear, but unlikely to be pleasant.

Publication of the report, under the limp-wristed title *Great Lakes, Great Future?*, created an uproar that lasted for several minutes, and then died, buried beneath all the stories that told us governments were spending too much money studying these claims.

The report pointed to forty-two Areas of Concern that had been identified by the Great Lakes Water Quality Board as far back as 1973. Detailed remedial action plans for eight of these areas had been drawn up in 1985. The cleanup cost was estimated to be at least "tens of billions of dollars." The plans left out a great many things that would have to be done, including expansion to meet new population growth. The report concluded that, expensive though the changes called for were, they could be made. "The public is now saying that the environment and the economy can be mutually supporting."

That was then; this is now.

In 1996 the International Joint Commission issued its *Eighth Biennial Report on Great Lakes Water Quality*, which indicated that we were, at best, treading water. Among other problems, programs to reduce toxins are "under stress from government restructuring and resource constraints, as well as regulatory review in Ontario."[28] At the same time, and in line with the see-no-evil, pay-for-no-evil-inspectors philosophy that has become so popular these days, the number of researchers is down by half since 1991.

One problem is that, while the Great Lakes Water Quality Treaty is Ottawa's responsibility, the actual implementation is assigned to Ontario, under the 1994 Canada-Ontario Agreement on the Great Lakes Basin Ecosystem. Ontario no longer believes in environmental protection — certainly not in spending money on it.

Dr. Peter Victor is dean of the Department of Environmental Studies at York University. He used to be assistant deputy minister in the provincial Ministry of the Environment, until "it got to the point where the ministry's own capacity to do science was so seriously diminished I didn't feel that I could agree with it." He described the Great Lakes Water Quality Treaty in these words:

> We have the agreement signed between the two levels of government, and that represents Ontario's contribution to Canada's obligations under the treaty. There are very clear, measurable targets in that agreement, but they were based on the assumption that the ministries of the environment would be much the same as they were, and would have much the same budgets. The targets could be reached, but they were a reach, and with the cuts, well, it's hard to see how they can be met.
>
> A case in point . . . the ministry used to have a fleet of five or six vessels to monitor the Great Lakes and, so far as I know, they were all mothballed or sold to save money. And you see the feds were doing much the same.[29]

Dr. Mark Winfield of the Canadian Institute of Environmental Law and Policy was more direct in his criticism: "Ontario simply turned its back on its obligations under the treaty, and Ottawa didn't do a damn thing about it."[30]

Not doing a damn thing about it has become a kind of mantra to describe modern governmental approaches to the environment — and always on the now-familiar grounds that we cannot afford to take action, although how we can afford not to take action is unclear. To help us keep things in perspective, the Ministry of Environment and Energy — which had budget reductions of $47 million in 1995–96, $149 million in 1996–97, and is slated for a further reduction of $201 million in 1997–98[31] — apparently decided to save money on an annual "state of the environment" report. This report was first prepared in 1992, but when journalist Martin Mittelstaed asked for a copy in 1997, the ministry denied it existed.[32] Then someone produced a copy, which indicated that all was not well on the environmental front. The ministry had begun work on a more comprehensive report for release in 1995, but it would have cost $250,000, so it was scrapped entirely.

Is there a pattern here? Don Evans, a chemist at the Dorset Centre, notes:

> We are dying the death of 1,000 cuts. We have been hacked and slashed so much that we are getting to the point where the whole structure will come down like a house of cards . . .
>
> . . . The problems are not going away, just the concern. Take acid rain, which is where this facility really made its reputation. What we are looking at is almost a resurgence of acid precipitation; there is still an incredible sink of sulphate in the environment and pulses of weak sulphuric acid entering the watersheds and hammering the biota [flora and fauna]. But our capacity to keep up with it is being destroyed. Now we're running into trace metals, especially mercury. There is a fairly large sink of mercury which is bioaccumulating in fish species — we believe this is from long-range transport, but we need to do much more work to know for certain.* Will it be done?
>
> We had to drop our study of the Lake Simcoe watershed, which is extremely important. First, they cut the conservation authorities, so we took on the job. Now they have cut us. We are talking about an area that produces hundreds of millions of dollars a year in revenue, and we are blind as to the degradation of the environment. How does that make economic sense?[33]

---

*A paper from the 1997 environmental science conference at York University had this to say about mercury: "Even after abatement has begun the mercury that is not in the biosphere will remain there for perhaps hundreds of years. The implication is that we are changing the biosphere in a fundamental and permanent way . . . the need for more information has never been greater."

When Evans and I spoke, the Ontario government had cut the conservation authorities. Now corporations can, for a $750,000 donation, receive voting rights on the board of Conservation Ontario, the umbrella group that represents the regional and municipal conservation authorities across the province. First to sign up was Dofasco Limited, which dropped in $1 million — to be used exclusively to promote Conservation Ontario's image — in return for voting rights on the board. In 1996 Dofasco had been named as one of the big polluters of the Lake Ontario basin.[34]

We are privatizing the entire process. The forestry division of the Ontario Ministry of Environment and Energy has lost 24 per cent of its budget and 40 per cent of its workforce. Standing on guard, in the future, will be the forest industries themselves, which have become the primary source of information on the state of the province's forests and on industry compliance with ministry requirements.[35]

In the mining sector, the province is now going around to the environmental groups, asking for handouts. In September 1997 the engineer in charge of cleaning up a heavily polluted mine site in eastern Ontario wrote to the Sierra Legal Defence Fund requesting financial aid for the project.[36] The mine was abandoned in 1961 and has been leaking arsenic, cobalt, copper, and nickel into the Moira River and groundwater ever since. In 1996 three tonnes of arsenic leaked into the river, according to a report to the environment ministry. But the ministry cannot afford to clean up the site, which is dumping poison into a river that drains into the Bay of Quinte, on Lake Ontario. Janet Fletcher, an environmental enthusiast, launched a private prosecution against the Ministry of Environment and Energy, which admitted: "It is truly a very, very dangerous site." The Sierra Club has declined assistance. The case continues.

We're giving the inspectors more clout

There are some signs that governments are beginning to feel the heat on the environmental front again. In December 1996 a revised Canadian Environmental Protection Act was passed which strengthens the enforcement process in two major ways. The first allows inspectors to enter premises without a warrant, if they believe the law is being violated, and to give polluters 180 days to comply with federal standards, or even to fine offenders on the spot.[37] (In the past, inspectors looking for violations could be, and sometimes were, charged with trespassing.) The second change guarantees anonymity for whistle-blowers who report serious environmental breaches and who, in the past, have often been rewarded for their efforts by being shown the door. In addition, the new law calls for the establishment of national emission control standards for engines and gives Canadians the right, for the first time, to sue for damage to the environment when the government fails to enforce its own laws.

These improvements have to be compared with years of neglect, downsizing, and abandonment. What good will it do to give environmental inspectors the right to inspect more vigorously if we have fired most of the inspectors? This process began in Ottawa, where, between 1994 and 1997, Environment Canada received budget cuts of $238 million; still to come are further cuts to the Environmental Protection Service's program to oversee waste management in the pulp and paper, mining, and chemical industries.[38]

Winfield points to one of the ironies of the downsizing process we are now going through. While Canadians have always prided themselves on their concern for the environment, particularly in comparison with the Americans, we no longer have any basis for pride: "The fact is that the Environmental Protection Agency has weathered the storm better than Environment Canada."[39] In part, this is an accident of American politics. The EPA is part of the executive branch, where President Clinton is determined to make his mark as a "liberal" president after his dismal failure in medicare, housing, and other areas. In part, too, American law works on behalf of the environment, particularly in allowing and encouraging an active, aggressive, and litigious population to launch class-action suits against polluters.

When we hit the point where we have to rank ourselves behind the Americans in providing state protection for the environment, we may have hit rock bottom. But no. We haven't talked about culture yet.

The Law of Unintended Consequences

Canadians still appear to be hemmed in by the
American ethnocentric notion that economics is
basically a matter of private ownership and the rules
of free enterprise . . . The undeniable success of a
public enterprise comes to appear, then, as nothing
short of magic.
— Hershel Hardin, *A Nation Unaware*, 1974

*In this part, we consider three areas — culture, transport, and science
— where the devastation incurred was never intended. Our decision
makers knew that a certain amount of pain was bound to follow when
funding was withdrawn from hospitals, schools, and the justice*

system, but they never intended to create chaos in these other sectors. Although they have spent much of their time denying that anything of consequence has happened, it has.

Curbing Culture

The technostructure embraces and uses the engineer
and the scientist; it cannot embrace the artist.
Engineering and science serve its purpose; art, at
best, is something which it needs but finds
troublesome and puzzling. The artist, by contrast,
still depends extensively on private patronage; he
has come, along with the rest of the community, to
accept the view that public support to the arts could
be dangerously repressive of the artistic spirit. It is
obvious that the resulting saving in public funds —
as compared with a society that sets the same store
by the arts as, say, moon travel — is very great.
— John K. Galbraith, *Economics and the Public Purpose*, 1973

*The building where the Canadian Broadcasting Corporation produces
its radio programs for much of the Maritime region stands on
Sackville Street, just behind Citadel Hill, above the pulsing hub of
downtown Halifax. From the outside it looks like an ancient warehouse that can't make up its mind whether to become an insurance
building or just fall down. On the third floor, which you reach by
climbing the stairs or waiting for the elevator — powered by a gang of
squirrels lashed to a treadmill on the roof — there is, on your right, a
long newsroom, containing the same rich mixture of newsrooms*

everywhere: sweat, spilled beer, abandoned coffee, and dying dreams. Should you turn left instead of right you will find yourself in a long corridor flanked by broadcast studios. The newsroom is a squalid mess, but the studios are neat and nicely furnished, well lit, and air conditioned, for the CBC knows you can heap more indignity on people than on broadcasting equipment before a breakdown results. I am sitting in Studio C talking to long-time broadcaster Don Connelly, who at first appears his usual cheerful, urbane self.

He is not; he is pissed off. He has been a witness, a far from silent witness, to the downsizing, hacking, cutbacks, regional disembowelment, and other indignities that have been heaped on the head of the national broadcaster, and he thinks it is all too much:

When the cuts first started in about 1985 there were a lot of people of a certain age here. They were glad to take the buyout and run, but the effect, because they were pretty good buyouts, was to reward the second rate, in some cases; they left. But later, when the real cuts hit, it was something else again. We lost many of the best people, we lost most of the young comers, we lost much of the ability to do the job, and nearly all of the ability to do it in the future. I remember they laid off one young woman who was really sharp in current affairs, and then they laid off the only radio drama producer in the entire region. That really hurt.

I don't know if we've passed critical mass or not. I can't tell from inside whether or not public radio — I know nothing about TV — can survive in this country. I do know that all the brown stuff is floating downhill, because all the guys who make the decisions talk the same language about downsizing and the need to be entrepreneurial and all that crap as those a-holes up in Ottawa.[1]

Since Connelly disavows any knowledge of what is happening in television, I raise the subject with Bill Cameron, a tall, humorous man with a quick tongue and a discerning mind, a television talking head who operates over on Bell Road where the television studios stand. Cameron puts it all in one sentence: "They are sucking the oxygen out of this place."[2]

You cannot keep cutting and cutting at the national broadcaster and expect it to do the job for which it was designed. As King Gordon once put it rather neatly: "Is it to be the State, or the United States?"

Obviously, since we refuse to fund culture adequately in this country anymore, it is to be the United States.

N o other advanced nation in the world has surrendered its culture to another nation as Canada has to the United States. No other advanced nation seems to prefer the artifacts of its neighbour to its own, to say nothing of its history, art, broadcasting, filmmaking, recording, publishing, and theatre. No other nation would think of licensing the right to sell souvenirs of its national police force to the Disney Corporation. If a Canadian sells a Mountie hat without paying Walt his royalty, he will find himself up to his own hat brim in writs flown up from Florida, where the motto seems to be: "The Mounties always get their cut."

There is no credible evidence that Canadians in general hold their nation in such low esteem. Nobody asked us if we wanted Walt to control the trappings of the RCMP, or Viacom to control the entertainment industry in Canada, or American broadcasters to rule our airwaves, or American publishers to dominate our newsstands and book stores. We had a culture which, by reason of our proximity to the giant mixmaster next door, required some national protection. Remove the protection, and we disappear into the mix. But it was never put to us in these terms. We were told that it was necessary to cut back funding to the cultural sector because of the crushing burden of debt that threatened to overwhelm us.

Once that lie was swallowed there was no way to disgorge it. The entire process of curbing the state's support of culture appears to be driven, once more, by the view held by a few Canadians — the few who make the decisions — that culture, while commendable, is too expensive for the public purse. It was all very well to hand out money to support the artsy-fartsy set when there was lots of money to spare, but, in these hard times, why not import? Importing, after all, promotes that other great good of modern times, globalization, and the combination of public penury and the free trade lobby is writing RIP on Canada's cultural coffin.

We are speaking here of a sector of Canadian industry that employs 900,000 people,[3] and, according to Statistics Canada, that contributes indirectly another 200,000 jobs. The economic impact of the cultural industry comes to $29.2 billion directly, and $42 billion if indirect benefits are added, or about 6.8 per cent of the total economy.

Government spending is much more than a catalyst in Canadian culture; it is indispensable. In 1992, the last year for which StatsCan performed this exercise, the three levels of government contributed more than $6 billion, of which about half came from Ottawa (see table 5 in the appendix for a breakdown of where the money came from and where it went). Private spending in aid of culture in the same year came to $135 million, or a little less than 1 per cent.[4] Governments contribute about $200 per capita per year to culture — or about the cost of dinner and an evening at one of the mega-musicals we stage, with American stars, directors, music, and scripts, at places like the Ford Theatre for the Performing Arts in Toronto.

The state intervenes on the side of culture both directly and indirectly. In broadcasting, it directly finances the national broadcasters, the CBC and Radio Canada, as well as provincial broadcasters. Of the $2.8 billion that flows into the cultural sector from governments, $1.7 billion goes to broadcasting. The state also governs broadcasting, both radio and television, and imposes minimum Canadian content rules, as well as limiting foreign ownership of Canadian broadcasters. In films, Ottawa backs Canadian film production by supporting Telefilm Canada and the National Film Board; indirectly, it sets regulations requiring television stations to carry a (varying and variable) percentage of Canadian films. In the magazine industry, there have always been direct postal subsidies — now fading fast — to ensure the survival of Canadian magazines, and such indirect aids as tax breaks for advertising in Canadian publications, and a prohibition on "split runs" — American magazines that carry only a tiny amount of Canadian content but demand the same advertising breaks. (More of this later.)

In the book business, the Book Publishing Industry Program

has provided direct subsidies to publishers, based on their sales of Canadian titles, as well as subsidies for "book-flogging," or, more formally, the Publication Development Assistance Program, which picks up hotel bills for author tours, among other things. Indirectly, Ottawa limits foreign control over Canadian book publishers — in theory, if not in fact. The Canada Council, established in 1957, funds the National Arts Centre, National Gallery, and National Archives, a handful of museums, galleries, orchestras, and ballet and opera companies, and hands out about $85 million a year in grants to artists.[5] For purposes of the Canada Council, an artist is a broad category that includes dancers, painters, sculptors, musicians, and even authors.

All of this activity merely means, to the foes of government, that we waste billions every year. To the rest of us, it means that, without vigorous state intervention, we would be in an even more parlous condition than we are. Whichever view you take, it is obvious that something is dreadfully amiss:

- In our movie theatres, 97 per cent of the screen time is devoted to imported films.[6]
- In television, 90 per cent of what we see comes from outside. A Canadian child will be exposed to 12,000 hours of viewing time before he or she turns eighteen, almost all of it American; the side-benefits will include 600,000 commercials.[7] North American children spend an average of four hours a day in front of the tube, almost as much as many of them spend in class. The child will see 8,000 murders, on average, and countless undressings, fumblings, rapes, and other experiences of enrichment. These figures are a couple of years old, now; we have to wait for the new figures to show how much of the four hours, or new hours, will go to the Internet. It is not astonishing that Canadians think their heroes are John Wayne and Davey Crockett, and have never heard of Madelaine de la Verchères.
- In our record shops, 89 per cent of the earnings in the sound-recording industry accrues to twelve foreign-controlled firms.
- On our bookshelves, between 70 and 75 per cent of the market is taken by foreign publishers.[8]
- On our magazine stands, four out of every five titles sold is an

American title. Seven out of ten Canadian magazines do not show up at all.[9]

What this dismal record proved to our overlords in Ottawa, apparently, was that we were spending too much to defend the national well-being. The result was a series of massive cuts whose impact is only now working its way through the system. Heritage Canada, the federal department that ought to be the keeper of the national flame, was cut, in the 1995 budget, by $676 million over three years.[10] Later, some money was put back in some sectors, a move the federal government called "new spending." That sounded better than saying "cuts to the cuts."

Mel Hurtig, the well-known nationalist, publisher, politician, and author, notes in his heart-wrenching book, *At Twilight in the Country*, that the cuts were not being made in a vacuum; other things were going on at the same time:

> A few days after Mulroney's government announced a $75 million cut in the CBC's funding, they also announced tax measures that reduced petroleum industry taxes by $578 million. When the Chrétien government chopped another $110 million of CBC money in Paul Martin's 1996 budget, they also gave another $422 million in tax relief to the petroleum industry.[11]

Obviously, if we are going to give the oil barons an even $1 billion while gouging $185 million out of the hide of the CBC, we must feel that the national broadcaster has too much money and the oilmen too little. But it ain't necessarily so.

We have an annual trade deficit in cultural matters of about $10 billion; that is, we import about $22 billion worth of movies, books, and records and we export about $12 billion.[12] Leaving aside such minor matters as whether we are about to disappear entirely, this equation represents a huge loss of economic activity and jobs. Moreover, culture is not one of the big-income areas. The average income from cultural efforts of a Canadian artist is just over $20,000; of a dancer, $14,400; and of a writer, $15,300.[13] StatsCan, where I got the numbers, points out that most cultural workers have to have other jobs to stay alive.

A number of sectors are worth looking at to see what has happened to us — broadcasting, films, books, magazines, even libraries — but none is more revealing than the sorry tale of the CBC.

The CBC is Canada's mirror

The CBC is Canada writ small, with all the bumps, warts, character, and potential for disaster — and greatness — that the nation itself contains. It is the nation's whipping boy — and its lifeline. It affronts us and defines us. It drives us to the telephone, bellowing with rage, and it pulls us to the edge of our chairs, crooning with delight. It is an aspect of this nation that sets us off clearly, irredeemably — and thankfully — from the United States, probably the only thing, aside from Elvis Stojko, that thinking Americans wish they had invented.

The CBC was born out of the sure knowledge that unless Canada took charge of her own airwaves, they would be usurped by the United States. At that time, being usurped by the United States was not the good thing people seem to think it is today, but a lamentable development. We all began from the same perception of reality: that the airwaves do not belong to any individual or firm, and that they are part of the nation, part of our common heritage, and therefore the responsibility of the state. Later, we worked out ways to discard this responsibility, sell it, or pretend it did not exist.

The Americans had three radio networks, which were linked from coast to coast. We had only a handful of private stations, operating locally. Across the border, licences were cheap and easy to obtain; in Canada, the government allocated frequencies stingily — when they could be had at all. When commercial broadcasting began in the early 1920s, six clear radio channels were left for Canadian use, under an international agreement. Then an American court ruled that it was illegal for any government to allot wavelengths in a free enterprise economy.[14] Private American broadcasters appropriated every clear channel on the ether, emitting signals that simply drowned us out. We trotted down to Washington, hat in hand, and asked the Americans if they couldn't, please, see their way to allowing us the use of a dozen channels through the International Telecommunications Union.

The Americans replied with a rude noise, but, after much delicate negotiating, finally agreed that we could have half of what we asked for, six channels, and they would take the other seventy-seven. We demurred, the talks broke off, and it became open season for Americans to beam their transmitters across the border, drowning out local signals. At this time, the total Canadian broadcasting power amounted to less than 50 kilowatts, while U.S. stations broadcast 680 kilowatts, so we were not going to win any contest of cross-border bombardment.[15] In Toronto, in 1925, there were seven radio stations. Three of these were owned by newspapers, the others by Bell Telephone, Eaton's, Marconi, and Westinghouse. They shared two broadcast frequencies, which meant they had to take turns on the air. Moreover, they were prohibited by law from carrying commercials, while the incoming American networks were already shouting the glories of soap suds, toothpaste, and floor wax. In 1925 the Toronto *Telegram* conducted a Radio Popularity Ballot, which listed seventeen U.S. broadcasters ahead of any Canadian broadcaster in the local market. The nation's vast distances and tiny markets defeated us, and we began to develop local offshoots of American networks to carry the message. In Montreal, CFCF became an NBC affiliate, while the station owned by *La Presse*, CKAC, joined CBS. In Toronto, the *Telegram* station, CKWG, became part of NBC, in order, as the newspaper explained, "to put programmes on the air which it would bankrupt any Canadian station to provide." These affiliates filled most of their airtime, naturally, with American shows.

Then, according to Sandy Stewart's history of Canadian radio, *From Coast to Coast*,[16] the CBC was created — by God. Not directly, but the churches began to launch their own radio stations, and that led to difficulties. A station owned by the Jehovah's Witnesses in Saskatchewan was rented out to the Ku Klux Klan. Howls of outrage poured into the offices of the minister of marine, Pierre-Joseph Cardin, who had been given responsibility for Canada's airwaves — ships, after all, have radios. Cardin immediately gave a frequency used by the Witnesses to Gooderham & Worts, a distillery, and that led to even more howls of outrage, from both the enemies of booze and the enemies of censorship.

J.S. Woodsworth, the feisty preacher who was then the member of parliament for Winnipeg North, rose in the House of Commons to put two questions to Cardin: Who had made him the national censor? And when, if he was going to censor the Witnesses, did he plan to take similar action against the Orange Lodge and the Catholic Church, both of which had broadcasting stations? Cardin decided to take the Canadian way out and dump the whole messy argument about controlling the airwaves into the lap of a royal commission. It was headed by Sir John Aird, president of the Canadian Bank of Commerce, and an implacable foe of almost any action undertaken by government.

Aird, however, became convinced that if there was to be any broadcasting in Canada by Canadians, it would have to have state support and sanction. When he visited New York and heard American broadcast executives describe Canada as part of their territory (much as American film distributors do today), he was affronted; and when he visited London and saw the British Broadcasting Corporation (founded in 1927) in operation, he was convinced.

It would cost a good deal of money to erect a transmission system and provide programming that could compete with the Americans. Private enterprise showed no inclination to spend any of its own cash. Both the Canadian Pacific Railway and the Canadian Manufacturers' Association had plans for national networks, but both, in the way private enterprise plans so often do, counted on the public coffers to put up the money; only the profits would be private. A government network was the only solution in these circumstances, especially since broadcasting would have to be provided in two languages and carried to remote corners of the country where no profits would be made. The Aird Commission reported in September 1929, recommending, in a mere nine clear pages of writing, "some form of public ownership, operation and control, behind which is the national power and prestige of the whole public of the Dominion of Canada."[17] There would be seven high-powered radio stations across the country, linked through a national system to be called the Canadian Radio Broadcasting Company. It would be financed, as the BBC was, by an annual licence fee of $3, paid by subscribers, and a $1 million annual subsidy from the public till.

The enabling legislation was introduced in 1932 by Prime Minister R.B. Bennett, and only one vote was cast against the bill. The CRBC was launched, and almost immediately fell flat on its face. For one thing, Canadians could not see why they should buy a licence to listen to Canadian broadcasting, even though the fee was reduced to $2 a year, when they could get the American programs free. For another, the politicians could not keep their hands off the controls, and, during the 1935 election, the CRBC cranked out a series of radio dramas featuring a Mr. Sage, who spent most of his time bad-mouthing the Liberal opposition. It turned out that the scripts were the work of the Conservative ad agency, and when the Liberals won the election, the CRBC was dismantled.

In its place, Prime Minister Mackenzie King erected a Crown corporation, the Canadian Broadcasting Corporation, which made its first broadcast on November 2, 1936.

For the next fifty years the CBC was praised, excoriated, fiddled with, and financed. Every few years, someone would set up a commission or board of enquiry to look into the corporation, and its members would always come away perplexed. For the first twenty-two years of its existence, the CBC was both the Crown corporation responsible for public broadcasting and the regulator responsible for all broadcasting, including the granting of licences and the processing of complaints. The private broadcasters didn't like this much; they thought it smacked of conflict of interest, although all it signalled was that the national broadcaster is not like other broadcasters. No one seems to take it amiss that the Bank of England performs a parallel role in banking. But nothing was done until Conservative leader John Diefenbaker complained that he was being ill-used by the network during the 1957 and 1958 federal elections. He was told to take his complaint to the CBC, which proved to be unsympathetic.

Diefenbaker won the 1958 election and promptly took action. The Fowler Commission, established to look into broadcasting in Canada, suggested dividing the broadcast functions of the CBC from its regulatory ones. In response, Diefenbaker created the Board of Broadcast Governors (BBG) and stuffed it with political appointees. It had two tasks: to press for more Canadian content on the airwaves, and to regulate the airwaves and hand out licences. It had little luck with either. The private broadcasters, Tories almost to a man, were outraged by the BBG's call for 55 per cent Canadian content. Since we were now in the world of television — the first broadcast in French, on September 6, 1952, was followed by the first in English two days later — the content rules were taking money out of the pockets of the private broadcasters who had backed the Conservatives in the first place. Their notion was always to produce programs at the lowest possible cost, even if that mean running nothing but imported schlock, and sell them at the highest possible gain.

The BBG had other matters on its mind. The patronage appointments undermined its authority to issue and control broadcast licences, and when the CBC refused to take orders from the regulator, there was no choice but to appoint another investigation. In due course it reported that what was really needed was a body to shore up Canadian content and to regulate the airwaves. The Canadian Radio-Television Commission (CRTC) was duly established in 1968, under a Liberal government, and headed by a staunch Liberal, Pierre Juneau (now saluted in the Juno awards). An aggressive gent who went on to become a prime ministerial aide to Pierre Trudeau, a cabinet minister (briefly), a Liberal candidate (disastrously), and then president of the CBC, Juneau possessed the ability to squeeze more and more money out of the government with each passing budget. He left the corporation defenceless against the charge that it was at least as much motivated by politics as the public good, and made it difficult to resist the onslaught begun by the Conservative government of Brian Mulroney in the mid-1980s.

Canada has had only three prime ministers who were clearly in favour of the CBC: R.B. Bennett, Mackenzie King, and, at least initially, Lester Pearson. Every other leader has regarded the national broadcaster with sullen disapproval or outright rage.*

---

*During the 1997 election campaign, Jean Chrétien blamed the CBC for making him appear heartless in a question-and-answer panel on the subject of unemployment. His handlers made the point to the press that the damn leftist loonies in charge of the CBC had had the temerity to find a questioner who knew how to ask an effective question.

Investigative journalism that hurts

In part, the increasing hostility of the politicians to their own broadcaster came about because, as the CBC became more proficient in news-gathering, it was always offending the powers that be. Investigation was part of its job, and no one said the powers had to like it. But the overall result was to make the funding of the national broadcaster somewhat problematic.

Pearson promised the CBC stable funding in 1965: it would know several years ahead what money it would have for capital as well as operating expenses. Thirty-three years later, stable funding is being promised again — but the corporation, in the meantime, has suffered what may be mortal blows, both in the way it is financed and in the way it is directed. Let us consider the second matter first.

The CBC's board of directors has always been heavily political, with party hacks far exceeding merit appointments. This imbalance did not matter so much when things were going well, for the CBC, like most corporations, is run by its management, not its directors. When the CBC comes under fire, however, this indifference becomes crucial — and disastrous. In 1985–86, when the Conservatives began to hack away at the government apportionment, causing the demolition of much fine regional programming and delaying the replacement of the corporation's mouldering capital plant, the directors seemed nonplussed. Mavor Moore, a long-time supporter of public broadcasting, was moved to observe:

> Appointment by patronage leads boards of trustees to abdicate up or down — to hand their power over to those who know the territory, the operating staff, or to give it back to the government of the day. The present CBC board of directors cannot, apparently, make up its mind which way to abdicate.[18]

It remained only to replace a gaggle of do-nothing directors with a gaggle of those who supported free enterprise, entrepreneurship, and competitiveness. The CBC presidency was given to Perrin Beatty, a high priest of Torydom, and the shaft was given to the rest. At the same time, and under the same auspices, the CBC began hiring and promoting executives who had anywhere from a modest to a non-existent attachment to the CBC's mandate as a public broadcaster. Most of them came from private broadcasting, and they thought of the dear old corp as just another competitor in the marketplace, so it was natural for them to organize television around commercials. They needed American programs to attract large audiences and lucrative ads. When they were confronted with the argument that the public network looked just like the private networks, they explained that, to have the ads, they had to have the schlock.

It became harder and harder to advance reasons why the public should put up money to fund another CTV clone. And, because CBC radio shared the shrinking budget and slinking leadership of the entire corporation, it, too, suffered along with the television network. Between 1985 and 1995, funding to the CBC was cut by 47 per cent and its staff was cut in half. There were protests, persistent but polite in the Canadian way, but they were nearly always mounted on behalf of CBC radio — with good reason. CBC radio is unlike anything else on the continent — U.S. public radio is not a patch on it — whereas CBC television, while it has some excellent programs, is absolutely indistinguishable, 90 per cent of the time, from the flood of formulaic junk that washes over the border.

Television producer John Kennedy, who spent almost his entire working career with CBC television, looks back on the early days this way:

> CBC-TV was great in its period of greatest growth — vitality, novelty, excitement, creativity. All the congenial conditions were there — keeping up with the Yanks and the rest of the world, and giving a tremendous impetus to creativity in a brand-new medium. It provided the country with a talent base that contributed to the growth of the entire communciations industry.
>
> The idea of the public broadcaster was great — and should continue. The CBC was the hothouse that provided the place where talent of all kinds could be employed — in all provinces — and on a local or regional or national stage, as required. And in as many languages as were deemed necessary.
>
> The public broadcaster brought the idea of "service" as a

primary goal. Get the signal out to everyone, everywhere. I think at first there was more concern with getting that signal everywhere because everyone would be paying for it. What programming that signal would carry was a secondary consideration.

The mandate was incredibly huge and undo-able. But by God, we tried. My early bosses seemed to me to be people of taste, culture and intellect who wanted good programming for many audiences, and spent a good deal of their time talking about how to accomplish it. Those reflective program bosses were listened to, and the organization was small enough and inefficient enough — and cheap enough — that commercial pressures and audience ratings weren't the top priorities.

Everything is so different now . . . [19]

Kennedy is describing the dilemma at the heart of the CBC: when it became responsive to commercial pressures and audience ratings, it lost its mandate. Why should Canadians pay $1 billion a year — or, now, $854 million — to fund what is essentially another private broadcaster? In 1996, when the federal government cut another $108.8 million from the parliamentary appropriation to the CBC, it was earning $250 million by flogging ads on television.[20] This money appeared to determine more than half the programming, which included vast segments of imported American shows.

The public broadcaster was put in place to do what no private broadcaster could do: to reflect the nation back to itself, and to carry its signals where no one else wanted to go. In theory, nothing has changed. The airwaves are still public, not private, property. The task of carrying a broadcast signal to the far corners of the nation, in a number of languages, is still a public, not a private, responsibility. The goal of serving a national purpose through broadcasting is still a federal goal — it doesn't even belong to the provincial public broadcasters, who were set up to provide educational broadcasting. The defensive purpose of building, operating, and financing a national operator, to keep us from being overwhelmed by private American broadcasting, remains at least as crucial as it was in 1932. All that has changed is that we no longer see any need to pay any money for it.

The CRTC as the national regulator

Broadcast regulation is, and always has been, quixotic, uneven, and highly political. The CRTC (now the Canadian Radio-television and Telecommunications Corporation), which was given the legal obligation to enforce broadcast rules and to see that licensees lived up to the lofty promises they made when they filed their applications, always seems to have other matters on its mind. The broadcast equivalent of "Of course I'll respect you in the morning" is "Of course my network will broadcast more Canadian programming, and of the highest quality, too." But when morning comes, the rascals have scampered off, leaving nothing but a crushed rose upon the pillow — until the time for renewal rolls around, when they turn up with candy and perfume and a new set of promises. No broadcaster, to my knowledge, has ever lost a licence for refusing to live up to the commitments made when the licence was issued or renewed. The CRTC simply issues papal dispensations after the fact and asks the broadcaster to try harder next time. When a broadcast licence comes up for renewal, no outsider is allowed to muscle in with a claim that he could do a better job. The licence holder reapplies, apologizes for what he did during the last term — or boasts about it — and walks away with his renewal.

Moreover, it never seems to occur to the people who run the CRTC that the national broadcaster should be given preference over private broadcasters when licences are under discussion. Yet we founded the CBC to do the job the private sector could not do; we poured billions of dollars, over the years, into its coffers; and it is an important instrument of public policy. But to the CRTC, it's just another hick with its hand out.

This view led the CRTC not only to license the importation of whole American networks on cable, when cable became the major force in the market, but to license more private Canadian stations in the major urban markets. And every time a new broadcaster appeared, the American content on Canadian airwaves went up once again. The creation of the Global network, for example, seemed to have been motivated by the CRTC's desire to see how many American game shows could be crammed on the air before something collapsed.

The licensing of pay television, in 1982, was handled in exactly the same way. The CRTC began by allotting licences to two national and three regional pay-TV networks. The expansion of pay TV has brought us shopping networks, movie networks, and even cartoon networks, onto which are tagged, from time to time, tiny slices of CBC programming.

It is the view of the CRTC's present chairperson, Françoise Bertrand, that the entire cultural sector will shortly be deregulated and that all Canadian content regulations will disappear. "It will. We all know that," she said.[21] With friends like Bertrand, the CBC has no need of enemies.

The CBC costs us about $28 per capita per annum to operate — about the price of three movie tickets per Canadian. If we cannot afford that — a frequent argument — we probably cannot afford the messy business of being a nation.

Publish and perish

At least broadcasting has escaped the direct charge that support to its programs constitutes unfair trade practice. Such accusations have begun to devil the film, magazine, and book publishing industries in this country.

For a brief period in the Mulroney regime, Marcel Masse, an aggressive nationalist, was in charge of cultural matters. As minister of communications, Masse was concerned in 1984 when Prentice Hall, a large American publisher, was taken over by Gulf + Western, a massive entertainment conglomerate that included Simon & Schuster and Paramount Pictures, soon after Mulroney's announcement that Canada was "open for business."[22]

Prentice Hall had a Canadian subsidiary, which was governed by Canadian regulations, so the question came up whether Gulf + Western would be allowed to swallow Prentice Hall Canada with no questions asked. At the time, we had a body, Investment Canada, since disbanded, which was supposed to rule on these matters. On July 6, 1985, Masse issued what came to be called the Baie Comeau policy: in an indirect takeover of this kind, Gulf + Western would have to sell at least 51 per cent of Prentice Hall Canada to Canadians within two years. Marci McDonald, in her book *Yankee Doodle Dandy*, details with loving rage what happened next. To make a long story short, not much. Masse's own department ignored the directive. Richard Snyder, the U.S. president of Simon & Schuster, came up to Ottawa to tell us that Canada had no right to interfere with what an American company did, just because it happened to take place in Canada. And our Washington ambassador, Allan Gotlieb, wrote a long memo which argued the American case with such vigour that "Masse felt Gotlieb had forgotten who he was working for."[23]

Shortly after that, RCMP officers turned up in Masse's riding with a warrant to search his campaign records, an incident, he suggested to Mcdonald, that may have been directly connected to the case. In any event, he resigned for three months while his records were ransacked, his name cleared, and he was restored to cabinet. By that time, the battle was over. In his absence, Gulf + Western had hired Frank Moores, Mulroney's friend and Ottawa's top lobbyist, to smooth the way. The takeover was approved on March 12, 1986, making Gulf + Western the largest presence in Canadian publishing.

Gulf + Western also acquired Ginn Canada, a large textbook publisher, after the Baie Comeau policy was announced and supposedly in place. (The Prentice Hall case was complicated by the argument that it was retroactive law.) In this case, Gulf + Western agreed to sell 51 per cent of the shares to Canadians within two years, and then simply ignored the promise. Two Canadian publishers tried to buy the shares, but were rebuffed. Then Gulf + Western announced, in March 1988, when the deadline was up, that no acceptable offers had come forward, so it was keeping Ginn.

The Free Trade Agreement, which was being negotiated at this time, had raised a lot of concern among certain groups about the viability of Canadian culture if it was left unprotected under the agreement. The government finally took the stand that "culture was not on the table."[24] As part of this arrangement, Ottawa agreed that it would buy any subsidiary in the cultural sector if, in the course of a takeover, it had forced divestiture on an American firm.

Accordingly, the Canada Development Investment Corporation, the Crown charged with handling privatization, offered to buy control of Ginn from Gulf + Western, a process that took three years. It seems there was another deal on the side, a secret understanding that if the Baie Comeau policy was changed, Gulf + Western would have the right to buy back the shares. It was never written down, but was one of those understood things. Matters were made more complex by the fact that Canada kept shedding communications ministers. Masse quit in rage and frustration. He was replaced by Flora MacDonald, who was in turn replaced after the 1988 election by Perrin Beatty. In January 1992 Beatty pronounced the Baie Comeau policy to be officially dead, instead of merely inoperative. Soon after, Ottawa sold its shares in Ginn to Gulf + Western for the same price it had paid for them,[25] and the whole notion that Canada had any control over its publishing industry was gone. The Liberals vowed that they would reverse this policy, but, once in power, forgot entirely about it.

In the same way, attempts to defend the Canadian film industry came to naught. Flora MacDonald made one valiant attempt in February 1987, when the free trade talks were coming to a boil. She announced new legislation that would establish a licensing procedure to ensure that Canadian films got more distribution. She had Mulroney's backing, for one flickering moment, and he raised the matter with Ronald Reagan. Mulroney asked the president how he would feel if "the Russians had 97 per cent of the screen time in the United States, and Hollywood had 3 per cent?"[26] Startled, Reagan said he would have to think about that.

Shortly thereafter, Jack Valenti, the American film industry lobbyist, landed in MacDonald's office and ticked her off for interfering in business. At the same time, another one of those side deals was stuck into the Free Trade Agreement. Although culture was not to be included in the agreement, the United States reserved the right, if Canada took any action in the cultural sector that harmed an American firm, to take retaliation in any field of trade against Canada.[27]

With this persuasion, no action has been forthcoming. When MacDonald's film bill finally reached the House of Commons, it had no teeth.

A similar arrangement was imbedded in Article 2005 of the 1995 North American Free Trade Agreement (NAFTA). There, we abandoned not only film but any cultural sector from any effective regulations that might protect it. A brief attempt to give preferential treatment to a Canadian speciality channel in 1995, by dropping yet another of the American country-music channels, was hastily abandoned by the CRTC when Mickey Kantor, the U.S. trade representative, threatened a full-blown trade war.[28] To the Americans, culture is the entertainment business, nothing more, and it is wrong, dumb, and unfair to interfere with the take at the ticket box, or anywhere else, on the fiddling grounds that we might want to preserve something of our own.

When the General Agreement on Tariffs and Trade (GATT) was washed away into the World Trade Organization (WTO) in 1994, this process was taken a step further. The WTO provides no mechanism by which culture can be protected in any way. Under the FTA and the North American Free Trade Agreement, its big brother, if we were dumb enough to try to protect ourselves, the Americans could retaliate. Under the WTO — and under the Multilateral Agreement on Investment (MAI), now being negotiated to govern financial arrangements among nations — the subject does not even come up. Culture is showbiz, that's all, and any arrangements about who spends money on what will be free of the taint of government largesse.

Let the market decide. Well, it's an argument, and it underlines the main argument of this book: we can let the market decide or we can interfere, by way of the state. There is no middle course. And, when we cripple the instruments of state intervention, we are not saving money. We are deciding that we can no longer afford to be a nation.

This debate, if it is one any more, flourished briefly when the Liberals made a pitiable attempt to protect the magazine sector in 1996. Canadian magazine publishers account for only 20 per cent of English-language newsstand sales,[31] so they get a little anxious when the Americans, as they did with *Sports Illustrated*, found a loophole in Canadian law. The law said that an advertiser could not write off, against Canadian income, money spent to advertise in a magazine that was not published in Canada. The reason was simple: an American magazine, with a market about fifteen times the Canadian English-language market, has a huge cost advantage over any Canadian publication. What could be simpler than to send the magazine across the border full of ads that were priced in a way that no Canadian publisher could match? It was this inequity that the law sought to eradicate — and did, for a time. But *Sports Illustrated* got the bright idea of beaming the contents over the border, publishing them in Richmond Hill, Ontario, and declaring itself, for these purposes, to be a Canadian magazine.

When Ottawa imposed an 80 per cent duty on profits gained through this technique, the Americans laid a complaint before the WTO, where culture has no protection whatever. They argued that no protection could be extended to any Canadian magazine, which was "a product," and nothing more.[30] They won, and Canada appealed the ruling, but it was a waste of time. Canada hastened to comply, removing all effective protection from the magazine industry.

If we own only 20 per cent of the market now, we haven't much to lose.

Bringing the libraries to book

We still have our libraries — so far. In Fenelon Falls, Ontario, the small village that serves as the metropolis where I live, civic authorities cut the library hours by 5 per cent, then cut the pay by 5 per cent, and then fired the only trained librarian on the staff because she was, well, a librarian. Professional librarians earn more than the hourly help, and even though this librarian offered to work fewer hours, she was let go. In Edmonton, people are charged a $12 annual fee just to belong to the library — a tactic that hurts only the people who really *need* that institution. The Edmonton central library was also renamed for an oil company president, to coax in a donation, thus implanting in the city's young minds how important it is to grease the cultural skids.

In Toronto the reference library on Yonge Street has been under so much pressure, with shorter hours, less help, and a smaller acquisitions budget, that you are as likely to get a snarl as a smile if you ask one of the hired help for help. So far, the library has lost 30 per cent of its budget, which meant cutting 140 jobs, trimming its collection, hacking its acquisitions of new books, and cancelling more than 1,000 periodicals.[31]

Libraries are used by 34 per cent of adult Canadians.[32] Yet the hatchetmen do not leave them alone because they themselves don't read books. Mike Harris, asked about the books he was reading, could only reply that he had read *Mister Silly* to his son.

Libraries receive very little support from the federal government, more from the provinces, and most from municipal governments. Table 5 in the Appendix shows that the towns and cities contribute more than $1 billion a year to libraries. This combination of circumstances means that when the axe began to fall, the people's representatives who had the most direct interest in the process were kept the furthest from the decisions. Ottawa cut the provinces, the provinces cut the municipalities, and they hacked the libraries, along with everything else.

In Ontario, where the economics of sadism prevail, the Harris government announced that it was going to cut the entire, meagre, $18 million per annum that it doles out to the library system. In late 1997, when it changed its mind and restored the money, librarians stood up at one of their meetings, and cheered.[33] When the most important custodians of our culture cheer because the government has agreed not to cut a sum that amounts to less than $2 per capita per annum, we are in trouble. In the meantime, the main provincial cultural funder in the province, the Ontario Arts Council, had $19 million lopped off its budget.

In the culture sector, we have had the same reverse generosity that has been applied elsewhere. The federal government, after five steady years of slashing grants to the Canada Council, suddenly turned around in 1997 and doled out another $25 million to that beleaguered organization. In 1992 the Canada Council's budget was $108 million; then it was hacked down, year by year, to $88 million.[34] In 1997–98 it will come in at $113 million, which, in constant dollar terms, is a little better — about $5 million better — than the 1988 level, for a population that has increased by about three million people. In the meantime, thousands of projects have disappeared, and quite a few cultural groups that would be eligible for the new money have disappeared. Others are grateful for the new help, but have very little reason to be. The National Ballet of Canada, for example, gets an extra $400,000 — but it lost $1 million per year in government support in the meantime. Are we to celebrate or grieve these late spasms of generosity?

The same pattern we have seen elsewhere has repeated itself all across the cultural sector: state aid, whatever its merits, is just too expensive any more. It has also been suggested that it inter-feres with the greater glory of our day, globalization. And we have bought the entire argument without ever seriously exam-ining its underlying premise, or asking ourselves what we really can afford as a nation.

In the next chapter, we will see how this approach sent our national transportation system into the ditch.

The National Dream Just
Went Off the Track

The national dream of iron horses, steel rails and
steam is dead. The national dream today is to try to
protect the integrity of social programs such as the
Canada Pension Plan and medicare. Railroads are
just another way of moving people and goods. They
don't get my heart going pitty-pat or anything.
— Transport Minister Doug Young, June 1994

*Lévis, the bustling municipality just across the river from Quebec City,
was named for François-Gaston, Duc de Lévis, the man who took over
from the Marquis de Montcalm when that brave but not overly bright
officer succumbed to his wounds shortly after the Battle of the Plains
of Abraham in 1759.*

*Today, in the middle of Lévis stands a splendid railway station. It
once served as the old Canadian National station, but was rebuilt, at
a cost of $3 million, to serve rail, bus, and even ferry passengers. But
here is the joke, which I think the old duke might appreciate as he
mutters: "Plus ça change, plus ça reste la même chose." The railway
line, unless somebody does something drastic pretty soon, will no longer
connect to the station.*

A decade ago, Canadian National applied to the National

Transportation Agency (now the Canadian Transportation Agency) for permission to abandon about 10 kilometres of track running to this station from the main line outside town. CN was not running any passenger traffic on the line any more — only freight. The way the law works, if you are transporting passengers, you have to go through an elaborate process to take a piece of railway out of service; but if you are hauling freight, it is much easier. Only VIA Rail was moving passengers, albeit on the CN track, so when CN sought to drop the line, it was given permission to do so. The idea was that another station would be constructed outside town, and the railway passengers could use that.

The Quebec government, which had put up a lot of money for the new downtown station, was displeased. Remove the trains, and much of the station's business would disappear. Quebec had been brought into the process by Ottawa on the grounds that there would be rail passengers, but that turned out to be just another broken promise. So Quebec blocked the suburban alternative by the simple process of refusing the planning permissions necessary to build roads and other facilities. The feds could build a terminal and get trains to it, but they couldn't get people in or out.

VIA came up with another location, out in Ste-Foy, but the only way they could get their trains there was to back them across the Quebec City bridge. The consulting engineers advised against that idea.

CN, however, would not give up and reapplied for permission to abandon its chunk of line. In due course, permission was granted, with effect as of February 1997. But the date came and went, after a local member of parliament and a provincial cabinet minister came out strongly against VIA's Ste-Foy scheme. There is still no decision. VIA has a mandate to bring passengers here, but no line. The CN has the line, but no wish to see passenger trains running over it. Quebec wants the station downtown. Ottawa wants it out in the suburbs. So Quebec and Ottawa block each other, and nothing has been settled for about ten years.

What we have here is Canadian transportation policy at its most typical; a process in which everything conspires to keep anyone from getting anywhere.

In contrast to the other areas of national life we have been considering so far, transportation in Canada is not something in which governments only recently came to play a large role. There always has been a "welfare state" when it came to the business of moving people and goods around, although it has never been acknowledged. When the attack on "government interference" came in this sector, it was seen simply as another area of society where private enterprise would act more effectively than the state. But the change is something far more than that: it is a reversal of the pre-eminence of the state for at least the past two centuries.

Getting large numbers of Canadians to and from the far reaches of the land seemed to call for public enterprise, for the very good reason that private enterprise shunned much of the work. If it didn't return a profit, and much necessary transport does not, the investors were not interested. From time to time government went through the motions of allowing private enterprise to move people while providing most of the funding, but in such situations the private sector usually ran around the outside, picking up the profits and complaining about government interference. In the latter part of the twentieth century, scornful of government and bedazzled by private enterprise, we have withdrawn much of the funding that made a national transportation policy work. As a result, travel is cheaper, better, and more comfortable for a few of us, but, for the majority, it is unreliable, inconvenient, and expensive. This is the thread that runs through transport history, beginning in the days when we moved about by water, through the grand days of railroading, and into our own time, where every mode of transportation depends heavily on government but nobody wants to say so. When the private entrepreneurs fell on their faces, or, as happened a regrettable number of times, disappeared with government funds tucked into their wallets, then, and only then, did we call in state enterprise.

The Welland Canal was private; the spending, public

Take the Welland Canal, the brainchild of William Hamilton Merritt, who was born in upper New York State in 1793 but came to Upper Canada when he was a lad of five. He fought on our side in the War of 1812 and was taken prisoner during the Battle of Lundy's Lane, near Niagara Falls. After the war, he got hold of a piece of property near the mouth of Twelve Mile Creek, on the high ridge that runs between Lakes Ontario and Erie. Walking about this land one day in 1818 it occurred to him that if someone were to carve a canal between the two lakes, it would be a whole lot easier to move the produce of western Canada, and the western United States, to market. A nice side effect would be a vast improvement in the value of his land, as well as a speedy way to ship the produce of the whisky distillery he owned nearby. One day he went out with a spirit level to work out the height of land to be overcome to gain water transport for his business. He measured it as 30 feet, though in fact it was 60 feet. Merritt was not a surveyor, but a shopkeeper. Except for this blunder of measurement, which made the task of carving a canal through the ridge seem much easier than it would prove to be, he might never have gone ahead with the project.[1]

Merritt, who had married the daughter of a New York senator and regarded the American way of doing things as the only proper way, was determined to build his canal, from Twelve Mile Creek to Welland, entirely with private capital. It would follow the example of the Erie Canal, he said, allowing his adopted province to "witness the same spirit of enterprise here that our neighbours, the Americans, possess to so eminent a degree." It would, moreover, be built "without taxing the country one farthing."[2] Actually, the Erie Canal was built almost entirely by state funding, but Merritt either didn't know that or chose to ignore it.

Merritt's company was incorporated in January 1824 by a provincial legislature grateful that the whole business was going to be paid for elsewhere, but, alas, it was not to be. As the work went forward, at much greater cost than anticipated, the government was gradually sucked into the financing. First, there was a land grant in 1825; then a series of loans in 1826 and 1827, until the project deteriorated into "a privately-controlled institution for the disbursement of public funds,"[3] a phrase that covers a regrettable number of Canadian undertakings.

In the meantime, the canal was a shoddy mess. Because of the need to scamp on construction, the banks were never properly protected against erosion and tended to cave in. No proper books were ever kept on the operation, although the rebellious William Lyon Mackenzie, who thought the whole process should have been handled by government in the first place, wrote that "economy and the Welland Canal are as far apart as earth and heaven."[4]

In 1828 the Deep Cut collapsed, necessitating another infusion of public funds, and when the canal opened in 1829, it immediately began to leak money. The locks and dams required continual, expensive maintenance, far above anything that could be covered by the tolls levied on shipping, so the government had to come to the rescue again, investing money into the company by buying shares. By 1836 the major shareholders of the Welland Canal Company were the governments of Upper and Lower Canada, which became the United Province of Canada in 1841.

By that time, even the massive infusions of funding — more than £400,000 — were not enough; the company teetered on the edge of bankruptcy and the waterway was still "a rickety, ramshackle affair."[5] The new province had to step in, dissolve the company, and take over the rebuilding of the canal, which was not completed until 1887.

The Rideau Canal, built between 1826 and 1832, was entirely a government operation. It was intended for military use in the event of war with the Yankees. The work was overseen by the Royal Engineers under Colonel John By, and the canal ran from Bytown, now Ottawa, to Kingston, and cost about £1 million, a huge sum in those days. But this figure was much less than the Welland cost in the end, and the facility was built so sturdily that many of its locks are still in operation today.

This comparison does not prove that government is more effective and efficient than private enterprise. But it surely allows us to consider whether the constantly reiterated argument to the contrary is open to question.

A mountain range of rascality

When "the mania for canalling"[6] turned into a mania for rail-roading, the same phenomenon of public funding and private building continued. The Grand Trunk Railway was first proposed as a government enterprise in the mid-1840s but was quickly turned over to a gang of thugs headed by the colourful Sir Francis Hincks, then the finance minister of the United Province of Canada.[7] Hincks went over to England to raise financing for the government-built railway envisioned in the legislation passed in 1850, but he got into the hands of an English contracting firm called Peto, Brassey, Betts and Jackson. Before long a private company was formed, the Grand Trunk Railway Company, and then this company gave Peto and colleagues the contract to build the railway.

Sir Francis came home with a smile on his face and shares worth £50,000 in the new company in his portfolio, shares that had been paid for by Peto. There was an investigation, but the Speaker of the Legislative Council, John Ross, who happened to be president of the Grand Trunk Railway, said that Sir Francis had done nothing wrong. He had no personal interest in the stock, the official report on the matter concluded, for it had been put in his name without his knowledge. If cabinet ministers were speculating in the railway, "everyone else who could do so was doing likewise." Sir Francis gave up his stock — and bought some more, but out of his own money. Peto and pals kept the contract to build the railway, and it remained a private corporation. The company was denationalized before it had even been nationalized; that would come later.

The Grand Trunk ran between Toronto and Montreal, and then on to the Atlantic, to get Canadian products overseas. It was capitalized at £9.5 million, of which about one-third was guaranteed by the government. The rest of the funds were raised on the basis of a prospectus written by three company stockholders, who were also cabinet ministers — Sir Francis, John Ross, and Alexander Galt. They promised shareholders annual dividends of 11.5 per cent, but these payments were never forthcoming.

Galt and a group of his cronies merged a dud railway called the St. Lawrence and Atlantic, at a nice profit to themselves, into the Grand Trunk, which then had to spend about £200,000 completing it. And so it went; the only people who gained on Grand Trunk stock were insiders, who made their profits mostly by siphoning off the money as fast as it poured in from the shareholders. The construction work on both the Grand Trunk and its subsidiary, the Great Western, which ran across southern Ontario, was scamped so badly that the lines were unsafe and accidents were common. In 1854 there were nineteen serious accidents on the Great Western; in one of these, sixty people died when a trestle over the Desjardins Canal collapsed: it should have been built of oak, but instead was built of cheaper pine.[8] During the investigation, the company directors explained that they could have done no wrong, so the tragedy must be laid at the feet of "Providence."[9] Among those killed was Samuel Zimmerman, the man in charge of construction.

The Grand Trunk was incorporated in 1853. By 1855 it was tottering, and by 1860 it was virtually bankrupt. It was a ward of the state from that time on, supported entirely by grants, subsidies, and loans. Yet it continued to be a private corporation, in name only.

Another of these private-public ventures was the Intercolonial Railway, which the Maritimers hoped would be funded entirely by Queen Victoria.[10] In 1846 the legislatures of Nova Scotia and New Brunswick sent a petition to London, asking Her Majesty to grant £3 million to build a line from Halifax to Quebec City through Saint John. The maintenance of British authority, she was assured, depended on construction of the Intercolonial. The queen was not impressed, although it was not until 1850 that her refusal was made definite.

Over the next seven years, various individuals and groups attempted to put together a series of railways. Others devised schemes to join the provinces to the United States, complete with a number of north-south railways. Finally, a line was built from Halifax to Truro in 1857 as a private track, but with government funding. Alas, "gross receipts were pocketed by conductors and station agents,"[11] and the company was soon in grave financial difficulty. New Brunswick started a private line as well, which, with the high-sounding title of the European and North American Railway Company of Saint John, proceeded to skim quite a few stock speculators, but to lay no tracks. The New

Brunswick government took it over, borrowed £800,000 from Baring Brothers, and managed to get a line from Saint John to Shediac by 1860 — about 125 kilometres. At the same time, another private line, the St Andrews–Quebec Railway, had laid about 80 kilometres of track. It was going to be a long haul.

When the delegates from the Canadas arrived to talk about Confederation in 1864, the Maritimers quickly pointed out that unless something was done to link their markets with central Canada, they might as well join the United States now, as wait to be absorbed, and the Intercolonial was made a condition of Confederation. Accordingly, the dominion government took on the task and, by 1879, had finished a railroad from Montreal to Halifax and from Saint John to Sydney, Nova Scotia. Canada had its first government railway. It did not make any money, but it made an important, if not crucial, contribution to the nation.

Our first transcontinental railway, our "national dream," was not a government railway, unless we look at who contributed most of the money. Historian J. Bartlet Brebner asserts that "the most casual view of the first six years of its financial history refutes any claim that it was a private corporation."[12]

The Canadian Pacific was also a condition of Confederation, demanded, this time, by British Columbia. In return for building a railway to the west coast within ten years from July 20, 1871, the Canadian Pacific Railway Company was given subsidies of $25 million in cash. It also had 25 million acres of land "fit for settlement" within 24 miles of the right of way across the prairies and a monopoly of "all rails running from the Red River to the United States border."[13] Of course, the $25 million was just the beginning; in the end, the Canadian government put up $261,500,000, or $120,000 per mile, to build the CPR, on top of another $245 million in loan guarantees. There were also tax and duty exemptions, mineral and timber rights, municipal terminal grants, and water facilities. The company's own contribution, in contrast, was about $100 million.[14] Despite this disparity of investment, the CPR never felt inclined to share any of its profits with its chief funder. Rather, the company was so corrupt that it brought down the Macdonald government in 1872. Sir John's undoing was a telegram he sent to John C. Abbott, the CPR lawyer, demanding "another ten thousand" in election expenses right away.[15] A contemporary observer, David Mills, commented: "Great railway corporations are the most dangerous enemies popular government ever had."[16]

But they were dangerous friends, too. Probably the most astute contemporary comment on these matters came from Sir Richard Cartwright, who broke with Macdonald over the Pacific Scandal and became the opposition finance critic. Detailing one of the many land deals that accompanied railway development, which he described as "discreditable, corrupt and scandalous," Cartwright went on to say:

> Every practical man knows perfectly well that in most cases of the kind which are coming before us, the facts are apt, as a rule, to be exceedingly well covered . . . In fact, Mr. Speaker, unless the thieves fall out, unless there is a quarrel over the division of the plunder . . . it is the rarest thing to obtain absolute and complete proof.[17]

Railway financing, he concluded, was "a mountain range of undiscovered, well-developed rascality." The difficulty the financiers faced in the case of the CPR was that the mountain range was discovered.

The Grand Trunk, and grand theft

At least the CPR got the railroad built from sea to sea and began to generate cash carting immigrants to the west and their produce to the east. This success set off stirrings of envy in the breasts of two other lines — the Grand Trunk and the Canadian Northern, which ran through northern Ontario and Manitoba. They wanted a piece of the immigrant action. The CPR was the Tory line, while the other two were owned mainly by Liberals. The prime minister, Sir Wilfrid Laurier, was also a Liberal. In the name of competitive free enterprise, he approved of the two other railways building parallel lines to the Pacific, and his government helped them along by building the National Trans-Continental line from Moncton to Winnipeg via Quebec City and leasing it to the Grand Trunk Pacific, the Grand Trunk's western subsidiary. In addition, the government would subsidize the other railways.

By this time, the government had committed itself to spending more than $100 million. Laurier's railways minister, Andrew G. Blair, argued that if the government was going to foot the bill, it should own the railways.[18] When Laurier dismissed this argument, on the grounds that everyone knew that private enterprise was more efficient than government, Blair resigned. The two new western lines were built, but badly, and quickly ran into huge debt. There was just not enough traffic to support three cross-country railways. Then the Grand Trunk repudiated its lease on the National Trans-Continental. Sir Robert Borden, who had succeeded Laurier, found himself lumbered with a railway he didn't want. A royal commission appointed to look at the railway situation suggested that Ottawa should take over the entire system. Borden refused.

Circumstances, however, forced his hand. The Canadian Northern was on the verge of bankruptcy, and if it went it would take with it the Canadian Bank of Commerce, which had loaned it all the money that didn't come from government. The government had little choice but to nationalize the Canadian Northern in 1917. Now Borden had two railways he didn't want. Two years later, he added a third, when the Grand Trunk ordered its subsidiary, the Grand Trunk Pacific, to cease operations. This closure would not only cost thousands of jobs but would swallow all the money the government had put into the venture — and was still putting in. By 1916 the government had invested $159,882,000 directly in the Grand Trunk Pacific.[19] To prevent disaster, to say nothing of political embarrassment, the line was nationalized under the authority of the War Measures Act, passed early in the First World War. Finally, Ottawa took over the Grand Trunk itself, which was virtually bankrupt, because its lines were necessary to make a continental railway of the pieces the government already owned. This solution led to a prolonged court battle when the Grand Trunk shareholders wanted to be paid for their shares, although an arbitration board held they were worthless.

The Canadian National Railway Act was passed in 1919. It cobbled the Grand Trunk, Canadian Northern, Grand Trunk Pacific, and Intercontinental into one sea-to-sea railway, which, because of the court cases, did not get rolling until 1923.

The Canadian National Railways began life with long-term interest-bearing debts of $2 billion — about $20 billion in current funds — and an annual deficit of $283 million.[20] Through application and hard work, it managed to push the debt up to $2.2 billion over the next fifty-four years; in many years its interest payments were $130 million a year, more than its operating costs. It never made money. This fact proved to many economists that government ownership always leads to debt. In truth, however, it showed the opposite: debt, when connected to an enterprise necessary to the public weal, often leads to public ownership.

Herschel Hardin put it this way in *A Nation Unaware*:

The CPR, built for political purposes, on government orders and design, as a monopoly by public money and mixed enterprise, came to be seen as a triumph of private enterprise, and the CNR, which took over two irresponsible, bankrupt private roads and other fragmentary lines and made them into a viable system, came to be considered a public enterprise white elephant.[21]

The People's Airline, more or less

We got a publicly owned airline by accident, or, more accurately, by a fit of absence of mind. In the early 1930s, in the midst of the Great Depression, everyone agreed we, like the Americans, ought to have an airline that could carry mail from coast to coast. The post office, then a government department, wanted to cash in on the money to be made by airmail, and an airline would provide much-needed economic activity and jobs. Moreover, the Americans were expanding their air services fast, so, if we didn't get an east-to-west service going soon, it would be overtaken, as broadcasting was then being overtaken, by the south-to-north movement led by the Americans. Canadian Airways, owned by James Richardson of Winnipeg, was the obvious private contender for such a project — his airline moved 122,000 pounds of mail, 1.2 million pounds of freight, and 10,000 passengers in 1928[22] — but it carried one insuperable burden: C.D. Howe couldn't stand Richardson.

Clarence Decatur Howe, the Massachusetts-born entrepreneur

and Mackenzie King's man-of-all work, framed and pushed through the legislation that established Trans-Canada Air Lines, but he always thought of it as a private corporation — his corporation. When an opposition MP reminded him that it was a public enterprise, Howe shot back, "That's not public enterprise; that's *my* enterprise."[23] In short, the major actor in the decision to create the TCA seemed blissfully unaware of the difference between a public and a private corporation and therefore did not, in any literal sense, rationally choose the public over the private corporate instrument. At first Howe proposed a joint venture, with the CNR acting for Ottawa, and the CPR and Canadian Airways providing the expertise and some of the financing, supported by subsidies from Ottawa to get the airline going. The CPR, however, refused to play. Sir Edward Beatty, the chairman, said that the government was in bed with his rival, the CNR, and he could not ask his shareholders to have anything to do with it.

Howe decided, in that case, to go it alone. The government would buy the majority of shares in the new airline, but would leave up to 49.8 per cent available for private interests. None of these shares was ever taken up, in large part because the post office, in return for offering a monopoly of its traffic to the new airline, insisted on a price structure where the return on capital could never exceed 5 per cent per annum. What emerged, almost by accident, was a thoroughly public airline.

By shrewd manoeuvring, the new TCA avoided the danger that it would return more than 5 per cent on its capital for quite a few decades. It took on the task of moving Canadians from coast to coast, of serving areas that it was uneconomical to serve, and of doing in the air what the railways had done on the ground — helping to bind the nation together. It did not, however, open up the North, as its spokesmen and cabinet ministers frequently claimed. Max Ward, in his autobiography, writes: "It wasn't TCA or Air Canada who opened the North, but private companies, including my own, every time. We were the ones who risked our lives, our equipment, our money and our reputations, not the government."[24]

In 1965 Trans-Canada Air Lines became Air Canada. It continued to expand, while continuing to bleed money as a government line until the 1980s. Most of us complained about the People's Airline, though we knew it was a lot safer than the American airlines because it spent the money to get the job done. (But in chapter 12 we see how the People's Airline was transformed into the Airline of Some Other People.)

Ward, whose Wardair Canada Limited was perhaps the best-run airline we have ever known, complains with some reason that government interference and obstructionism kept him from ever making money. He believes, however, that Canada can afford only one airline, if that. He says government should get out of the business and let one private airline rise to the top, without interference. That one efficient airline will, in the end, take over the market.

But how does a privately owned air giant possess more magic than a publicly owned one? Government will still have to set the rules, not only for safety, but for routes, international accords, and even prices. All international airlines belong to organizations that control the pricing structure, and all involve intergovernmental agreements.

The part of Ward's argument that is irrefutable is that air traffic is a natural monopoly. The competition brought on by deregulation in the late 1980s succeeded in providing airfares for some people — those who could afford to winter in Florida, or flit over to France for the weekend — that were so low that they could not possibly make money for the carriers. As a result, the world's airlines, between 1990 and 1993, lost $20 billion, while constantly cutting services to smaller, outlying centres. The bargains, as usual, are for the well-heeled. The airlines are performing exactly the same cross-subsidizing that they accused the national carriers of doing. Instead of using profits from mainline traffic to carry people to and from the hinterland, however, they are using business customers, who cannot use the low-rate charter fares, to subsidize the Florida-flitters. This may make sense for the airline corporations, but not for the nation as a whole.

A fair share of the $20 billion deficit was lost by Canadian airlines — more than $2 billion[25] — until Air Canada succeeded in sloughing off its public service traffic into small markets where the airline was a necessary, but unprofitable, link. On Air Canada, now a private line run by a man from South Carolina, you can fly to London, England, from Toronto much more cheaply than you can to Regina, although Saskatchewan is less than half the distance. And if you want to fly around the Maritimes, be prepared to dogtrack all over the place on schedules designed to fit the airline's needs for aircraft in Toronto, Montreal, and other high-traffic centres.

How did this $20 billion free-for-all benefit the majority of citizens who never fly? More important, how will we gain in the future, if the air is ruled by an increasingly small number of increasingly large companies? Ward says they are the inevitable future of air traffic, especially at today's aircraft prices: the Boeing 747s that Ward bought in 1973 for $24 million now sell for more than $170 million. To Ward, the lesson is clear: "Air transportation is, of necessity, pricing itself out of the mass market, even while the world is relying more and more on air travel."[26] If that is so, how can we move Canadians and their goods economically in the future? Perhaps railways are again the answer.

A necessary mess

Earlier in this chapter we left the railways, with the CNR chugging along, laden with debt, and the CPR, laden with public subsidies but no debt. They were both surrounded by thickets of regulation, including mandatory rate equalization, and subsidies. The Crow's Nest Pass Agreement of 1897, for example, which exchanged a subsidy to build a branch-line through the pass for a reduction on freight charges, became a permanent fixture of Canadian politics. Everybody bitched about it, but it remained part of the price structure for the CNR as well as the CPR. Successive governments, which were run by free enterprise adherents, and a succession of royal commissions looked at the heavy government interference in railroading. They always concluded that it was messy, but necessary.

The railroads were done in by three factors: the automobile, the airlines, and the abandonment of the notion that we needed a national transportation system that worked for most of us, not just some of us.

The automobile age, when it hit us in the period immediately after the First World War, was remarkable not only for the freedom it gave us to go from point to point without a schedule in hand but also for the huge infusion of public funds it cost to provide this private transport. Highways are built mainly by governments — they always have been, always will be. In 1919 government spending on roads, bridges, and ferries came to $22.2 million; forty years later it was $1,067 million, or forty-eight times as much.[27] In 1997 it was $11.3 billion, or about five times as much as we spent on all other transport modes combined.[28] This money continued to multiply, because no one thought of it as government spending, even while other transport modes were being savaged. Today, Canadians make 88 per cent of their overnight trips by car[29] and always think of them as "private trips," but, in fact, they are supported by huge government infrastructures, including the roads and bridges, the traffic police, and the roadside picnic sites.

The British North America Act gave the provinces control of roads, ensuring that we would have ten uncoordinated and completely autonomous regimes at work even in the 1950s, after highways had become the way we moved the majority of Canadians and their freight about. The Trans-Canada Highway, built with federal subsidies that covered up to 90 per cent of the cost in some areas of the country, and opened from Victoria in the west to St. John's in the east in 1965, has no consistency. Anyone who has driven its entire length knows that it ranges from a modern, safe, broad band of commerce — across most of Ontario and Quebec — to a narrow, dangerous slash of roadway, particularly in parts of New Brunswick. Once this highway was built, the federal government virtually withdrew from funding highways. By the end of the 1980s, Ottawa was contributing less than 4 per cent of national highway expenditures.[30] If it ever had any idea of a national highway policy (such as the brief, spectacular, Roads to Resources Program of the Diefenbaker government), it had vanished.

Canada is one of the few major industrial nations without any program to fund highway maintenance and improvement. The inevitable result has been a sad, and dangerous, deterioration in the national highway system. Canada has 900,000 kilometres of highways; 25,000 of these, including the Trans-Canada and other interprovincial and major north-south links, are considered to make up the national system. The Canadian Automobile Association now estimates that 50 per cent of the system is below standard, and this evaluation does not mean merely potholes; many lanes are too narrow for today's traffic, thousands of kilometres have shoulders that are inadequate, and 700 bridges are in need of urgent care.[31] The potential repair bill is $16 billion and rising. The longer the work is put off, the more it is going to cost.

Cutting the ties that bind

In short, a nation that depends on transport has very little in the way of dependable public transport. We have never acknowledged that government activity, whether expressed by outright ownership or merely by subsidies and regulation, is central to the process. Since the cuts to government began, no one has ever stopped to think what the effect might be on the ties that bind. No one has ever stopped to ask, what is the best, cheapest, and most efficient way to move people and goods? The answer would be, by train. Instead, the only question that seems to have been asked is, which mode gets the most direct subsidy from Ottawa? That answer is also the railroad, provided you leave out of the equation all the costs of building and maintaining the highways and airports — which is precisely what is done.

The railways have been trying to get rid of their passengers for decades. As competition from the highways and airlines cut into their traffic, they quickly realized that moving freight was more profitable than moving people. The CNR (now usually referred to as the CN) and the CPR were both making money out of hotels, communications, real estate, and even a little something out of freight. They were losing, steadily, on the passenger services that their contracts — and subsidies — required them to keep up. They began allowing the passenger services to run down, while asking to be freed from the pestilent passengers.

In 1977 they got their wish, with the establishment of VIA Rail Canada Inc., a Crown corporation that took over all the passenger service from the CPR and CN. It began operations on April Fool's Day 1978 with passenger equipment that was, on the average, twenty-five years old, over lines that it did not control itself, and which its godparents were busy closing down as fast as they could get approval from the Canadian Transportation Commission (later, the National Transportation Agency, now the Canadian Transportation Agency). CN was given a $900 million writedown of its debt to government and a new lease on life. (We will meet this giveaway again in chapter 12.) VIA was given a declining business, a lousy reputation, and several rail-yards full of decrepit stock, for which it paid $67 million.[32] In all, VIA received less capital funding over its first two decades to run a national passenger service than the government blew in its lamentable attempt to construct a single international airport at Mirabel, outside Montreal, at a cost of more than one billion dollars.[33]

The first serious cuts in lines and money to back passenger service had come in the 1960s. They led, of course, to a drop in passengers and a growth in losses on both major railways. Then came the "reforms" of 1977, instituted by Trudeau's transport minister Otto Lang, which slashed passenger subsidies again and transferred the problem into the lap of VIA Rail. While other government-backed railways in the United States and Britain were responding to the need for cleaner, more energy-efficient transport by investing heavily in new services and infrastructure, VIA Rail kept losing passengers.

Harry Gow, a professor of criminology at the University of Ottawa, whose real passion has always been railroading and who speaks for a bumptious railway lobby called Transport 2000, puts it this way:

> It's like kicking a chicken around the farmyard and then when it gets too miserable, you go after it with the axe. The kicking has occurred with the huge government grants for air and road infrastructure. It was obvious for years that the federal government was willing to put enormous amounts of money into airports and roads without a thought to the railways. They'd give operating grants to rail, as a sop to the political opposition that was bound to come without them, but really the whole process was undermined, and the position of passenger rail made insupportable, because there was no adequate, long-term investment. Then they chopped the chicken's head off.[34]

Between 1981 and 1988, 3,210 kilometres of railway track were abandoned in Canada[35] — including all the lines in Newfoundland and Prince Edward Island and much of the trackage in Nova Scotia. Hundreds of towns and villages across the country lost their rail service, and many of the towns and villages, as a result, simply disappeared.

Then Mulroney's Conservative government brought out the axe. In 1990 half of VIA's remaining network was declared redundant — including the daily transcontinental, the *Canadian*, which followed the old CPR route. Then VIA's operating grant was sliced by more than half, from $800 million to $350 million a year. Most regional services were gone, along with the southern transcontinental route from Montreal to Vancouver. If you wanted to cross the country by train, it would cost you about twice as much as by plane, on the three days a week when the northern route remained open.

The Liberals, as is their wont, denounced this savaging of the national dream, and then outperformed the Tories. In the summer of 1994 Doug Young, Chrétien's transport minister, announced that all rail subsidies would be eliminated by the year 2005. The 1995 federal budget began the process, cutting support to VIA to $274.5 million (CN received just under $95 million and the CPR $3.3 million)[36] and promising to eliminate all support within a decade.

The CN and the CPR, freed of the incubus of passengers, concentrated on making money by hauling freight. Between 1987 and 1994 they reduced employment by 32 per cent, increased productivity per employee by 59 per cent, and began to make a huge dent in truck freight traffic. In 1994 alone, their combined freight traffic went up 13 per cent, and the two lines had an operating income of $790 million and profits of $422 million.[37] To those who said, "Wait a minute, you guys took on the job of hauling passengers, too," the two, now private, lines replied, "not interested."

As part of the grand new world of privatization, which hit CN in 1995, the Crow Rate (more properly, the Western Grain Transportation Act) was lifted in 1995.[38] Rather than the government paying part of the tab to move western grain to market, the farmers would now pay the whole cost themselves. In the winter of 1996, western farmers were hit with $35 million in "demurrage" costs because they couldn't get their grain to the ships waiting in port on time. The railways had an explanation: it had been cold on the prairies, and heavy snow fell in the mountains on the way to the coast. Verna Thompson, writing in the *Western Producer*, was not impressed: "Cold weather on the prairies and heavy snowfall in the mountains are facts of life in Western Canada, something that happens every year . . . The Crow is dead, farmers are paying more to ship their grain, transportation problems still plague us. And the government seems unable or unwilling to do anything about it."[39] More likely it is unconcerned. It has turned the whole problem of transportation over to the private sector.

But it cannot be allowed to do so. When highway safety inspectors are fired, trucks begin to lose tires and brakes and to kill people. When air traffic controllers are pulled out of the towers, or the towers are shut down entirely, air safety comes under threat. When the money to maintain bridges is cut back, they threaten to fall down. Then we rush in and spend more money to make up for the savings. We cannot turn this process into a series of private enterprises, for every time government withdraws, safety suffers, and we are not stupid enough, yet, to form a public policy based on the idea of sacrificing a few hundred, or thousand, of our people every year to enhance the profits of some private enterprise. We do it, but we don't admit it, yet.

We can substitute toll highways for public highways, but, as Ontario found when it built its billion-dollar Electronic Toll Highway (ETR) north of Toronto, while the private sector can run such a facility, it needs government to provide both the finance and the oversight to make it work. The ETR is the old CPR — with whitewalls.

The opening of the first section of the new road, scheduled for December 31, 1996, was delayed until October 14, 1997, because of serious concerns about its safety. These concerns surfaced when the Ontario Provincial Police finally drove the route and declared that it presented a number of problems which, if not corrected, might kill motorists.[40] It turned out that the 36-kilometre section of roadway had never been examined by provincial highway inspectors; it was self-inspected by the contractors. It also turned out that a number of changes had been made, with savings of $300 million, but which presented a number of design difficulties that had to be overcome before the road could be opened. However, by the time that occurred, what had been contemplated as a public-private partnership had become a deal in which the public purse put up the money and took most of the risk. The private entrepreneurs were to have put up a good portion of the $930 million price tag (the price before the new safety measures were taken), but it was much cheaper if the province carried the load, so that was done. The consortium that built the highway will run it for thirty years, then turn it over to the government. If it goes belly up, most of the cost will be borne by the Ontario government. The profits, if any, will go elsewhere. The provincial auditor summarized the arrangement in a single stern sentence:

> We observed that, although cited as a public-private partnership, the government's financial, ownership and operational risks are so significant compared to the contracted risks assumed by the private sector that, in our opinion, a public-private partnership was not established.[41]

The huge costs contributed by the Ontario people to fund this new speedway for the well-to-do might have gone quite a way to ease some of the problems of the city to the south, where the Toronto Transit Commission and GO (for Government of Ontario) train systems are threatening to collapse. On January 15, 1997, the province announced that it was cutting $718 million in transit spending and passing responsibility for this function over to the municipalities.[42]

Public transit is cheaper, safer, environmentally cleaner, and much more efficient than the car, especially in terms of fuel consumption over what the experts call "seat miles" — the number of miles multiplied by the number of seats. A private car is about twice as efficient as a jet aircraft, a bus three times as efficient as a car, and a train twice as efficient as a bus.[43] Now that we know this, we put most of our public money into airplanes and highways.

In the same way, trains are far more efficient, safer, and cheaper than trucks for moving freight, so we starve the trains. A study by Transport Concepts, an Ottawa research group, showed that the "overall average cost of inter-city trucking in Canada is 2.15 cents per net tonne kilometre." A tonne kilometre is the equivalent of a seat mile, except that it measures the cost of carting a tonne of freight, instead of a person. The same cost by rail is 0.51 cents, or less than one-fourth. Pollution is about one-fifth on a train for the same freight carried on a truck, and the accident rate about one-seventh.[44]

Where is the sense in this? Every major form of transportation in Canada has its infrastructure — roads, bridges, terminals, ports, canals, airports — provided by government. Only the train is required by government to build, maintain, operate, and even police its own infrastructure. Then it gets hammered because it cannot make money doing so.

We have created a transportation policy that encourages the private automobile, in the first place, decades after we knew that it was the most inefficient, polluting way to travel. In the second place, we give a helping hand to the (now) private airlines, even as they cut more and more services to the regions. We are getting rid of all support for the railways, although they still make more environmental, energy, economic, and safety sense than any other form of transport, simply because they are a "government thing."

Every form of transportation is a government thing; we just don't know it, or, more accurately, we have just forgotten. By the time we find this out, again, it may well be too late. The whole country will have come to a (private) standstill.

10

Curiosity Killed the Budget

There is nothing more antagonistic to original thought than business efficiency.
— E.W.R. Steacie, president of the
National Research Council, 1957

Our research programs were focused on technologies which are crucial to our nation's competitiveness . . . But this reorganization was only one component of a broad plan of revitalization and renewal for the NRC. Another important element was a plan that encourages individual and institutional entrepreneurship in order to maximise opportunities for the transfer of knowledge and the commercialization of technology.
— Arthur C. Carty, president of the
National Research Council, 1997

The sign on the front of the building says "Nuclear Physics," but there are no nuclear physicists here in Chalk River any more. It is a long, two-storey structure, and across the front are ranks of empty windows, staring blankly at the Ottawa River. Beside the main door are two nubbins of metal where a plaque was once attached, proudly proclaiming the site of TASCC (pronounced "task"), the Tandem Accelerator Super-Conducting Cyclotron. The machinery is still in a mammoth concrete bunker attached to this building by a concrete-block tunnel. TASCC was unique in the world and an invention of the

198

physicists who no longer inhabit these structures. The authorities took down the plaque because it was embarrassing to have $100 million worth of equipment sitting around once Atomic Energy of Canada Limited, the Crown corporation that was once so proud of this facility, cut off the funds.

If you ask the public relations people in Ottawa about TASCC, they will tell you there is no point in driving all the way to Chalk River — about 200 kilometres — because there is nothing to see. "It's just a bit of rubble," I was told. "Most of the equipment has been placed elsewhere, at universities, and they may even have taken the building down." But one of the sad lessons we learn in life is that PR persons do not always tell the truth. Two buildings are still standing here, one brick, one concrete, lonely but proud, and, while much of the ancillary gear has been scattered, along with the seventy-eight men and women who worked with it, the tandem accelerator and the cyclotron are still here. You can't get in to see them, though. Notices at each of the three doors state, "For Entry, apply to Security," but Security just shrugs and says, "Those buildings are closed."

TASCC, just so we understand what we have closed down and written off, was mainly a research tool. It did not pay for itself, but it was an important research tool. There is only one copy of one AECL bulletin left on the premises to tell us about it — the rest have been scrapped — but it waxes eloquent:

In the early 1970s when scientists at Chalk River Nuclear Laboratories (CRNL) began to look for a way to accelerate particles to higher speeds, they didn't know where their search would end. But they did know that if a solution wasn't found, scientists throughout Canada would find it increasingly difficult to keep pace with other world laboratories as they upgraded their facilities for heavy ion physics . . .

The subsequent design and construction of Chalk River's TASCC facility was an exercise in creativity and resourcefulness to challenge the best of science and engineering. The cyclotron produced its first beam on September 12, 1985, and physicists carried out their first experiment using the new machine on March 3, 1986. TASCC is one of a handful of machines in the world to carry out research with a broad range of high-energy heavy ion beams. It is the only one that does so

with a tandem accelerator injecting ions into a supercon-
ducting cyclotron . . .

. . . These superconductors are perfect conductors of electricity at very low temperatures — near absolute zero — and,
in cyclotron technology, their use as pioneered by Chalk River
is a major breakthrough.[1]

*Damn. We don't have a whole lot of major breakthroughs in
Canadian science, but we are continually told that we need more of
them, to stay alert, to compete, to move with the world's heavy hitters
. . . to keep pace, as the brochure says. Heavy ions may not be as sexy
as rock music, but they have their place in the world of science.*

*This is what TASCC did: scientists put some material that they
wanted to use for study at one end of the tandem accelerator, where it
was vaporized and its atoms made to accept additional electrons.
Now they had negative ions of the material. The negative ions were
next steered into the tandem accelerator, where they were accelerated,
and then fed into the cyclotron — which is another accelerator, but
circular. The tandem accelerator looks like the tank on the back of an
oil truck, only bigger; it is about 24 metres long, 4.5 metres high, and
bulges in the middle, where the two — thus tandem — accelerators
dwell. The cyclotron is an octagon with a circle inside. Its major component is an electromagnet that measures 1.5 metres in diameter and
provides a magnetic field of 5 Telsa — or, in lay terms, a hell of a
powerful magnet — which was used to hustle the ions along still
faster. By the time they emerged from the cyclotron they were moving
at speeds up to 100,000 kilometres a second, fast enough to jostle
the nuclei of all kinds of other substances they were used to bombard.
The beam of particles allowed the AECL scientists, and visiting
experts from all over the world, to study the composition of various
kinds of atomic nuclei and the forces that hold them together. By
using super-conducting magnets, the scientists were able to keep the
beam of ions very tight and controlled, and, among other things, that
meant they didn't need a big facility. The whole process started with a
group of physicists trying to work out how they could get their
research tool without spending more money than AECL was willing to
pay. TASCC was the answer, and, as the brochure said, it led to a real
breakthrough, internationally:*

TASCC enables scientists from across Canada to contribute and collaborate on par with other world laboratories in studies of high-energy nuclear collisions. It is through analyzing the results of these sub-atomic collisions that nuclear physicists can discover more about the fundamental structure of matter and the forces that hold it together.

Not any more, they can't. We had built something unique, right here in Canada, and had done it very cheaply. We were providing our scientists with exactly the kind of advantage that everybody keeps telling us we must have. R&D, or Research and Development, is the buzzword for every after-dinner speaker in the land who talks about industry, trade, science, or any combination thereof. We had made a world breakthrough in R&D, so we shut it down.

Why? It's the old story: no mon, no fun. The federal government, in its wisdom, hacked $74 million out of the R&D funding it gave to AECL, and AECL, in a bit of a sulk, said, "Well, fine, if you don't want to pay for it, we won't do it," and shut down every project that didn't have a direct connection to selling the CANDU (Canadian Deuterium Uranium) reactor.² The CANDU is going through a hard time these days, what with seven of Ontario's nineteen CANDUs out of service, but if you can sell a CANDU, there's money in it — at least in theory. In reality, we seem to lend most of the dough to whichever dictator wants to buy one, such as those we unloaded to tyrants in China, Romania, and the Republic of Korea. Anyway, the theory is that the CANDU will some day bring us vast amounts of money for the billions invested, and, in the meantime, it will provide jobs.

TASCC, in the main, added to our knowledge, not our pocketbook. It cost about $10 million a year to run, and, while the scientists were able to get some of that back by examining materials for space programs, for example, it was never going to be a money maker, or a job creator with the potential of a CANDU.

Still AECL was proud of TASCC's impact on science, generally:

A major research facility like TASCC generates both direct and indirect benefits beyond the actual physics results. The demands of front-line research not only bring into the laboratory state-of-the-art technologies, detectors, and data acquisition electronics but also lead to the development of new technologies useful in other fields.³

The tandem accelerator had other practical uses. Through a process called Accelerator Mass Spectrometry, it was able to determine the age of bone from a skeleton found near Taber, Alberta. It had been claimed that the bone was 35,000 years old, but Accelerator Mass Spectrometry tests put the age at 4,100 years, shedding new light — and some controversy — on the claims of very early human habitation in the new world.[4]

We can't go lavishing money on projects that merely make us wiser, better informed, or potentially richer and more competitive. If a faciltiy doesn't bring in the bucks, right now, shut it down. TASCC was used to measure chlorine-36 and iodine-129, which are radionuclides resulting from atomic reactions, but that didn't bring in any cash, either; it was just part of the fearful chase to find ways to deal with atomic waste and emissions. No, not interested.

Another closed-out project was FusionCanada, which was delving into the possibility of fusion energy as a viable, environmentally sustainable energy source for the twenty-first century.[5] If anybody comes up with this energy source, it will create opportunities undreamed of. But we are no longer interested. Maybe if EXXON wants to chip in?

At the same time as it shut down TASCC, AECL withdrew funding from the Neutrino Observatory in Sudbury, Ontario, where we are exploring the origins of the universe. Who needs to know stuff like that? Amazingly, this project is surviving — so far.

The clever and knowledgeable woman AECL has sent to walk me around the facility is thinking of designing a tour to look at all the bits and pieces that have been closed down since AECL decided it would concentrate only on CANDUs, but she doesn't want to talk much about TASCC. "There seems to be some controversy about it," she says.

Just along the road from the TASCC facility is a huge hole in the ground, where two MAPLE reactors are being installed to produce medical isotopes, used to diagnose and treat diseases. But here's the joke — these two reactors in the middle of AECL will be owned by a private company, MDS Nordion, although AECL will be responsible for their operation. We're going to privatize most of the profits, while lending the company $100 million to do the work. Most of the world's supplies of a number of crucial medical isotopes have been produced, since 1975, at AECL's National Research Universal reactor here, but it is reaching the end of its useful life. So the job will be taken up by MDS Nordion, the company through which AECL sold the products.

An agreement to lend $100 million to this project came into effect on April 10, 1997.[6]

As I stand here, with a wind that started somewhere in the high Arctic blowing up my coat and a fine sleet befogging my glasses, I can't help wondering, Am I missing something? Are we really crazy enough to shut down a unique facility like TASCC because it doesn't make money, and then turn around and let the money represented by medical isotopes drift off?

Oh my, yes.

John Hardy and Arthur Carty are both scientists with international reputations, but quite different approaches, which reflect the tug of war currently going on in Canada's science community. Dr. Hardy is a large, cheerful, loquacious, bearded, arm-waving sort of man who wears sweaters to work. He is one of the world's leading experts on cyclotrons and was, until recently, the man in charge of the TASCC accelerator. He says outrageous things. For example: "Canadian research facilities are dropping like flies before government deficit cutters who can't tell the difference between an expenditure and an investment." Or:

> What we were doing with the cyclotron and what other people in basic research are doing is securing the country's future; not in a direct line, because there are no guarantees with basic research, but, in general, historically, basic research develops the new ideas and the new brains, the people, the students, who will be making the practical applications and the economic success of the future. And if you get rid of your basic research, you're getting rid of the investment that secures your future. What counts here is not saving a penny today, but making sure your country as a whole can deal with its future financially. Basic research is what gives you the means to earn money and be competitive thirty, forty years from now, and Canada is just turning that in, ploughing that under . . . The cyclotron is not a big factor in itself, but it is a sign of what we're doing in every sector of scientific research.[7]

Hardy has been cast into the outer darkness, like Lucifer. When he began raising public hell in April 1997, about the cuts that were crippling his program, he was given twenty minutes to clear out his desk and go. Now he lives in College Park, Texas, where he has taken his expertise to Texas A&M University, which is glad to welcome him in.

Dr. Carty is the president of the National Research Council in Ottawa. No arm waver or sweater wearer, he is a tie kind of guy. His academic background is in chemistry, but he has had many years of administrative experience, which may explain why he sounds like a brochure from the C.D. Howe Institute and appears more or less resigned to the gutting given to science over the past few years. The NRC is the linchpin of scientific research in this country, yet it has been hit with cuts of $76.2 million, out of an annual budget of $483 million in 1994.[8] I ask him how much it hurt, and he replies:

> I am not trying to underestimate the difficulties, but there were some benefits. Certainly a budget cut of that magnitude really makes you think whether you're effective, efficient, whether you're focusing in the right areas. It clears the mind a bit, if you like.[9]

The prospect of hanging is also reputed to concentrate the mind, I quip, and he allows himself a faint smile. I ask him for his reaction to a quotation from a Canadian scientist, and I read him the remark of E.W.R. Steacie about business efficiency being antagonistic to original thought. He looks out the broad window and down on the rolling lands, dotted with purposeful buildings, that mark the NRC's vast tract of land off Montreal Road in Ottawa, and replies: "I'm not sure of the context in which that was said, but I would just simply point out that there have been a number of Nobel prizes won by people working in industrial environments."

Perhaps he suspects I have sandbagged him with the ravings of some left-wing nut, so I tell him the quote is from Dr. Steacie, who held Carty's present post between 1952 and 1962, and remind him that he is a recent recipient of the Steacie Award for chemistry. He raises his eyebrows, rolls right over that, and goes on: "What we need in Canada to my way of thinking is a balance between fundamental basic research, on the one hand, strategic research, which would be focused medium to long-term, and applied research."

When I press him about the kind of damage to fundamental research that appears to be driving Canadian scientists like Hardy across the border, he tells me that some of them may be disappointed in conditions in the United States. But a recent academic study, I remind him, noted that any single major research school in the United States — Stanford, Washington, Michigan, Johns Hopkins — receives more research funding than all the universities in Ontario, where most of Canada's research takes place, put together.[10] He changes tack:

> Over the last few years we have allowed our public sector funding to slip and to slip quite badly. Indeed I don't know of any country that has allowed its publicly funded research to slip more than Canada has . . . There has been a steady increase in industrial R&D of about 4 to 5 per cent per annum, whereas government research has been going in the opposite direction at about the same rate.
>
> The solution is to reinvest, but I don't just say in curiosity-driven research, I say a balanced investment, that would require an investment in the universities, a reinvestment in NRC and other government labs as appropriate.

"Curiosity-driven research" is shorthand for research that is not directed at a specific target, or backed by an industrial "partner" that shares the bill and gets to cash in on the results. Curious research is the kind of fooling around in a lab that led Robert Boyle to produce his epic studies on gases, when he might have been working on alchemy, transmuting lead into gold, as many of his colleagues at the time were doing. It is also the kind of fooling around that led to the discovery of insulin, and that prompted the NRC in 1963 to set up a site in Algonquin Park called "LGM," for Little Green Men. The astronomers were picking up radio signals from outer space, so they hiked off to see if they were being produced by extraterrestrials, or LGMs. Alas, no, they were merely signals emitted by neutron stars — stars collapsing in on themselves after using up all their fusion energy — and that discovery was made, in the end, by scientists in Cambridge, England. No inventions resulted, although the scientists had a fine time indulging their curiosity.

Carty is in favour of curiosity-driven research, although you would never know that by looking at the material produced in the NRC's annual reports. However, what the NRC seems now to be doing — certainly what it talks about almost incessantly in these reports — is its aid to, and partnership with, industry. There is nothing wrong with that. A good many projects are under way, especially in the field of biotechnology, in which industry and government both have a stake, and to which both contribute large dollops of research money.

Where is the unbiased research to come from?

If most university research is now tied to industry, and if the NRC is preoccupied with "clients," "entrepreneurship," and "maximizing commercial opportunities,"[11] where will the independent research, the heart of the NRC, come from? In 1996 the NRC took in more than $60 million, in cash and kind, from private partnerships with various companies,[12] and it hopes to do better than that in the years ahead. Isn't that flirting with a conflict of interest?

For the first and only time, Carty gets a bit shirty with me, but only to the extent of thrusting his words out through clenched teeth: "We're not being dictated to or dominated by industrial contributions, and I don't intend to let that happen." Fine, but why does the 1996 NRC annual report, under Yearly Collaborative Biotechnology Research, show that, of the $33 million the council spent on cooperative ventures with clients, $26 million, or 79 per cent, went to studies shared with pharmacological companies — hugely profitable concerns that ought to be able to pay for their own research? "The biotech industry has come from nowhere in Canada," Carty replies, "and I would suggest to you that this is one example of a sound Canadian investment in a sector which is starting to pay off . . . That's not all big companies." He notes that there's a "tremendous demand for biotechnology," which may be true, but hardly explains why the NRC is selling its services to any passing corporation when it ought to be getting on, for example, with climate change. Carty dismisses that one: "Global warming is mainly looked at by Environment Canada." But shouldn't we have an active program, run by independent scientists, to tell us if Environment Canada knows what it's talking about?

According to Carty, the NRC has become active in promoting industrial research because Canadian industry cannot do the job itself. I am later told by Tom Holder, a senior scientist who used to work with AECL and now works with NRC, that scientists in government sometimes have to speak in bureaucratese "to preserve what they can of the pure research programs."[13] Holder is an expert in materials research, which has some practical applications. The NRU reactor at Chalk River has been used to check for metal stress on the U.S. *Challenger*; an atomic probe can detect problems long before cracks appear, without having to cut the metal apart. Thus, when AECL decided to close down everything not connected to the CANDU, Holder was able to move the program over to the NRC by emphasizing its cash-flow potential:

> I was able to sell them on the notion that we could get back as much as 25 per cent of our budget by doing work under contract for outsiders, and we do. We're only costing our masters about $2 million a year, and it is a lot easier to come up with $2 million than the $10 million John [Hardy] needed for TASCC. When AECL was dumping us, Carty took us in and put us in the Steacie Institute, which is where he has put most of the pure research. He is doing his damnedest to keep them from taking everything away.

So what it comes down to is this: we can keep some science going as long as we keep our heads down and make the right noises about building "alliances with governments, private companies and universities."[14] We must not say anything about wanting to find things out just for the hell of it, or, like John Hardy, just because of a naive contention that most research will, in the end, justify itself — if only by making us smarter and better informed, and providing us with the next generation of scientists.

The NRC's proud record

The NRC is still doing basic research, mainly through the Steacie Institute for Molecular Sciences, and it has always had, as part of its mission statement, "to undertake, assist or promote scientific and industrial research."[15] But the balance has shifted away from curiosity-driven research to Contributions to Canadian Firms to Develop, Acquire and Exploit Technology, which came to a little over $83 million last year.[16] The NRC's annual reports say nothing directly about how much money goes to the Steacie Institute, and the spending patterns are almost impossible to follow. Carty explains that this reporting conforms with "government methods — we are not holding anything back."

The NRC was formed in 1916 to promote scientific and industrial research, investigate and improve standards of measurement, operate and administer astronomical observatories, and maintain a national science laboratory.[17] It has always prided itself on the practical applications of science, such as work on controlling wheat rust which benefitted Canadian farmers. In 1945 Dr. Henry M. Tory, one of the early chairmen of the council, noted: "The saving in one year as a result of the rust control research project was sufficient to repay to Canada the total cost of the National Research Council from its foundation to the present time."[18] Tory was an interesting man, a Maritimer who was educated in theology and mathematics and who spent many years as an educator before he was appointed to the NRC in 1923. He had the usual problem of convincing parliament that it was worthwhile investing in the curiosity trade, and his attempt to found a National Research Institute was killed by the Senate. He established a program in basic refractories (mainly for telescopes and other optic instruments) which led to the development of a vigorous industry that shipped goods to thirty other nations. Then he was abruptly sacked by Prime Minister R.B. Bennett, who scorned intellectual curiosity and disliked Tory personally.

During the Second World War, the NRC established twenty-one new laboratories across the country — including a nuclear laboratory in Montreal, a plant for explosives research at Val Cartier, Quebec, and radar and aeronautics establishments in Ottawa. The Council invented a "jammer" to disrupt the flights of German radio-controlled glider bombs, and, as early as 1940, began the work on atomic energy that led to the establishment of Atomic Energy of Canada Limited. Dr. George C. Laurence, an NRC researcher, conducted the first experiments in Ottawa by bombarding uranium with beryllium neutrons in a pile constructed in a wooden bin lined with paraffin.[19]

After the war, money was much harder to come by. Every time parliament showed signs of reducing the annual appropriation requests, the argument was made that Canada needed research in all areas if it was to remain competitive internationally. But, like every other aspect of government, scientific research was hit by the downsizing craze in the 1980s. The same politicians still make the same speeches about the need for Canada to be in the forefront of scientific research, but the wallet has been withdrawn. Canada is the only nation in the Group of Seven which has cut research funding. The prospects became worse when many provinces followed Ottawa's lead and performed their own reducing operations on provincial research funding institutions.

The NRC is far from the only Ottawa victim. The Medical Research Council, the major source of funding for health sciences study in this country, abandoned or cancelled 500 projects in 1997, as the direct result of a $32 million cut in federal funding.[20] This is the money that goes to support researchers in universities and hospital-based institutes who generate the ideas that lead, quite often, to medical breakthroughs — and, just as often, to the development of products that can be sold for profit. In a speech at Calgary on December 3, 1997, Dr. Henry Friesen, head of the council, noted: "If Canada is going to be competitive, we're going to have to spend as much as our competitors do on basic research." But Americans spend more than eight times as much, per capita, as Canadians do in this area. Seven years ago the disparity was four to one. Again, the federal government in the United States is responsible for 72 per cent of basic research funding; in Canada, the figure is 22 per cent.[21]

We are heading rapidly in the wrong direction. During 1998 federal government support for medical, scientific, and social science research will be lower than it was in 1985, according to the House of Commons Committee on Finance. At the same time, funding at the U.S. National Science Foundation has risen 30 per cent, and that at the National Institutes for Health, the

American counterpart to our Medical Research Council, by 80 per cent.[22]

We have already seen what the cuts to Canada's Health Protection Branch have done to that body, where funding is being cut in half — from $237 million in 1993–94 to $118 million by the year 2000.[23] Then there is the Natural Sciences and Engineering Council, which provides grants to individual researchers and groups for specific projects, not all of which have to be linked to an industrial application. One scientist who has just been turned down for one of these grants complained:

> There are two problems; the first is that you seem to spend about half your time filling out applications and forms — I know it's all necessary, but it also drives you crazy — only to be turned down because the money has run out. The second is that if you are aiming for anything substantial, anything over, say, $100,000, and you don't have an industrial sponsor you can sign up to carry part of the cost, forget it. Not every idea worth exploring interests the corporate sector.

We're losing many of our best and brightest scientists

The cuts have led to the exodus of some of our best and brightest scientists and have prompted a stern warning from Dr. Bodo Stavric, a world-renowned food scientist who left the country in September 1997:

> The situation is not very promising for Canadians. Somebody can be functional without one finger. You can be operational without a leg. But if you cut and cut, the body is there but it's not functional.[24]

Another recent science exile was Alan Hidebrand, the Canadian geologist who gained international fame for proving that a giant meteor struck the earth at about the same time that the dinosaurs disappeared. The Geological Survey of Canada, a branch of the Natural Resources Department, which has accumulated five decades' worth of material, is shutting down its research into meteor craters just as worldwide interest in the subject is perking up. "It's a question of priorities," according to the official spokesperson for the department.

At about the same time, we lost astrophysicist Scott Tremaine, who predicted moons around Uranus seven years before they were actually seen by a *Voyageur* spacecraft. He left the University of Toronto for Princeton, where he will receive more research funding. He told Warren Gerard of the *Toronto Star* that he and his wife both agonized over the decision to go:

> The decision we made to leave was a joint decision and reflected the fact in her case that the teaching load she had and the support service she was able to get simply meant she couldn't adequately pursue her research career . . .
>
> . . . What's clear to me is that the general situation at U of T is very bad in the sense that we are not competitive with the best American universities. The federal government funds are not on the scale you need to conduct world-class research, and general cuts in the provincial funding have led to higher teaching loads, reduced services and real problems in paying competitive salaries.[25]

Canada now spends less on research and development than any of its competitors among the Group of Seven industrialized nations except Italy.[26] While the prime minister pledges that "the government is determined to do more to support innovation and risk-taking in Canada,"[27] the reality is that his government has presided over the sharpest cuts to research in our history.

The 1997 federal budget announced, with much fanfare, a new program to pump $800 million into the Canadian Foundation for Innovation. The main purpose of this independent corporation:

> to provide financial support for the modernization of research infrastructure at Canadian universities and colleges, in research hospitals, and in associated not-for-profit research institutions and organizations in the areas of health, environment, science and engineering.[28]

There are a number of catches to this program, the most important being that the money — about $180 million per year over five years — will be allocated entirely outside the control of the government. Indeed, that is the program's boast: "Members of the research community and the private sector, not the government, will be responsible for spending decisions."[29] Are we crazy? As Thomas Walkom puts it, "Why does Paul Martin want to give my $800 million to a group of people over whom I will have absolutely no control?"[30] Another problem is that the money has to be matched by other players,[31] especially the provincial governments, which have cut back their funding in these areas, and the universities, which must, in turn, line up private-sector partners. Ontario hacked $280 million out of its support to universities just before Ottawa announced its new program.[32] The research bodies that need the cash may well find that they cannot have it, because they cannot come up with the matching funds.

The real world of research is scrounging funds

The real world for many university researchers revolves around two main tasks: applying for grants, instead of doing the work the grants are supposed to support, and repairing broken-down equipment, which cannot be replaced because there is no money.

Many universities are now levelling user fees on scientists for the basic materials they require for their experiments.[33] A researcher in chemistry described one of these cuts to me:

> I no longer have any time to sit and read and think, and reflect. I am too busy trying to scrounge equipment, or scrounge money, or trying to fight off the pencil-pushers who now run this hell hole, to sit and think. And that's a bloody shame.

We have also cut back on many international programs, such as the Human Frontier Science Program, the Ocean Drilling Program, and the Climate Change Program run by the United Nations. We have eliminated our contributions to the Commonwealth Science Council and the International Institute for Applied Systems Analysis. Most astounding of all, we have cancelled our membership in the North Atlantic Treaty Organization Science Program.

It is not as if industry is stepping in to do the research on which so much of the future depends. Statistics Canada figures show that fewer than 1 per cent of Canadian firms conduct any

R&D in this country; and, of the 3,500 firms who actually do such work, about 1 per cent accounted for half the research done.[34]

We have operations like the Technology Canada Partnerships program, which is run through Industry Canada. Through repayable, interest-free loans, it helps companies support projects that have a technology base and that promise new products and jobs. It pumped $87 million into Bombardier Inc. to help it launch a new regional jet aircraft. Bombardier's total R&D bill for this project will come to $349 million.[35] The company makes a lot of money, so we are left with the question: Why should the Canadian taxpayer ladle out money, when the company has so much already?

The answer to that question is that we hope to lever more money into R&D, and therefore into jobs and investment, with these handouts. In all, Industry Canada has approved $400 million worth of these partnerships, which include $147 million to help Pratt & Whitney Canada complete a new turboprop engine; $57 million to help de Havilland Inc. develop a new version of its successful Dash 8 aircraft; and $30 million to Ballard Power Systems Inc., of Burnaby, British Columbia, to help develop a stationary fuel-cell-driven powerplant.[36]

The NRC's version is called the Industrial Research Assistance Program, which ran 240 projects all across the country in 1996–97. Most of the money — about $25 million — went into electronics, food, and agriculture and computer software projects.[37]

To dismiss these handouts as mere giveaways to companies that should bear the cost themselves misses the point: government hopes for, expects, and sometimes actually gets a return on its investment through taxes paid by the companies whose R&D it sponsors. If we want more research done in this country, there is no instrument so effective as a little bribe to the private sector to get it to participate. If the private sector gains by this arrangement, so do we all.

But this kind of bribe does not promote research in areas that the private sector won't touch. No manufacturer is going to be lured into an in-depth study of the ravages of acid rain caused by his smokestacks — even if the government offers to put up part of the cash for the work. There is no lineup at the doors of the

NRC, Industry Canada, or the NSERC for partnerships to probe into pharmaceutical costs, or whether we are swallowing pills unnecessarily. The reason governments went into research in this area in the first place was because some of the drug companies were arrant liars, fakers, and cheats when it came to research reports on their own products.

Similarly, no aircraft firm is going to join hands with Industry Canada to try to determine whether we would be better advised to spend a few hundred millions on urban transit than to give it to Bombardier, de Havilland, and other aeronautics firms. But if you have a university-based project on what a good idea it is to spend more on aircraft engines, we can probably accommodate you.

One of the major issues in environmental science these days seems a simple matter, but it is not: What size of particles spewing out of smokestacks will cause the most harm to human health? Will very tiny bits of matter do as much harm, or more, than the kind of output that can be readily filtered out of the stack? No private firms want to back this kind of research — nor do any of our publicly owned power firms — but if we can't sort this out, we cannot set standards for the release of particulates.

We expect university and government researchers to take on certain kinds of projects, but it is no longer so. Dr. Peter Victor, dean of environmental studies at York University, told me:

> The assumption is that when you cut the funds to universities and other independents, that somebody else will pick up the slack, but I can't find anybody who's doing that, and the more basic the science and the more long-term and long-range the investigation, the less there is in it for the private sector. Why would they put money in that? Why should they put money in that?[38]

He suggests that many people in industry, despite all their complaints about big government, want government to stay on the job of scientific investigation:

> I never heard business complain about that part of government activity, never. They wanted the government to be doing

the science . . . For example, the Ministry [of Environment and Energy] has a wonderful environmental lab, and, when I was in the department, one thing the private sector did not want was that that major lab should be turned over to the private sector. They wanted a government lab that would do the more difficult testing, that would develop new tests, that would provide quality assurance testing, and to do that you had to have a full lab.

The private sector was saying, "We recognize a valid public role here."

But it is not a role that is being fulfilled with vigour. Victor points out that when the ministry went through one of its rounds of recent cuts, it fired the only man on staff who had real expertise in nuclear radiation:

The argument was, well, that's a federal responsibility. Even if one accepted the Atomic Energy Control Board [which is the federal government's watchdog on these matters] as everything it should be, when we are the province with sixty per cent of its energy coming from nuclear, with the mothballing or whatever going on with so many CANDUs, one would expect the ministry to have at least one person with expertise to know what's going on.

If Canadians want to walk away from the expense of funding basic research, curiosity-based research, and research aimed at telling us whether we are being led up the laboratory aisle by private researchers, we will find ourselves back at the hewers-of-wood stage. I know of no Canadian who wants that. But it is what we are apparently going to get as our political masters respond to whatever happens to provoke the latest outbreak of news coverage.

The curious case of the doomed monkeys

Consider the case of the doomed monkeys. When the Health Protection Branch of Health Canada decided to get out of doing its own experiments in toxicology and to turn the job over to private labs, it was left with 115 macaque monkeys, specially bred to serve in such experiments. A news story broke on television, complete with pictures of the monkeys, which said that they were going to be slaughtered within a few days because there was no further use for them. The ensuing screams of outrage brought Health Minister Allan Rock out before the cameras to announce a reprieve while the matter was studied. Rock was followed by a scientific panel mounted by the Royal Society of Canada, which reported that the monkeys, if they were not to be used any more, should be given a decent home — pensioned off, if you like.[39] That was done, but two points seem to be missed in this huge kerfuffle.

The first is that, in the ordinary course of events, when the experiments were concluded, the monkeys were to be killed — one by one, instead of 115 at a time. Saving their lives didn't do anything to make use of the years of work, funding, and research that went into the projects they were used for — mostly in studies of dementia and other diseases related to aging — and it didn't save any money, either. This reprieve did nothing to help us come to grips with the vexed question of whether we have the right to slaughter animals for research. It showed only that if we try to slaughter too many cute animals at the same time, and word gets out, all hell breaks loose. The second point is that, in the fuss over the monkeys, we seemed to miss the far more important issue that we were closing down the most important area of expertise we possessed on health safety — to save money.

We cannot afford such savings, any more than we could afford to save the money we spent on TASCC. If a trading nation like Canada decides that curiosity is just an expensive hobby, we will lose our best scientists, our best brains, and, in the long run, our best opportunity to survive and thrive.

And Now, a Word from Our Sponsors

In our day, the ultimate result of conservative economic policies is to provide cheap labour to fuel the expansion of more fast food outlets, T-shirt shops, brightly packaged deodorants, faster cars, louder radios, and more eye-glazing "specialty" TV channels. In the vast and heroic sweep of mankind's evolution, we seem to be going backwards.
— David Ross, executive director,
Canadian Council on Social Development, May 1997

Two groups of people have sponsored the process that is now taking place, only one of them intentionally. The first group are our financial overlords, our new robber barons, who bestride the world on behalf of globalism. They have paid for the studies, advanced the electoral expenses, and funded the propaganda of unfettered multinational enterprise that has led to the dismantling of the state and the triumph of "free" trade. The other heavy investors, although not willing ones, have been welfare recipients, psychiatric patients, the old, the young, the female, the unemployed, the disabled — the disadvantaged of all sorts. They have paid a good deal more in money and pain than our new robber barons, but have received few benefits from the new system.

The New Robber Barons

Indonesia has one of the best mining laws in the world . . . Thank God it's a dictatorship. If it were a democracy, this [the Busang gold find, then being explored by Bre-X Minerals] could be tied up in court for years.

— Unnamed Canadian mining company president, *Globe and Mail*, December 14, 1996

There is a large sign on the side of a building on 14th Street South West in Calgary which reads, simply, "One Nineteen." It replaces an older, more impressive, sign that used to read, all in capitals, "BRE-X," in letters of bright gold. These letters were 1.5 metres tall and shone with 23-karat luminosity. The sign cost $30,000. It was taken down when tests proved that the Busang gold discovery, whose anticipated value had propelled the company shares to $286 each in October 1996, and to $0 each in May 1997, was faked. The samples cited in the stock-boosting process had been fiddled with; the gold had been added later, naughtily, and then the fabulous find had been reported. The billions of dollars it promised were nothing but an airy dream. Not that this catch prevented people from making money. Many made millions when they sold their shares before the regrettable news filtered out. Bre-X was, as the authors of one of the quickie books on the subject remarked, "a fable for our times."[1] The moral *was clear: Get in, buy low, sell high, and get out before word of the racket became general knowledge. In the end, $3 billion worth of share value was vaporized on stock exchanges within a few days;[2] but no one knows how much was made and salted away by insiders and lucky guessers before the crash.*

Now I am confronted by a comely young woman in top-hat, tails, and striped trousers on a street corner. Around her neck is a strap that supports an open box containing a pile of fake Bre-X stock certificates. She waves one of them under my chin and, with a dazzling smile, offers to sell it to me for the knock-down price of $10.

"Ten dollars for a Bre-X share? It isn't worth spit."

"Well, no, sir, it isn't a Bre-X share. Just a copy."

"Why should I pay ten dollars for a copy of a share that isn't worth anything in the first place?"

She heaves a sigh. She has been asked this before.

"It was my boss's idea," she explains. "He lost a lot of money, hundreds of thousands of dollars, on Bre-X shares, so he had this notion of making a copy and changing the colour a bit — see, it's nice and red, the lettering. You could give it to a friend for a joke, or just have it framed and stick it up on the wall. Isn't it pretty?" She pauses. "I sell quite a few of them every day."

I pick up one of the shares. It is pretty.

"The real shares are being sold as souvenirs," she urges. "People are paying $28 each for them."

I want to make sure I have this right. "People are paying $28 each for shares of a bankrupt firm which aren't worth anything, and you're willing to sell me a copy of a share, still worth nothing, for $10?"

"That's right. You save $18 dollars."

"But it still isn't worth anything."

She sighs again, a well-if-you're-going-to-take-that-attitude sigh, takes back her (worthless) share copy, and moves off.

The incident reminds me of the caper pulled by Jay Gould, the American robber baron. He nearly cornered the gold market in 1869, but instead precipitated a gold crash that wiped out many fortunes. But not his. He and a group of colleagues got out in time and made millions, while the rest took a bath.[3] "Diamond" Jim Fisk, one of Gould's partners, pronounced the proper coda for this kind of brisk business: "Let everyone carry out his own corpse!"

The old robber barons, men like John D. Rockefeller and Andrew Carnegie, J.W. "Bet-a-Million" Gates, Jay Gould, J.P. Morgan, Daniel "The Great Bear" Drew, and "Diamond" Jim Fisk, were both revered and reviled in their time, from just before the American Civil War to just after the First World War. They were revered because they made huge amounts of money and because they formed what one of their biographers, Matthew Josephson, called "the new nobility of industry and banking."[4] They represented capitalism triumphant and untrammelled. They were sharp traders, visionary builders, princes of international commerce. They didn't even blush when the business press of the day referred to them collectively as "the Lords of Creation."

The robber barons were reviled because they were not nice in their methods. Most of them bribed, cheated, stole, committed frauds, and ran roughshod over the laws of every country where they did business. When Commodore Cornelius Vanderbilt, the shipping buccaneer who founded one of the great fortunes of all time, was advised that what he was doing was illegal, he replied, "What do I care about the law? Hain't I got the power?"[5] The barons bought and sold legislators, used the U.S. National Guard as their personal enforcers to break strikes, forced thousands of workers out onto the street, and caused many people's deaths by poisoning them with tainted meat or having them murdered for daring to strike — as happened at the Rockefeller-owned Colorado Fuel & Iron Company during the Ludlow Massacre of 1914.[6]

Canada had its own robber barons, but we are such a polite people we never called them that. Mostly, we called them "milord," as with James Dunsmuir and George Stephen, two great rogues who were raised to the peerage as a result of, or despite, their swashbuckling ways. I have written about them as "Maple Leaf Rogues," but it doesn't have the same sting.

What brings the robber barons to mind these days, besides a new crop of books designed to show that they were good guys after all, or, if not exactly good guys, that their activities led to good things for the economy overall,[7] is a feeling that they could step into the boardroom of one of our modern megacorporations with no questions asked. They might be advised to butt out the stogie, but, apart from that, they would feel right at home. What made the robber barons was a set of ideas very like those which are now being promulgated by our finest business schools, but which had been laid aside for a few careless decades:

- Moral principles have nothing to do with running a business. They clutter up the economy, preventing corporations from operating with maximum efficiency.
- State interference is bad, not only for the corporations against which it operates, but for business, generally, and thus for the nation.
- There is nothing wrong with using the public purse to finance business, co-opting public servants to crush opposition, or relying on national diplomacy to open foreign markets to our goods.
- The "free market" is the only effective mechanism for the distribution of wealth, the setting of prices, and the acquisition of raw materials. It follows that anything that interferes with the free market is a hindrance to sound economic policy.
- If some of us get rich enough, the general economy will benefit in two ways. First, we will be able to form the large pools of capital necessary for global expansion, which is a good thing in and of itself. Second, we will spend some of our riches, thereby providing employment for the rest of the economy.
- The nation state is an outmoded concept. What is required for the efficient operation of a modern economy is what J.P. Morgan called "a community of interest." In this scenario, corporations act together to assure the smooth running of trade, both at the national level and around the world. The "community" had no sense of citizenship. As Morgan's biographer noted: "The idea of democracy evaded him."[8]
- The law is an ass.
- And, as Mark Twain said about Jay Gould: "The people had *desired* money before his day, but he taught them to fall down and worship it."[9]

The new robber barons receive our reverence, but not our revilement. We have convinced ourselves, with some help from our think-tanks, that we were wrong when we tried to interfere with the entrepreneurs who create so much wealth. We surrounded them with restrictions, and told them it was bad to fix prices, rig markets, smash unions, avoid taxes, or move jobs to other lands after having received large subsidies to create them here. When Massey-Ferguson, the farm-implement manufacturer, decided to relocate in the United States after accepting $200 million in Canadian government subsidies, there was a fuss, but it soon passed. Massey simply tranformed itself into something called Varity, then merged with Lucas Industries PLC of Great Britain, and re-emerged as LucasVarity PLC. Along the way, 63,000 employees lost their jobs. Victor Rice, the chief executive officer, explained his technique to a gathering of fellow lords at Davos, Switzerland, in February 1997. "Don't hesitate about people decisions," he said.[10]

We have now learned that this must be the right approach and that it was wicked of us, not to say futile, to try to restrict people like Rice, who only want to make things run smoothly in the cosmo cosmos. We were wrong to put up labour laws and other artificial barriers, which hindered them and kept them from creating the wealth that would make us all comfortable — well, perhaps not us personally, but it would make them comfortable, and we could take comfort from that. Besides, when they have spent enough on big cars, luxury yachts, huge houses, and foreign travel, they will hire us to cut the lawn.

Like the old robber barons, they are movers and shakers. There is nothing timid, weak, or backward about them. They know what they want and, by God, they go right after it. They may have to make deals with dictators from time to time, but at least dictators get things done. They don't waste a lot of time on environmental surveys, boiler inspections, labour laws, bureaucratic forms, and all that drudge. You hand over your bribe one day, and you can get your drills in the ground the next.

Moreover, like the old robber barons, this new bunch probably represents the Divine Will. Rockefeller had a simple explanation for his fortune: "God gave me my money."[11] Of course, our generation doesn't cite God directly. We refer rather to the new deity, "the market," or its virgin offspring, "the free market," in whose name activities that might otherwise seem a trifle greedy and self-serving are justified. To interfere with the representatives of the true faith is probably to trifle with matters best left alone. They will look after things better than you or I, or any government, can do. This is the way George F. Baer, one of the nineteenth-century tycoons, explained his labour policy during a strike: "The rights and interests of the labouring man will be protected and cared for by the Christian men to whom God has given control of the property interests of the country."[12] Or, as Dr. Michael Walker of the Fraser Institute, says: "The success of the wealthy is important for the maintenance of the unfortunate."[13]

The new robber barons are not as overtly rough and crude as their forebears, thanks to the shoals of lawyers, public relations people, pollsters, advertising executives, consultants, and hangers-on who draw large salaries to smooth the way for them and keep them from blurting out too blatantly what is on their minds. When you get reports of them saluting the joys of dealing with dictators, for example, you never get the actual name of the tycoon. Cornelius Vanderbilt would have scorned such evasions; he was a blurter. Once, when he was in Europe a group of his associates took advantage of his absence to grab one of his properties. He dropped them a note that said:

Gentlemen:
   You have undertaken to cheat me. I will not sue you, for [the] law takes too long. I will ruin you.
   Sincerely yours,
   Cornelius Van Der Bilt[14]

He did, too, although it took awhile. A new robber baron would not write anything like that down and tip off the enemy. He or she would just do it — or send out a bar-full of lawyers to do it.

Contemporary robber barons are smoother than their predecessors in another way, too: they don't run roughshod over the laws of the land. They just send in their lobbyists and get inconvenient laws changed, in the name of global competition. If that doesn't work, they pack up their capital, hoist their sails, and move to a country where they are appreciated and where there are no effective laws to curtail them. If Vanderbilt, Gould, and Rockefeller had enjoyed the mobility of capital that is the most valuable asset of the modern corporation, what couldn't they have done?

A fire in Thailand

If these same old-world tycoons had been able to massage public opinion the way modern media permit, they might have been able to avoid criticism altogether. Consider the case of the conflagration — the worst industrial fire in the history of capitalism — that swept through a toy factory on the outskirts of Bangkok, Thailand, on May 10, 1993. Thailand, like Malaysia or Indonesia, is one of the new offshore havens where our cosmocorporations can go to find a more amenable atmosphere than is provided by short-sighted governments in North America. In these lands, men are men, and regulations are flexible. There are rules, of course, but few pay any attention. A regrettable side effect is the occasional accident, like this fire. We can think of it as part of the price of obtaining the kind of efficiency required to operate effectively in the new global economy.

Officially, there were 189 dead in the Bangkok fire, all but fourteen of them women, most of them young, some of them in their early teens. Another 469 were injured, but both figures were probably vastly underestimated. Three buildings collapsed at once, incinerating many bodies, so an exact count was rendered impossible. The Kader Industrial Toy Company of Thailand, which made Bugs Bunny, Bart Simpson, Sesame Street, and other toy favourites for the international market, employed 4,000 workers at monthly wages of US$120 to US$160, wages that ensured that they would never be able to afford any of the toys for their own childen.[15] When the fire broke out, hundreds were trapped because the main exits had been locked to make sure that the hired help didn't steal any of the toys, and the narrow stairways, which were the only escape, either collapsed under the weight of bodies or became so clogged they were useless. By law, these stairways were supposed to be 5 to 9 metres wide; in fact, they were 1.3 metres wide.[16]

The *Washington Post* carried the story on page 25 of its editions of May 11.[17] The *Wall Street Journal* thought it important enough to rate a niche on page 11. The *Financial Times*, daily newspaper of the global economy, ran a small item on page 6. In Canada, the Montreal *Gazette* noted, in a page 9 story on May 13, that "many Canadian toys come from Thailand," while the *Financial Post*, getting to the important stuff, carried a headline three days after the fire, which brought us the reassuring news: "Thai death factory owners say they won't lose money."[18]

In 1911, when there was a dreadful fire in a shirt factory in Manhattan and 147 immigrant women died, there was a huge uproar. The investigation that followed led to the launching of a number of unions in the garment industry.[19] We have come a long way since then; the conveniently facile coverage of the Thailand tragedy provoked very little outrage, even though the story had a strong North American angle. David Miller, president of the Toy Manufacturers of America, who represents many of the companies for which the toys were being made, commented that Kader, which had experienced three other factory fires before this one, was "extremely reputable." Moreover, he said, "The responsibility for those factories is in the hands of those who are there and managing the factory."[20]

This is one of the great things about globalism: whenever anything goes wrong, responsibility is always deposited somewhere safely offshore, while profits go wherever taxes are the lowest. Another great thing that comes up in this same incident is that, if workers get uppity, owners can move out from under the unions, if any, to some place where they can get themselves a little elbow room. It probably would have cost two or three times as much to produce those cute dolls in Canada or the United States, where there are all these labour inspectors and red tape, than it did in Thailand, where they understand the need for business efficiency. Rockefeller would have been green with envy. He had to call in the troops to break unions, and attracted a lot of nasty press.

Still, in general outline, the old and new robber barons have many things in common, including a yen for what used to be called "rationalization" but now has been dubbed "the merger." Same procedure, really; you move in on a company whose shares are undervalued, or which is sitting on a pile of unspent earnings, take it over with borrowed money, pay off the loans with the treasury or the income of your new acquisition, and then either break it up, by selling off the assets for as much as you can get, or "downsize" it, firing most of the workers and reminding the rest that their jobs are at risk too. The whole process makes labour negotiations go more smoothly the next time around. You explain that you are doing this to save the company and make it ready to meet competition — which, if you are really clever, you have just eliminated by buying it up. Granted, there will be an outcry from some of those who wind up on the street, but their tragedies are just a part of the necessary process of economic progress. In Canada in 1997, $100.9 billion was laid out in private funds — nearly all tax-deductible — to promote such mergers; that is, an amount equal to about two-thirds of the federal government's total spending of just over $160 billion was blown away to allow corporations to buy other corporations.[21] In 1998 the figure will be much higher, especially if the bank merger mania, which began with the proposed $40 billion merger of the Royal Bank with the Bank of Montreal, comes off.[22] This was quickly followed, in April 1998, by a similar merger announcement from the Canadian Imperial Bank of Commerce and the Toronto-Dominion Bank, which wanted to be joined as a $47 billion giant.

Frederick Lewis Allen, the biographer of J.P. Morgan, called the process of one company swallowing another "a device for the manufacture of millionaires";[23] we call it "restructuring," which has a nicer ring to it. Same thing. George Pullman, the railroad-car magnate, fired one-third of his workforce in 1894 in one of these exercises and cut the wages of the rest by 25 per cent. When the men went on strike, every newspaper in the land warned that they were attacking "property rights" and assured them that what was being done was only for the good of the company — the good of the workers — in the end. Sounded just like a *Globe and Mail* editorial of today. When U.S. president Grover Cleveland marshalled troops to crush the strike but was asked to keep out of it, he replied: "You may as well ask me to dissolve the government of the United States!"[24]

Merging is not the only way to make a lot of money; there are fortunes out there for the really creative non-merger. Cast a brief glance at what happened when Falconbridge Ltd., the giant

Canadian mining company, went through a non-merger with a rival. Falconbridge had offered just under $4 billion to take over Diamond Fields Resources Inc. and its huge holdings at Voisey's Bay in Labrador.[25] Falconbridge made its offer in February 1996; Diamond Fields looked at it, saw it was good, and signed some papers. Then along came Inco, Falconbridge's chief rival, and offered $500 million more than Falconbridge had. Diamond Fields tore up the first deal and accepted Inco's offer. Diamond Fields had put up $28 million as a "commitment fee," and Falconbridge got to keep that. In addition, it received $78 million for a "non-completion fee."

The whole saga was written off as a business expense, and shared with the taxpayer. At least all this money isn't being wasted on food, shelter, and clothes for the poor, the elderly and the disabled — who don't do a damn thing for global competition.

Downsizing with Chainsaw Al

While many of the activities of our new robber barons are reminiscent of the bad old days, the process of throwing workers out of the corporation to bring down costs is no longer handled with the same irresponsible verve, or panache, as it was back then. But there are some regrettable exceptions. One of these exceptions came to public notice in the case of "Chainsaw" Al Dunlap, one of the heroes of the new economic order. *Time* magazine described him as "a talkative, roll-up-the-sleeves corporate turnaround specialist."[26]

He was named CEO of Scott Paper, the international giant, in 1994. He proceeded to cut the workforce by 35 per cent, unload billions of dollars worth of assets, and then sell the firm to its rival, Kimberley-Clark. By that time, Scott's shares had tripled in value, and Chainsaw Al, via generous stock options and grants, tucked away US$100 million for his work. Then he moved over to Sunbeam Corp., whose earnings were in decline. Sunbeam's stock price jumped 50 per cent the day he signed on.*

---

*Alas, the *Wall Street Journal* reported, on June 14, 1998, that Chainsaw Al was dumped in turn when Sunbeam Corp. rang up a loss in its second quarter of the year. He had slashed about 12,000 jobs at Sunbeam, but was unable to deliver a fat profit, as promised. At this writing, he is working for a fat severance package, instead.

Chainsaw Al is not altogether approved of by the gang when they gather around the water-cooler. When posing for a photograph that was to capture the essence of the new nobility, Al wore criss-crossed bandoliers across his chest and brandished an automatic weapon, like a latter-day Zapata. His posturing was described as crude, and even Al later admitted, "That was a dumb idea."[27]

It helps a lot to say, "Gosh, we're sorry, but owing to circumstances, we have to fire quite a few of you. Nothing personal, just the inscrutable working of the market." This was the approach Bell Canada took when, after the first half of 1997, it found itself earning only $372 million (up 9 per cent from the previous year). It fired 2,200 employees, even though it had promised three months earlier, when it had slashed 10,000 workers under a three-year restructuring plan, that it wouldn't try to hack its way to better profits.[28]

When Eastman Kodak Company slashed 10,000 workers from the payroll in 1997, it actually apologized. "We are embarrassed by this year," Kodak chairman George Fisher said. "We are clearly mad at ourselves, for the most part, that we got ourselves into the situation we find ourselves in today."[29] This embarrassment and anger did not go as far as to provoke the downsizing of the executives who made the decisions that created the situation.

The justification is always the same: if the corporations flourish, the nation will flourish. Only if the corporations have the profits to allow expansion will they hire more workers, and only if they are able to make money will we be able to prosper. Or, as our bank presidents like to remind us each winter when we chafe at the release of their obscene profits: "Our profits are your profits."[30] Between 1989 and 1995, Canadian corporate income rose by 6.5 per cent, while the average Canadian family income dropped by 3 per cent.[31] Our companies are doing much better, but the rest of us are doing much worse. It's not that the companies are intentionally out to despoil us. They are out to make themselves rich, by whatever means, and if that means we are despoiled, well, so be it.

It was against precisely this kind of corporate behaviour that we built up the modern state's bothersome bureaucracy, for reasons that John Kenneth Galbraith understood:

From the free operation of the market there is injustice, pain and hardship, which no society, either from compassion or wisdom, can tolerate. This we accept; from this acceptance comes the complementary role of the state.[32]

Not any more; the state is a bloody nuisance, and so we move around its encircling strictures in a way that would have left the old robber barons shaking their heads with admiration. We call it "globalism," "international competition," or, most mendaciously, "free" trade. Let's take a look at how it works out, in the next chapter.

12

The High Cost of "Free" Trade

The economic concept of free trade (that is, trade which is unfettered by government-imposed trade restrictions), is unlikely ever to be achieved between two sovereign countries.
— Royal Commission on the Economic Union and Development
   Prospects for Canada (Macdonald Commission), *Report*, 1985

The newspaper photo shows a boy about seven years of age, with a humongous hammer hoisted over his shoulder, staring straight into the camera. He looks old. He's a kid, all right, with spindly legs and arms, scruffy hair, a dirty face, and clothes in tatters, but his eyes look old. It's a sucker picture, of course, taken to make us feel sorry for the little guy, who, after ten or twelve hours of whacking away at rocks in this quarry, probably goes home and eats two, or even three, crusts of bread. Well, not bread, the picture was taken in Mexico. He probably goes home and has a few tortillas. We are not to be taken in by his woebegone looks. The truth is, he should be proud of himself. He is one of the foot soldiers of progress. When he breaks rocks for a few cents an hour, he is contributing to global competitiveness. If you want to crack rocks, a necessary job for building purposes, and you want to do it cheaply, you can't afford to employ unionized labour. Of course, you can use machines, but they cost quite a lot, and moving them around is also expensive. So, as long as we can keep child wages low enough, it's still productive to use them to whack rocks. Look at it this way: if the boy was getting anything like a living wage, it would make more sense for the construction company to bring in a machine, and then the youngster wouldn't have any job at all. The big advantage this little guy has over your children and mine is that he's not wasting his time in school. He's contributing to the global economy, right now.

However, with any luck, the way things are going, our children will soon be standing next to this one, looking old, and joining in the fun of contributing to free trade.

In economic terms, free trade has a specific meaning. It refers to commerce carried on without the hindrance of import duties, export bounties, domestic production subsidies, trade quotas, or import licences. There are no tariffs and no Buy Canadian (or American, or Japanese) policies, especially in government deals. In theory, free trade is wonderful. It may be hard to point to a single instance in history where it has actually worked, but that does not diminish the fact that, in theory, it is wonderful.

Free trade exploits the economic concept of comparative advantage. David Ricardo, a stockbroker and self-made millionaire, came up with this concept in 1817,[1] and it seemed to make sense. Each nation, or each region of a nation, should concentrate on what it can produce most cheaply; it should then exchange these goods with others for the things it cannot produce so efficiently. Canadians drink orange juice, but we are not renowned for our orange groves. Rather than spending money to erect greenhouses, it makes more sense for us to bring juice in from the United States, Mexico, or South Africa, and save our energies for making maple syrup.

Similarly, we are not as good at producing television sets or computers as the Japanese. There is a benefit to us, and to them, if we import these products and export, say, newsprint, to Japan. The illustration Ricardo used was similar: if Portugal could produce cloth with the labour of one hundred men, and wine with the labour of eighty men, and if England could produce the same amount of cloth with eighty men, and the same amount of wine with one hundred, it would be advantageous to both to trade English cloth for Portuguese wine.

The same argument applies to regions. Saskatchewan grows wheat better than Newfoundland does, but Newfoundland provides cod more efficiently than Saskatchewan — or did, until the supply ran out. Canada as a whole is an efficient producer of forest products, steel, and petrochemicals; Taiwan can make cheaper textiles and computer chips. If goods are allowed to flow back and forth between regions within a nation, and between nations, consumers will benefit from cheaper goods, and everyone will benefit because the jobs lost in one place to imports will be more than made up in another place in exports.

Free trade brings other benefits, too. If there are barriers to foreign competition, domestic corporations will be able to charge higher prices. They will also be able to afford to be less efficient, for there is no alternative. But protectionists do not accept these arguments. In unveiling his National Policy, Sir John A. Macdonald asked: "What can be more reasonable than to so adjust the tariff for revenue purposes that it will enable us to meet our engagements, and to develop our resources, the duties falling upon the articles we ourselves are capable of producing?"[2] He promised he would provide government income, and work, by erecting a tariff wall around Canada behind which manufacturing could flourish, without competition. Foreign firms would be forced to establish plants in Canada to obtain access to our markets, and they would provide jobs. Macdonald vowed, in the 1878 election campaign in which he pushed the National Policy, that protection would bring an influx of 30,000 skilled workers to Canada to staff the new factories.

In a way, it worked. But there were, as always, some winners and some losers. A number of industries, such as sugar processing, which had decayed, sprang back to life behind the tariff wall Macdonald erected. The cotton industry blossomed, with some mills returning 100 per cent on their invested capital in a single year. However, it soon became clear that manufacturers were using this protection to raise prices, and many firms collapsed in the recession that began soon afterwards in 1883. The next year, 6,000 jobs vanished, while wages plummeted. It was not exactly what Macdonald had promised.[3]

Over the years, we learned that free trade can provide both the positive advantage of greater efficiency and the negative advantage of curbing price-gougers through foreign competition. We also learned that a protectionist tariff is a tax borne by consumers, in the form of higher prices. However, free trade does have its own inherent disadvantages as well. Consider the theory again: there is a comparative advantage in specialization. There is, in particular, the advantage of huge production runs. You can make electric mixers more cheaply in a plant that turns out a million a year than in one that turns out a thousand. You can make cars "cheaper by the million," too. This system is known as "the economies of scale."

So, economics argues that we should serve North American markets with a few huge factories that export their products all over the world. But if there are to be only a handful of factories in North America, where will they be situated? Not in Canada. In the case of automobiles, they will almost certainly be built in the United States, homeland of the giant automakers. To prevent such an imbalance, Canada and the United States created the Auto Pact in 1965. The agreement set down, in rigorous detail, the conditions under which cars and parts are permitted to move back and forth between the two countries free of tariff. These clauses include a requirement that three-quarters of the vehicles sold in Canada must be manufactured here, and complex rules about the amount of Canadian content that the vehicles must contain if they are not to draw down a financial penalty.

The Auto Pact is touted again and again by its proponents as an example of the advantages of free trade. But it is, in fact, an example of the opposite. It illustrates the need to control the conditions under which manufactured goods pass across the border. If free trade in autos and parts were what the designers had in mind, all they would have had to do was remove the tariffs from existing legislation. It was, and remains, the tariff system, not free trade, that makes the Auto Pact work for both nations.

If we push the economies-of-scale argument to its logical conclusion, a few giant factories run by a few giant firms are all that is required to supply not only home markets but the markets of the world. And these factories will not be placed in Canada. The trend has already begun. They will be established in Taiwan, for cheap labour; in China, for an absence of any human rights restrictions; in nations where friendly political regimes offer bribes and anti-union laws; and in the United States, because of the pressure on political leaders to provide jobs in their home constituencies.

The factories will not, as a rule, be in Canada. If there were no barriers to trade in the world, and only economic considerations were to guide international commerce, then, before long, every nation would be an economic province within a single empire. Probably an American empire; possibly Japanese, or European. Never Canadian. Our role in such an empire would be the one Abraham Gesner, a founder of the modern petroleum industry, saw in 1849. We would supply wood and water, raw materials and energy. Oh, yes, and markets.

The global corporation is not the stateless wonder it likes to think it is, and the home government of the most aggressive global corporations — the United States government — plays hardball on behalf of its own corporations, which also happen to be the major contributors to its political parties. And it wins. When the Free Trade Agreement was put in place in 1989, opening our markets to the Americans, we soon discovered that their markets were not nearly so open to us because, wherever we had a comparative advantage — in softwood lumber, for example — they simply bent or broke the rules to establish tariffs, or non-tariff barriers, on our products.

Another of the difficulties of the theory of comparative advantage is that we live in an uneven world. It would be much better if there were some sort of balance: if the Americans were efficient in the production of automobiles, but not electronics; if we were whizzes with electronics, the Japanese with steel, the Germans with furniture, and so on. But once established, a large industrial nation has an enormous advantage over its competitors in many fields, if not all. The Japanese produce radios more cheaply than we do; but they also produce computers, microchips, and hundreds of other products better than we do. The Americans, backed by a home market that gives them a huge economy of scale, are better than we are at producing not only toasters but also textiles, ballpoint pens, and much more. It isn't hard to work out which goods Canada can produce more cheaply than the United States — and the Americans still have tariff or non-tariff barriers on most of them: manufactured steel, fish, softwood lumber, and cedar shingles.

A nation whose factories are more efficient than those of its competitors will dominate the market and use its profits to take over and dominate other industries. An advantage gained by making widgets, let's say, allows the widget corporation to invest in mining, real estate, and beer. It can then establish branch plants in the target nation, and they will squeeze out local competition. Canada was once the third-largest automobile maker in the world, in its own name. Now there is no such thing as a Canadian car; there are only Canadian-made American cars, or Canadian-made Japanese cars, or Canadian-made cars from other countries.

We need more jobs

There's little in global markets for the consumer, either. Once dominant, the market-leader will control prices to increase profits, punishing the consumer in the name of the maximum profit obtainable for the shareholder — which just happens to be the intruding corporation itself.

The argument for the removal of barriers to trade is based on the supposition that world markets will provide huge increases in productivity. So they do. But our problem is not productivity. We produce far more products than we can absorb. All the beer sold in Canada could be furnished by a single plant, and probably would be except for the intervention of provincial governments to prevent that happening.

We don't need more things; we need more jobs. There is nothing in the argument for free trade that will produce more jobs beyond the constant claim that they will, somehow, exist. The collapse of the manufacturing sector in Canada in the wake of the signing of the Free Trade Agreement wasn't real, apparently; it was just a rumour started by a bunch of people waiting around for unemployment cheques. After the Free Trade Agreement came into force, its boosters always regretted that there was no way, really, to show whether jobs were being lost as a result. Factories were closing, certainly, but was that because of free trade, or other factors? Tom d'Aquino, spokesman for the Business

Council on National Issues, which oversaw the spending of $5 million by Canadian corporations to back the deal, dismissed any idea of trying to measure whether jobs were up or down as mere "scorecardism." He told Linda Diebel of the *Toronto Star*:

> It's really a very, very difficult thing to do. It's really going to be difficult to be terribly specific. I squirm and get terribly uncomfortable, and sometimes even angry, when people opposed to the deal come up with their scorecards. It's not responsible.[4]

In an attempt to offset this drivel, the Canadian Labour Congress compiled a list of plant closings directly tied to the agreement:

> Northern Telecom — moving production of telephone switching equipment from Aylmer, Quebec, to Georgia — 650 jobs.
> Silvaco — closing Ingersoll plant, shifting production to New York State — 125 jobs.
> Albright and America — closing chemical plant in Long Harbour, Newfoundland, and moving plant to Lee Creek, North Carolina — 200 jobs.
> Canadian Coleman — closing Etobicoke facility, work transferred to Kansas and Texas — 214 jobs.[5]

It went on for pages and pages and was, all in all, pretty boring. But what it showed was that 72,000 jobs were lost — jobs that the union knew about because the losses affected its members — in the first full year of the Free Trade Agreement. The union might as well have saved itself the effort. Our newspapers were either puzzled by the fact that it seemed to be so difficult to figure out if jobs were being lost or gained, or overjoyed because Canada was exporting more. Yet the numbers were telling us that, while new jobs were being created in Canada, our relative position was constantly slipping backwards. As Mel Hurtig put it:

> Since the FTA was implemented, Canada's population grew by some 2.7 million, yet full-time employment is still back about where it was in 1989. During the first seven years of the FTA,

full-time employment in Canada grew at less than one-sixth the rate for the previous seven years.[6]

In the years before the Free Trade Agreement, Canada's unemployment was roughly the same as that of the United States; now it is about double. In the first three years of that treaty, Canada lost about one-quarter of its manufacturing jobs.[7] Its heartland collapsed, plummeting real estate values and causing a sharp drop in the gross domestic product. In 1988, the year before the deal, the GDP grew by $54.3 billion; in 1991, it grew by only $7.0 billion.[8]

To believe that making our corporations larger will result in more jobs is to believe in the tooth fairy. Globalism is all about shedding jobs in one nation and replacing them in another, cheaper nation, not about creating them. The International Labour Organization released a report in January 1998 which underlined this effect. Leading multinational corporations, including General Motors Canada, Ford Canada Limited, General Electric, Allied Signal, United Technologies, Rockwell International, Dupont Chemical, and 3M, slashed 18,462 jobs from their Canadian operations after the Free Trade Agreement went through, and created 47,045 jobs in Mexico between 1990 and 1996.[9] Multinational corporations have grown sevenfold in sales in the last generation, without any increase in employment.[10]

Our opinion makers were not impressed. If we were exporting more, we must be making more. So, we must have created more jobs. A typical response was the lyrical editorial in the *Globe and Mail* of February 1997. Looking back on the employment issue it enthused:

> Since 1991, Canadian exports have increased by 90 per cent, and they have more than doubled to the fearsome United States. Our imports, meanwhile, have grown by only 71 per cent, creating the biggest trade surplus in Canadian history last year: $34.1 billion on exports of $267.1 billion.[11]

True, there was a huge gain in Canadian exports to the United States, but it had nothing to do with the removal of tariffs. By 1987, 80 per cent of Canada's exports to the United States entered duty free, and another 15 per cent faced duties of less than 5 per cent. In effect, we were going through this whole nation-gutting exercise to avoid tariffs on 5 per cent of our exports to the American market.[12] Moreover, most of the export gains came in only two areas — autos and auto parts, which still carry tariffs that can be avoided only by complying with the rules; and resources, for which there had been no tariffs when the deal went through.

The export boom came about because of the collapse of the Canadian dollar. Our exporters had, and still have, an advantage of about 40 per cent when shipping into American markets; by the same token, Americans face a 40 per cent hurdle coming into Canada. Without this advantage, the devastation of our industrial heartland, which lost about 25 per cent of its jobs, would have been much worse. The collapse in the dollar, in turn, came about because, while we have been shipping out more manufactured goods to the United States than ever before, we have also been shipping out more profits, patent fees, management costs, and interest on debts than ever before, as Americans take over more and more of our infrastructure and send the takings home. Our trade balance is positive, but our current account balance, which reflects travel, business services, and investment income balance (the interest and dividends paid to foreigners) is negative, and getting larger every year.

In 1995, when we had a trade surplus of $28 billion, we had an investment income deficit of $41 billion and a current account deficit of $13 billion.[13] We borrow to cover this annual deficit, and we are getting deeper and deeper into debt, especially to the United States, with every passing year. We now owe more than $339 billion to foreigners, most of it to Americans. Why don't we get excited about that? Because to do so would be to acknowledge that free trade involves trade not only in goods but also in services, dividends, and management fees, and that, overall, we are heavy losers in the process.

What's more, a good deal of this increased trade, as with most trade in the world these days, consists of corporations moving their own goods from their own factories to other factories they also own, for the best price advantage. We aren't selling them tractors, they are selling themselves tractor parts, at prices they arrange internally, and taking off the profits wherever it suits them best. About 40 per cent of global trade, according to one American study, consists of the intrafirm trade of the subsidiaries of the cosmocorporations. Another 20 to 30 per cent is managed directly by governments, on behalf of their own corporations. Lawrence B. Krause, international relations professor at the University of California in San Diego, aggregated all the different ways in which trade was massaged and concluded that only about 15 per cent of global trade was genuinely conducted in free-market circumstances.[14] If prices go down for consumers, it is a temporary and illusory relief because income always goes down faster than prices. A staggering 70 per cent of all international trade is controlled by a mere 500 corporations, many of which are much larger, in terms of assets, than nations.

When Gordon Ritchie, Canada's ambassador for the free trade negotiations, wrote a book ten years after the deal, he was still ambivalent about its results. On the one hand, he considers free trade and "open" relationships to be good; on the other, he thinks the Americans are so aggressive in their dealings that he calls his chapter on the triumph of their protectionist policies "Thugs and Bullies." Here is his summation in his final chapter:

There is no question that Canadian society has grown closer to the American model over the past ten years. Our increasing wealth has not been evenly shared and the disparities of income have become more pronounced, particularly between those with jobs and those without, between the old and the young. Our cities have become more violent and the cancer of the drug trade more pervasive. Our politics has generally moved farther to the right at the national and provincial levels. Governments at all levels have reduced their spending, even on such vital areas as health and education.

I deplore these trends, but it is much too facile to attribute them to increased American influence because of the Free Trade Agreement. Many of these problems arise from mistakes entirely of our own making.

These "mistakes" turn out to be only one mistake — "massive" overspending in the 1970s and 1980s. Then, he concludes: "Free trade can be used as a powerful instrument to advance Canada's political, social and economic interests in a challenging and competitive world."[15] How? Ritchie doesn't say, except that "these arrangements must be properly managed." I hope Ritchie is going to write another book to tell us the answer. John A. Macdonald, who was no fool, thought free trade too expensive for Canada for just the reasons Ritchie discovered more than a century later; but at least John A. learned something from the exercise.

The Free Trade Agreement, like its offspring, the North American Free Trade Agreement, is not a free trade deal at all; it is a sectoral trade arrangement. We have joined the club not to open it to the crude masses, but so we can invite in the presentable and exclude the rest. You do not sign on to a fraternity to rub elbows with the unwashed. The entire process is driven by the need to open markets for corporations, not to provide opportunities for people. These larger sectoral markets provide the environment in which corporations can accumulate financial surpluses on a vast scale, but they leave nations exposed, specialized, and vulnerable. Control of the economy is transferred from the state to financial and commercial interests. Nations lose the power to direct their own political future and to serve the needs and priorities of their own people.

With both the Free Trade Agreement and the North American Free Trade Agreement, Canadian objectives, such as environmental protection and decent labour laws, were swept aside. The Americans complained bitterly that our medicare system gave Canadian firms an unfair advantage. So it does; medical insurance for American workers costs up to $10,000 a year each. We are in the process of responding to this complaint by destroying medicare. That is no accident.

Corporations, not nations, gain as tariffs drop

Even if the theory of comparative advantage worked, and all nations benefitted, they would no longer be nations. We would have the Principality of Pepsi Cola, the Earldom of Exxon, and the Empire of IBM. Nations do not gain as tariffs drop; corporations do. Ask anyone from the Third World. The rich get richer and the poor starve. In some African nations, poverty-stricken people spend up to 25 per cent of their incomes on cigarettes pushed at them by an industry that sees its own home markets shrinking.

British economist John Maynard Keynes made the key point when he wrote:

> If nations can learn to provide themselves with full employ-ment by their domestic policy . . . international trade would cease to be what it is, namely, a desperate expedient to main-tain employment at home by forcing sales on foreign markets and restricting purchases.[16]

Every nation of sense will try to reduce the barriers to interna-tional trade to the maximum extent consistent with its own situation, first, to keep its own corporations from soaking the consumers, and, second, because there is a degree of greater effi-ciency obtainable through the free movement of goods. But for Keynes the "maximum extent" possible was a matter of practical calculation, not economic cant.

Liberalized trade is what people and nations of prudence and sense aim for; free trade is a crock. One of the more revealing, but less noted, sentences in the Macdonald Commission report of 1985, which set off the movement towards the Free Trade Agreement, underscores its impracticability: "The economic concept of free trade (that is, trade which is unfettered by gov-ernment-imposed trade restrictions), is unlikely ever to be achieved between two sovereign countries."[17]

The model of the European Community, often held up for our approval, has nothing to do with our situation. If that union proves anything, it is that a regional trade bloc can be success-fully formed — and used as a battering ram in world markets — only when partners of more-or-less equal strength come together. A second condition is that the partner countries each possess vig-orous manufacturing sectors capable of taking advantage of the markets opened by the union. Neither of these conditions applies to Canada. We are not more-or-less equal to the Americans; together, we made a stew with one rabbit and one horse (and the Mexicans threw in an ass). As for the Canadian manufac-turing sector, we only give it houseroom; it belongs to others, mainly Americans, who own or control most of our dominant corporations.

The North American Free Trade Agreement simply led us further down the garden path. It was sold to us as an opportunity to compete, and so it is. Our wage slaves get to compete with Mexicans, whose hourly wages are less than one-tenth of ours. Custom Trim Ltd., a corporation which has a plant in Waterloo, Ontario, and another plant in Mexico, pays workers in Ontario $12.22 an hour and in Mexico, 71 cents an hour.[18] It is no mystery where the company is hiring, and where it is laying off staff.

The *daily* minimum wage in Mexico is now the equivalent of $4.72 Canadian,[19] but the purchasing power of that wage has been cut by 30 per cent because the Mexican peso was devalued in December 1994. Canadian workers are losing jobs, Mexican workers are losing purchasing power, and we are in a race to the bottom that has no apparent end.

When electronics workers in Malaysia tried to organize, to improve wages ranging from US$130 to US$150 a month, the government, at the prodding of its multinational partners, immediately banned all independent unions. Then some of the companies moved to Vietnam, where the pay was about 10 per cent of that in Malaysia, or to China, where the minimum wage in the new industrial zones around Shanghai was established at the equivalent of US$24 a month. Companies use their own workers anywhere in the world to undercut workers at home, as Swissair did when it began shipping 20 million airline tickets to Bombay for processing by Indian computer specialists who make one-tenth of Swiss salaries. In Germany, Daimler-Benz conducted an international bidding contest for its new small-car plant, and in the process extracted cutbacks from its union totalling DM 200 million (about CAN$160 million) and eliminated 80,000 jobs.[20]

The preferred instrument for exploitation these days is a duty-free zone, such as the *maquiladoras* along the U.S.–Mexican border, where labour and environmental laws are a joke. These zones can be created by whatever government wants in on the action. Canada is going to have its own local model, if all goes well, in New Brunswick. The provincial government sold the option to develop a 400-hectare parcel of land which it had expropriated in Lorneville, just outside Saint John, to AMW Holdings Ltd. of Toronto, for $1, in December 1997.[21] This new duty-free facility will allow us to compete with other similar zones in Asia, the United States, and Mexico.

When our overlords tell us we must compete with others in the new global economy, they mean we must compete with a moving target. Cutting our pay to the Malaysian level won't do, when companies can still skip off to Shanghai.

But aren't these companies competing in the same rough way? No, what they are doing is the opposite. They buy out the competition and control the markets. They fire workers, bump up productivity, and then give themselves huge raises out of the results. When Ford Canada dumped 8 per cent of its workforce, it created 11,688 new jobs in the *maquiladoras*. Productivity at Ford Canada went up by 88 per cent. The company responded by allowing wages in the remaining Canadian jobs to grow by 33 per cent, while executive compensation jumped by 645 per cent, according to the International Labour Organization.[22]

The result of the triumph of "free" trade has not been an increase in wealth, but a huge and growing disparity between rich and poor. In 1960 the ratio between the incomes of the world's richest and poorest was 30 to 1; by 1993 it had soared to 60 to 1. Billionaires are being created at a rate never seen before. At last count, the world boasted 358 of them, and together they owned more than countries totalling 45 per cent of the world's population earn in a year.[23]

For ever-expanding corporations, what these new treaties mean is the availability of a pool of cheap labour and the removal of all those pesky environmental laws, labour laws, safety rules, and other detriments to the bottom line. If the corporations get caught, and a fuss is made over the way they treat their workers, they can always say it was all a misunderstanding, or that they are obeying the local laws of whatever dictatorship they have happened to wind up in. Look at Nike, for example. When the leaked copy of an audit of a Vietnamese factory that makes shoes for Nike showed that workers were being paid slightly more than US$10 a week to labour in a plant where they were exposed to carcinogens, Nike's public relations people swung into action. The fact that there had been an audit and that Nike had taken steps to improve the working conditions showed that "our system works," they said. From here on, the workers would follow a new Nike code — "no more than 60 hours a week of work." Oh, yes, and Nike had also "complied with Vietnamese labour laws."[24] What a relief.

The MAI makes corporations into nations

It is not a matter of surprise that our business community, by and large, embraces free trade, despite its demonstrably dismal record. Corporations get the raises, while their workers get the pink slips. Nor is it a surprise that this same community favours our immediate embrace of the newest venture into free trade dogma, the Multilateral Agreement on Investment, or MAI, which first appeared in draft form in January 1997.

We have seen that free trade has become a process to enhance corporations, rather than nations or people. The MAI takes this process one step further, under the auspices of the Organization for Economic Co-operation and Development, and makes corporations into nations.[25] The MAI proposes to make every trading nation treat every foreign corporation exactly the same way as it treats every homegrown corporation.[26] If Canada tried, for example, to impose any restrictions on foreign imports because they came from companies that violated human rights, labour relations, or environmental rules, that would be illegal. If our government were to do anything that one of the multinationals thought interfered with its interests — which is, come to think of it, a pretty good definition of the role of government in many circumstances — the corporation could sue, and collect, on the grounds that a government was trying to protect its own people. Under the World Trade Organization rules, only a nation can bring another nation into court on these matters; under the MAI, any corporation that thinks its rights have been, or are about to be, or might be, interfered with can tie up the process for years. For example, if a nation, as it were, Canada, passed a law banning all tobacco advertising, the tobacco companies could haul it into court on the grounds that it was in violation of the non-discrimination clauses of the treaty, and keep the case going for years.

Richard Gwyn calls the MAI "a charter of rights for absentee landlords."[27] He is right.

The treaty proposal, while conferring huge benefits on private corporations, does not confer on them any additional responsibilities; there is nothing in it about labour standards or environmental protection. The restrictions are all heaped on what is left of the nation state. We couldn't give any grant, loan, tax incentive, or subsidy to any Canadian company without making it available to Walt Disney et al. Nor could we limit the right of Sony Corp, or any other foreign firm, to bid on any privatized public infrastructure, social good, or cultural transmission. In fact, under the draft treaty, any provision of goods by any government to its citizens is a monopoly, subject to strict controls. Such social goods as medicare or public education would have to be priced "solely in accordance with commercial considerations."[28] However, and here's the best part, monopolies of knowledge by corporate copyright are given a special exemption. They are classed as non-monopolies.

The MAI aims to end, once and for all, all our loose talk about protecting indigenous culture. Canadian content rules would be forbidden, as would any form of restriction on the foreign ownership of cultural industries. Even if we were able to put in place a series of exceptions to protect Canadian cultural and social programs, the treaty contains a clause requiring us to eliminate all "non-conforming measures," ensuring that any safeguards are temporary.

In the negotiations, Canada is seeking forty-eight reservations in the areas of culture, environment, and social policy. However, these restrictions are all subject to "roll-back" provisions. If some of them are granted, they will be removed, one by one, just as similar exceptions under the Free Trade Agreement and North American Free Trade Agreement became null and void. Linda McQuaig argues, with characteristic clarity, that the proposed treaty is "a one-way street in which capital-holders are given the power to challenge the laws of democratically elected governments and governments are given no powers over them." The end result, she suggests, will be unavoidable: "If the MAI comes into force . . . the impotence of democratic governments will not only be a reality but one enshrined in law."[29]

The MAI, or Madness Associated with Industry, was to have been signed and then made public, but someone leaked a copy of the draft. Now our government is saying not to worry, everything is still negotiable. That's what it said about free trade at first. Then it became "Oops, can't change anything now, too late." The storm of protest that broke out after the details of the negotiations became public gave the federal government pause. Then the Americans announced that they would not accept the new deal unless it was renegotiated to wipe out any possibility of cultural protection, and the French said that they would not sign without much stronger cultural protection. So the whole process was put on hold until the end of 1998, and this delay led to a number of stories in the newspapers suggesting that the MAI was dead. Not dead, not even wounded. As I write, the likelihood is that the whole process will be moved away from the OECD as sponsor to the World Trade Organization, which seems a more natural body to deal with trading issues. But if you believe the international financial community is going to let up on this chance to give cosmocorporations the power of nation states, I have some shares in Bre-X you might want to buy.

An old *New Yorker* cartoon had a parent trying to feed veggies to a kid, with the line, "But it's broccoli, dear." The kid replied, "I say it's spinach, and I say to hell with it." The MAI is spinach. To hell with it. It makes J.P. Morgan's "community of interest" into a global trade treaty and removes from the argument the nation state, which alone stands between the new Lords of Creation and their prey — the rest of us.

Private Parts

Canadians still appear to be hemmed in by the
American ethnocentric notion that economics is
basically a matter of private ownership and the rules
of free enterprise . . . The undeniable success of a
public enterprise comes to appear, then, as nothing
short of magic.

— Herschel Hardin, *A Nation Unaware*, 1974

"Once upon a time," the senior bureaucrat said, shuffling the papers on his desk, *"there lived in York County — that's just north of here — a heroic pig. His name was Drake."*

"Why Drake?" I asked.

The senior bureaucrat frowned. He did not like being interrupted. We were sitting in his office on the fourth floor of a government building in downtown Fredericton, New Brunswick, and he had already made it clear that he ought not to be talking to me, that he did not want to be quoted by name or identified by rank, and that he was pressed for time. He cleared his throat.

"Possibly he was named for the Elizabethan admiral, who was also bold and venturesome. May I continue?"

I begged him to go on.

"Once, when the young Drake was rooting around the barnyard, Arabella, the farmer's daughter, fell into the millpond. Quick as a

flash the porker dashed across the yard, threw himself into the pond, and pulled the little girl to safety."

"Gosh," I said.

"On another occasion, the farmer — his name was Henry, not that it matters — became trapped underneath his tractor, which he had overturned by driving too fast. Drake crawled under the wreck and propped it up, allowing Henry to scramble free."

"Some pig," I ventured.

"Then there was the time when the toolshed caught fire, trapping the farmer's ten-year-old son, William, behind a wall of flame. Nothing could be done, the blaze was so fierce. And then, just as the roof began to crash down on the boy, Drake rushed inside, allowing the collapsing structure to bounce off his broad back. He was lightly burned, but the lad rolled free, unharmed.

"It was not long after this incident that one of Henry's neighbours dropped by and noticed that Drake was limping around on three legs. The fourth was gone entirely.

"'What happened to Drake?' he inquired.

"'Well sir,' the farmer replied, 'when you get a valuable pig like Drake, you don't want to eat him all at once.'"

The senior bureaucrat raised his eyebrows. I raised mine back. I said it was an interesting story, but I had asked him about privatization.

"This is about privatization," he said.

They are bears for privatization in New Brunswick. Jails, schools, hospital services, cafeterias — almost anything owned by the public has been priced, packaged, and sold to the private sector at breakdown prices. The process reached its climax when a Chicago-based company, Andersen Consulting Ltd., was hired to oversee a $60 million project to reform and privatize the province's justice system. It was called the "Justice Enterprise," and, to make a long story short, it finally sank beneath a barrage of angry memos in the spring of 1997, with not much accomplished except that Andersen Consulting walked off with a fee of $2.9 million for its trouble.[1]

Months before that, opposition members had raised concerns

in the legislature that a number of Andersen's similar enterprises in the United States had set off a series of lawsuits against the company. In fact, the New Brunswick deputy minister of justice, Paul LeBreton, had already written a memo describing the enterprise in pointed language. "Planning ourselves into bankruptcy," is the way he put it then, noting that the consulting giant had yet to meet either the budget or the deadlines for the work.[2]

Other bureaucrats complained that the company's proposals were vague, soft, and hard to understand. There was, for example, this bit of advice from the consultants from the Windy City:

> The Justice Enterprise is not a formal entity. It is a virtual grouping of the collective services offered by all organizations that play a role in the justice system. New Brunswick Integrated Justice does not propose that such an organization should exist in a formal sense. However, since the Enterprise viewpoint is frequently the layman's view of the justice system, significant benefit can be derived for all contributors, from assessing the performance of the overall justice system as though it were a single enterprise.[3]

I have no idea what this means, and neither, apparently, did the people who were paying the bills, so they finally pulled the plug. Andersen Consulting was able to bear the blow, however; not only was it walking off with $2.9 million but it still had a contract to redesign the Department of Human Resource Development the Andersen way, with proposed savings to the taxpayer of $85 million. If the plan worked out the way it was supposed to, Andersen would take its fee of $16.5 million. Just after the Justice Enterprise deal collapsed, Andersen was also hired to work for the Harris government in Ontario. Again, it will be paid a portion of the money it saves.[4] The lesson, it seems, is that we must privatize government enterprises because, as everyone knows, private corporations are efficient and governments are bungling.

Despite the teachings of history, we still rigorously divide our notions of economic efficiency into two watertight sectors: the public economy and the private one. This segregation allows us to accept with equanimity that the one sector, public, can be starved while the other, private, is loaded up with goodies from the same purse that has snapped shut on the public sector.

The reality is much closer to the view of economist Robert Reich, who was labour secretary in the Clinton administration from 1993 to 1997:

> Every major industry in America is deeply involved with and dependent on government. The competitive position of every American firm is affected by government policy. No sharp distinction can validly be drawn between private and public sectors within this or any other advanced industrialized country; the economic effects of public policies and corporate decisions are completely intertwined.[5]

What Reich is describing is the way the economy actually works, not the way it functions in the columns of the *Wall Street Journal*, the *Financial Post*, or the *Globe and Mail*. Let's take some examples. When Olympia & York Limited, the development company owned by the Reichmann family of Toronto, wanted to take over Gulf Canada Limited, the nation's second-largest integrated oil company, the federal government facilitated the purchase by allowing the Reichmanns to use a tax technique called the "Little Egypt Bump," named for a famous Chicago belly-dancer. This ploy resulted in a tax savings to the corporation, and thus a tax expenditure to the people of Canada, of somewhere between $500 million and $750 million.[6] Paul Reichmann, the company chairman and the very soul of free enterprise, said there was a lot of exaggeration about these figures. John Turner, the Liberal leader, claimed the giveaway was $1 billion, but Reichmann countered that it was only $500 million, spread over five years, "with another $50 to $60 million saving after that time."[7] Well, thank heavens, I thought we were talking about real money.

When the Bronfman family of Montreal wanted to rearrange its finances by moving more than $2 billion worth of assets — including shares in Seagram's — out of the country without paying capital gains tax, they were the beneficiaries of two secret rulings made in advance by Revenue Canada to allow the move.

Auditor General Denis Desautels noted in his annual report that the manoeuvre resulted in the loss of what could have been "hundreds of millions of dollars in taxes."[8]

When AT&T Canada Enterprises Inc. announced plans to establish a call centre in Halifax in mid-1997, the province offered to give the company $12 million over five years to help with start-up expenses. Instead of recoiling in horror from this obvious example of big government pushing in, the company accepted the money. When reporters wanted to know whether AT&T would have established in Halifax without the cash, Premier Russell MacLellan told them they shouldn't ask such a question because it was "unfair."[9] Why? That is surely the nub. Ladling millions of dollars into the laps of companies like AT&T, which is not noticeably short of funds, may be a perfectly intelligent thing to do. AT&T is providing 1,000 jobs in return. But we need to know whether the bribe was necessary.

When the government of New Brunswick charged a Toronto conglomerate a meagre $1 for the option to develop a duty-free zone on 400 hectares of land the government had assembled, it was not allowing the market to decide. It was greasing the skids for one firm at the taxpayer's cost.

Only after they have the giveaways tucked safely into their wallets do most of our entrepreneurs make those speeches about getting the government off the backs of the people.

The government is broke, so let's give corporations money

These transactions, and scores of others like them which transfer monies from the cash-poor public sector to the cash-rich private sector, are defended on the grounds that they are perfectly legal and proper ways of doing business. And so they are. That, surely, is the point. When the government donates hundreds of millions of dollars to private entrepreneurs while hammering down its social welfare expenditures, the issue raised is not whether governments should play a role in the private sector. They do play such a role — a crucial role. The issue is more focused: Why should the same governments that shred the safety net, because there is no money for it, transfer money instead to private corporations?

The answer lies in the perceptions that we are fed every day by our media. According to Allan Gregg, the nation's best-known pollster, writing in *Maclean's* magazine: "People increasingly have decided that governments are simply not an important force in their everyday lives." It's quite possible that Gregg's pollsters did not interview the Reichmanns, the Bronfmans, or Revenue Canada. Anyway, a nationwide survey they conducted for *Maclean's* and the CBC through his company, Strategic Counsel, Inc., proved that Canadians were resigned to the new ways of doing things:

> In a continuing but deepening trend, overwhelming majorities expect the society of tomorrow to be a poorer, more violent place, where full-time work will be harder to come by, and people, by necessity, will be more self-sufficient. As for promises by Chrétien and other political leaders that universal health care and social programs such as unemployment insurance and old-age pensions will be maintained, poll respondents are either ignoring those assertions, or simply do not believe them.[10]

Shredding the social safety net is, apparently, a matter not for outrage but for resignation. There was an astounding coincidence in these findings, which *Maclean's*, doubtless for the best of reasons, did not share with its readers. These views were precisely the views of the Conservative Party for which Gregg was both an important pollster and a key adviser. His polls were turning up the same view of the nation that had been laid before the populace in the 1993 election, which had led to the most massive defeat of a political party in the annals of Canadian history.[11] Now he was repeddling these rejected views as the wisdom of the common man. Possibly the voters were not the same people as the respondents to the poll; possibly polls tend unconsciously to turn up the results that are in accord with the sympathies of the folks who publish the results.

Are the media feeding us their own platefuls of propaganda under the heading of "findings?"

Let's privatize

As people accept this propaganda as fact, they see the privatization craze, which has engulfed every level of government, as the working out of the public will. It is common sense. That is why the conversion of billions of dollars from public assets to private assets, which is the practical effect of many of the privatizations in Canada and around the world, has taken place against a background of thunderous applause but little study. Since we know that private enterprise will run things better than those second-raters in government can ever do, and since we know, thanks to Allan Gregg and friends, that most of the supports that made life in Canada better than in other lands are doomed, we raise no complaint when national treasures are sold off, one by one, and when Air Canada, Petro-Canada, the Canadian National, our airports, our port authorities, the Digby ferry, and everything else that is not actually nailed down become private entities.

Such privatizations usually result in huge instant benefits to the purchasers. The shares of Canadian National doubled after the company was privatized and now are worth more than three times the original price. That price was no doubt made possible by the fact that the government wrote off $900 million of CN's debt just before the sale in 1995. The sale brought the government $2.1 billion, although the company's assets were then listed at $6.1 billion (and long-term debts at $1.6 billion), making the purchase one of the great bargains of our time. The year after the sale, in 1996, CN went from a loss of $1.09 billion to a profit of $142 million, on revenues that were just about the same — $4.098 billion in 1995 and $4.159 billion in 1996.[12] This increase was not a miracle of private management, but of debt erasure; it was an act of government. A lot of people, but not the people of Canada, made huge profits. Canadian National is now 70 per cent American-owned, and doing very well indeed. So, the effect of this privatization was to take $900 million from the Canadian taxpayer and make a lot of Americans rich.

The railway is now, in effect, an American railway with a Canadian connection. In February 1998 it bought Illinois Central Corp., which owns the railroad for which Abraham Lincoln once acted as legal counsel, for $4.3 billion. The new conglomerate will be run by Hunter Harrison, chief executive officer of Illinois Central.[13]

The private sector owners also gain because one of the first things that happens in a privatization is that whatever union was protecting the workers (or, from management's point of view, forcing the company to pay excessive wages and provide benefits) is shed. When the Digby ferry was passed to a private firm in March 1997, all the workers had to reapply for their old jobs. Those who were hired got their jobs back in much worse condition than before. The federal government had made no provision in the sale for workers to keep their union.[14]

In Manitoba, a modest victory

Creating profits on the backs of the hired help doesn't always go smoothly. In Manitoba, home-care workers went on strike when they discovered that their union had been removed from them in the course of privatization, and they won a modest victory. Manitoba had established home care in 1974 because it is much cheaper, and better, to provide service to the long-term sick, elderly, and disabled in their own homes than in expensive hospitals. By 1996 the program was serving 17,000 people and receiving rave reviews as "one of the best long-term care systems in North America."[15]

Then someone got the brilliant idea of unloading the whole system onto the private sector, a move that would allow wages to be cut. The highest-paid workers were getting $10.50 an hour, and the treasury board calculated that these rates could be cut by 40 to 60 per cent. In addition, 3,000 workers would be fired from the public payroll, to scramble on the private one as best they could. Figuring they had nothing to lose — and, with the surprising support of most of their patients — the home-care workers walked out all across the province and stayed out for five weeks. The government, whose polls told it that it was making a big mistake and that the public did not look kindly on its efforts to save money at the expense of the ill and elderly, finally compromised; the hired help were given two years of job security, and the privatization process was applied only to growth in the service, not to pre-existing jobs.

This rare victory was brought about, according to Doug Smith, who reported on the strike for *This Magazine*, "because the majority of the public opposed privatization from the outset."[16] Making a profit for a private firm by reducing the meagre wages of home-care staff and cutting services to the most vulnerable in society did not play well. However, far more often, the public is either indifferent or hostile when unionized government workers — fat cats, all of them, according to the cant — face the axe. We have been well schooled.

However, if you think about it for a moment, the reason we created so many government corporations in the first place was because of necessity. We didn't believe in public enterprise, but we were almost always forced into it by circumstance. Ontario Hydro, for example, was brought into being because at the time there seemed no alternative. Coal was the usual fuel for Ontario's factories, but a disastrous and bloody strike in the Pennsylvania coalfields in 1902 (J.P. Morgan owned the fields) led to an abrupt quadrupling of the price of a ton of coal.[17] All over the province, factories shut down because of events taking place across the border.

The coming alternative for coal was electricity produced by hydro, or "white coal" as it was called. But Ontario had only one major source close to the industrial heartland — Niagara Falls. If the falls were developed by one of two competing syndicates (an American one controlled by Morgan, and a Canadian one backed by Sir Henry Pellatt, the fey financier who built Casa Loma in Toronto), the winner would have a monopoly on electricity. Ontarians knew where that would lead — to higher prices.

No one was suggesting a government monopoly, but it seemed prudent to set up a commission to look into the matter. Adam Beck, a cigar-box manufacturer from London, Ontario, and a Conservative member of the provincial parliament, was named chairman of the commission, which, to the astonishment of all, proposed a government monopoly that would be run by himself. And it was.

Since its launching in 1911, Ontario Hydro has grown into something of a monster, so now it is to be broken into three parts and sold to the private sector. Well, not all of it. The way it appears to be scheduled to happen, there will be one company to produce electricity, a second to distribute it, and a third to inherit the mountain of debt now rising around the ankles of the old corporation. The public will get to keep the third one. So, we will have three monopolies instead of one. We will sell the pig one leg at a time. How will that help? The huge advantage of the government-owned utility was that it could, and did, pool the costs of generation and transmission, so that they remained the same, regardless of the distance a customer lived from a generating station or the cost of generation at any plant. But a government policy paper on the subject makes it clear that under the new, privatized system the pooling system will be junked. Private companies will develop new generating facilities, at one end, and act as agents, marketers, and distributors at the other end.[18] Large corporations will get special bulk prices, small consumers will get stung, and added to the system will be a layer of profit that has to come from somebody. Guess whom?

There is a hidden menace in the midst of this proposed privatization, and it has to do with the question of who would pay for a nuclear meltdown. In the process of erecting nuclear facilities all over the country, the industry came under the Nuclear Liability Act, which limits the liability of any of the major Canadian nuclear operators — Ontario Hydro, Hydro-Québec, and New Brunswick Hydro — to $75 million. This limitation is based on similar American legislation; but, across the border, nuclear operators are often private concerns; in Canada, they are public, so the $75 million limitation — a risible amount if there ever were to be such a diaster — was not important. Public utilities would make safety their first priority every time. However, if nuclear plants are privatized, this cap will suddenly become important. The public purse will have to pick up most of the costs for a system it doesn't own and for which the rules are likely to be quite different. The highest priority will be making a profit, not safety.

The Wheat Board — grist for the privatization mill?
The Canadian Wheat Board came into being because of the greed and unrelieved rascality of the grain companies, the banks, the railroads, and the private elevator firms. Before its establishment, farmers, lured out onto the prairies to grow wheat and babies,

took their grain to an elevator, where it was graded and priced by the operator, a grain company employee. The farmer could accept the price, which often did not cover the cost of raising his wheat, or take it back home. He could not ship it because the CPR, which moved most produce, would not allow that. The wheat had to be sold through grain merchants in Winnipeg.[19] When the crop came in each fall, the price fell because the market was glutted. Again, the farmer could take what was offered or haul his grain home. The banks added their own twist by refusing to lend money for more than three months and making the loans come due at harvest time. If the farmer didn't sell, he could lose his farm; if he did, he had to take whatever price was offered.

Because of the strong feeling that government interference was both wicked and wasteful, it took until 1935 to get the Wheat Board established, and until 1943 to make it the sole purchaser of prairie wheat and barley, as well as the "seller, banker and shipper." Now there is a strong movement under way to break it up, sell it off, and get rid of it, although a 1995 study showed that the economies of scale attributable to the Wheat Board's size and muscle "generates an additional $265 million per year in wheat revenue for farmers, thereby enhancing Canada's competitiveness."[20]

Why would we want to get rid of a board that adds $265 million to Canada's farm wallet and doesn't cost the taxpayer a cent?* It's not because banks have become kinder, railroads softer, or grain companies (nearly all of them American) less avaricious, but because the Americans don't like it. They complain constantly about it and want it replaced by a free enterprise system like their own (which, incidentally, receives far more government support, by way of export aids, than our grain does). The Americans demanded an audit of the Wheat Board in 1993 because they were sure it would show that our wheat producers

---

*In 1995–96 the Canadian Wheat Board, according to its *Corporate Abstract*, was worth $8.2 billion and had revenues of $5.9 billion for the year. Its net income was $0.0, "to reflect the fact that all proceeds from sales, less marketing costs, are passed back to farmers." Its loans from government during the year were $0.0, and its "Funding from Canada" was $0.0. It is a gold mine. Well, a wheat mine.

had an unfair trading advantage. It cost $200,000 — paid by both governments — and showed nothing of the sort. The next year, North Dakota Senator Kent Conrad suggested that 300 nuclear missiles in his state should be targeted at Canada because of our wicked ways.[21] In 1998 the Americans were back at it again, demanding yet another audit of the board. The intention is to wear us down, and there is every chance that it will succeed, as similar bullying tactics have so often succeeded in other sectors of trade.

Americans sell wheat the way they sell most agricultural commodities, on rigged markets, which they choose to call free markets. The exchanges that dominate commodity prices are loosely run, and fortunes are made by "wash trading." This practice, in which contracts are sold back and forth among the members of a syndicate to force up prices, is illegal but common. The exchanges are self-regulating, although the U.S. Commodities Exchange Authority, which was supposed to oversee the regulators, commented that it could not "rely to any great extent on exchanges carrying out their responsibility for maintaining adequate surveillance over the trading activities of floor brokers."[22]

A brief attempt was made to clean things up when James M. Stone was brought in as chairman of a new body, the Commodity Futures Trading Commission. He gave up, and subsequently declared: "An excess of speculation, like gambling everywhere, tempts the cheaters, nurtures the fast-buck artists, then forces them into political activity to protect their franchises."[23] It was Stone's experience that, under the American system, any attempt to clean up the trading simply brought in the political fixers, and that was the end of it. That is not what the enthusiastic proponents of privatizing the Wheat Board say. They insist that it would be more efficient to go back to a "market-based" method for moving grains in today's economy. But there never was a free market in wheat, and there never will be. The only issue is whether it is better to have some public control over the way the grain moves to market or to leave it all to the hucksters.

Just as the Wheat Board was formed to meet a public need that private enterprise could not or would not fill, so were Air Canada, Canadian National, Petro-Canada, and dozens of other Crown corporations. The needs of the public remain; nothing has changed but the cant. And these enterprises are all now privately controlled.

In Britain, the privatization of water supply systems has led to huge increases in rates and decreases in service. Never mind, ideology demanded the reform, and it was put through. In all, the government of Margaret Thatcher dumped $50 billion worth of assets onto the market, usually at a fraction of their value. Some of these sales, such as the sale of Jaguar, the car firm, led to great success; many more, such as the sale of British Petroleum, Britain's largest company, were disasters. Between 1979 and 1983 the government sold shares worth £827 million in three batches. Those shares would have netted it £1.93 billion by way of dividends on mammoth profits in the next three years alone.[24] After British Telecom was privatized, the polls soon reported that 63 per cent of the respondents believed services had either become worse or failed to improve. British Gas was privatized, and the price at the pumps went to the highest in the Western world, despite the North Sea reserves that ought to have brought them down.[25] When Harold Macmillan was the Tory prime minister, he said that selling off state assets made no more sense economically than selling off the family silver. But he was one of Thatcher's "wets" and the deals went through, creating not public wealth, but huge commissions, fees, and stock gains for the investment firms that managed the sales.

None of the British privatizations created such opposition as the sale of the water supply. It set off a series of prosecutions of the new private companies. They simply pay the fines for environmental damage and forge ahead. In 1996, on average, a water company was found guilty of violating environmental protection laws once every three weeks.[26] The cost of water to consumers rose at three times the rate of inflation in some areas. Broken pipelines leaked as much as one-third of the water flowing through them.[27] The problem was that the aging infrastructure had been neglected for years — part of the cutbacks — and the new owners were reluctant to remedy the situation. In some towns, there was water rationing; in others, trucks had to haul in water when the pipes burst. At Harrogate, in the Yorkshire Dales, so many trucks were needed to perform this task that they cracked the highways around the town. While the company executives were drawing down the usual large salaries, more and more of their customers who couldn't pay the fee were cut off. The British papers reported stories of parents carting the kids to public washrooms to give them a bath.[28] Water companies responded with a solution that shows the ingenuity we have come to expect. The Severn Trent Water Company sent out a notice advising customers to "pave over their lawns" as one way to conserve the precious fluid.[29]

We can see how one of these capers works in Canada by looking at the Manitoba Telephone System. Within forty-eight hours of the shares of this once-Crown corporation being issued on the market, 5.7 million of them were sold, earning the company an instant $18 million profit. Six months after the sale, Manitoba Telecom Services Ltd., (as it was renamed) migrated out of the province. Then most of its shares were taken up by institutional investors, although one of the key rationales given for the sale had been that it was "more democratic for individual Manitobans to own shares in their company than for all Manitobans to own it collectively."[30] Then the non-Manitoban, institutionally controlled company jacked up the local consumer rates by $3 a month, on top of an earlier increase of $2 a month. Thus we see how competitive free enterprise reduces costs to the consumer.

Well, perhaps we do have too many Crown corporations, and perhaps there is something to be said for private firms stepping into some of them. But the problem we face is that, as in so many matters, we are being led by ideology, not by sense. Selling water systems to private enterprise just because we think private is better than public makes no more sense than it would to nationalize the banks, in hopes that they might provide better service — a step that failed dismally in France. Public ownership in itself does not bestow magical benefits on any sector of the economy; the argument for public ownership is that there are tasks that must be done — such as running a transportation system that serves everyone, not just the centre of the nation — tasks that private enterprise has given up on because it cannot make money with them. We can either subsidize private enterprise to do the job or create a public firm to take it on. If the public firm makes money, over time, it may well make sense to turn the job back to the private sector, provided it is willing to undertake the entire job for the benefit of the public and not just skim off the cream.

That is not what is happening today. As it appears to work now, if a particular government enterprise fails to make money, then we get rid of it because we cannot afford it. However, if it makes money, we get rid of it to reduce the public debt. We call this selling the pig's other leg. Among the first candidates for privatization by the Harris government was the Province of Ontario Savings Office, a small network of banks that makes a steady, if not spectacular, profit every year. The Savings Office was created by the United Farmers of Ontario in 1919 because they hated the banks. It has been operating ever since, and now operates twenty-three branches and five agencies across the province, where it pays more on savings accounts and guaranteed investment certificates than do the big chartered banks, and never charges monthly maintenance fees.[31] It is to be sold, even though it makes money.

The responsibilities that government ownership carries with it were spelled out in the case of Air Canada. When it was created, the airline had a clear national mandate: "Air Canada was established by the Parliament of Canada as the national airline to provide essential air transport, cargo and mail services across Canada."[32] Nothing was said about making money, although that might be a bonus. The airline's main job was to make the country work. In 1988 the Mulroney government unloaded 30.8 million shares, while still holding on to a majority of the company. In July 1989 the other half was sold, and Air Canada became "a fully publicly owned corporation." In plain language, Air Canada became a wholly *privately* owned corporation that happens to be traded publicly. Private individuals can buy the stocks.

Today, the company has a new objective: "Air Canada has been pursuing a strategy of selective growth with the objective of achieving the market position, alliance partner network and cost/productivity performance necessary for long-term success."[33] Now that it has been sold, Air Canada is being run by an American CEO for his purposes, not ours. Making money is all very fine and I salute it, but it has nothing to do with the reason we created a national carrier in the first place.

Of all the daft privatizations on the menu today, perhaps the looniest is the proposed selloff of the Liquor Control Board of Ontario. Its sale was promised in the Tories' *Common Sense Revolution*, but has been delayed, although we are assured it is still on the books. In 1996–97, the LCBO returned a profit of $730 million to the public purse. That was up from $680 million the year before. Over the last decade, it has returned $6 billion to the Ontario taxpayer. It had an increase in sales of 5.8 per cent in a period when sales in the Ontario market as a whole grew by 0.1 per cent. At the same time, expenses were cut from 18.9 per cent of income to 16.1 per cent.[34] But the government is determined to sell it off because, as we've been told, government enterprises aren't run efficiently and don't make money.

The one dollar bribe

Why would we do anything so silly as to sell off a profitable asset? For the sheer pleasure of allowing ideology to swamp common sense, or perhaps the titillation of the "one dollar bribe?" Most government assets are carried on the books for $1. If you sell a government-owned asset into which you have poured, say, $500 million over the years to build it up and keep it going, and to help it fulfil the public function for which it was created, it has a net worth, on the government books, of $1.

If you sell it for $100 million, which is $400 million less than you have put into it, you show a bump in government revenues for the year of $99,999,999. Honest. You blew off a half billion dollar asset for 20 per cent of its worth, and you get to claim a profit of $100 million.

If you are a private person, or a corporation, and you invest in something that you expect will bring you a benefit, it appears in your reckoning as an asset, and you spread the cost over years, perhaps decades. The mortgage on your house is a good example. However, that is not the way the government keeps its books. If it puts up a school, builds a road, or invests in a railway, the cost is written off in one year, and it becomes part of our overhanging debt, whereas the asset is carried on the books, usually, at $1. This is accounting madness; but worse, it deludes us into thinking we are broke when we aren't, and convinces us that public ownership is a drag. Imagine the effect if Imperial Oil wrote off the entire cost of its oil wells, refineries, and pipelines in a single year; gas would cost about $10 a litre. But that is exactly what our governments do when they build a new university — which is one of the most productive expenditures any government can make — and cost it in a single year.

The federal government was able to show the sale of Petro-Canada as a profit of $154 million, and that of CN as a profit of $171 million, even though the sales were made at hundreds of millions of dollars less than the government's investment in these plants.[35] If we were to sell the Canadian interest in the St. Lawrence Seaway, an asset that has absorbed hundreds of millions of dollars and whose value is immeasurable, we could pass it into private laps for $10,000 and show a gain of $9,999. The Wheat Board causes the private market to salivate because of its $8.2 billion in assets. Think what a bump the government could get by unloading these two at, say, one-quarter of their worth.

The federal deficit is reduced, on paper, by losing money. You take a public asset, which is performing a crucial task, and sell it because you are driven by ideology. When Ottawa sold its air navigation system for $1.5 billion in 1996, it was able to lower its deficit by that figure (minus the one dollar). The new company, Nav Canada, immediately set about closing down facilities, including air traffic control towers, to save money. Fredericton, New Brunswick, had one of the towers that got closed; the airport in New Brunswick's capital is now run from Moncton, 200 kilometres away.

When an Air Canada regional jet slid off the runway at Fredericton on December 17, 1997, and skidded into the trees, thirty-five of its forty-two passengers were hurt. It was a miracle they weren't all killed, but no fire broke out. At least twenty minutes went by between the time of the crash and the arrival of the first rescue crews. It might have been much longer; the fire crew (one man) at Fredericton quits at midnight, unless asked by an incoming pilot to stay on. Nav Canada company spokesmen wanted everyone to understand that there was nothing to worry about, that everything was done that could be done, and that having a control tower in Fredericton would not have made much difference. Maybe; but Tory MP Elsie Wayne struck a nerve when she noted: "This is exactly what we said would happen [as a result of the cutbacks] . . . Here you are flying into Fredericton and somebody in Moncton is telling you whether you can or can't land."[36]

Deleting air traffic controllers in many Canadian airports (there are none in Charlottetown, or Saint John either) is a hard sell, and a lot of people maintain that with privatization, cuts designed to improve the bottom line are bound to make safety a likely casualty. Without our bizarre accounting system, where totally fake profits are made from selling valuable assets, many of these sales would never be made.

It gets worse; not only do our accounting tricks overstate the take from privatization but they massively overstate the public debt whose burden leads us to dump our assets. As the *Canada Year Book*, StatsCan's biannual roundup, used to explain it in every edition:

> The statement of assets and liabilities is designed to disclose the debt, which is determined by offsetting against the gross liabilities, only those assets regarded as readily realizable, or interest — or revenue — producing. Fixed capital assets, such as government buildings and public works, are charged to budgetary expenditures at the time of acquisition or construction and are shown on the statement of assets and liabilities at a nominal value of $1.00.[37]

In recent years, this description of our cockeyed system of measuring debt has been deleted from the *Canada Year Book*. William Krehm, an economic theorist and the publisher-editor of *Economic Reform* magazine, has written several letters to StatsCan requesting an explanation as to why the change was made, but he has had no reply.[38]

The Americans began very quietly to restructure their government books in January 1995, by setting off physical investments as capital costs and showing them as assets on the books. The change applied over the three previous years (1992–94), reduced the national debt by $618.5 billion, and allowed Bill Clinton to claim he had made massive inroads on the national debt.[39]

Even the group up in Ottawa is beginning to question its approach. The auditor general recommended a change to "capital budgeting" a decade ago. It took a while for word to percolate through the system, but now, according to the *Public Accounts of Canada*, bible of the public sector:

> The federal government is gradually moving towards full-accrual accounting, whereby the cost of acquiring physical assets is spread over the asset's [sic] useful life through annual depreciation charges, and thus the true cost of such assets will be more accurately recorded in the future.[40]

What this block of wooden prose is telling us is that the government has finally figured out what a bizarre accounting system it has been running for years. We are also being told that officials will "gradually" stop cooking the books.

Whether this change will end the rush to privatization remains to be seen. Since so little of the decision to privatize has anything to do with sense, probably not. However, it will remove the temptation to sell off valuable assets in exchange for a temporary and imaginary bump in the budget. What it will not affect is our readiness to use fantasy as a tool to justify the destruction of other aspects of the responsive state, as we will see in the next chapter.

14

Suffer, Little Children

To pretend we can erode government and
governance with impunity may be convenient to
some. But the price to be paid would be high, in the
form of social unrest, polarization and inequity.
While a few would gain, many would lose. And in the
end, we all would lose what binds us together; the
commitment to the public good and its pursuit, one
of the defining features of Canadian society.
— Charles Caccia, MP, December 16, 1996

*There was a faint but irritating noise in the alleyway that ran below
the bedroom window of the hotel where I was staying in Winnipeg. I
couldn't make it out, but it reminded me of something from my childhood, a sort of clanging bump. It was not regular: there would be a
series of clangs and then silence; then, a minute later, or maybe five
minutes later, more clangs. I pulled the pillow over my head and tried
to go back to sleep. No luck. Then I remembered: Kick the Can. When
I was a kid growing up in Montreal we used to play a kind of game
that started by kicking a can down the alley. Whoever was It had
to retrieve the can, bring it back to base, look for the hiders, and
bring them back to base. If another kid could get in and kick the can
again without being spotted, all the prisoners were freed and the
work began again. The noise was like the one I was hearing now,*

except that it was accompanied by shrieks and giggles. Was some ghostly crew playing kick the can at 4 a.m. on a cold October day in Winnipeg?

Wearily, I got up, dressed, and went downstairs. When I reached the back alley, a single man was there, under the lone street light, kicking a juice can. He would kick it against the wall of the building, hobble after it, then boot it again. I thought he was wearing black runners, but then I realized, with a bit of a shock, that they weren't runners at all. His feet were bare — and they were black with dirt, not race. When I came down the alley towards him, he paid not the slightest attention.

"Hello," I said.

He looked up, but didn't say anything. He was wearing an over-coat, torn but serviceable, a pair of ragged pants that peeked out below, and three or four sweaters. He had a wool cap on his head. I couldn't see his face clearly, but he looked to be in his mid-fifties. He had a straggle of chin-growth that only his best friends would call a beard, and showed a lot of grey.

"Lose your shoes?" I asked.

He still didn't say anything, but he stuck out his hand. I put a doubloon into it. He waggled it. I came up with another doubloon.

I couldn't get a word out of him and I concluded he was probably a mental case. He refused my offer of breakfast with a shake of his head — good thing, I had no idea what might be open at that ungodly hour. When I asked if he would like me to get someone to help him, he glowered, then stalked off down the alley.

I went back into the hotel. A few years ago, I reflected, people like him could always find help, or help would find them. No longer. We have been forced by the shortage of funds to take down the series of protections that guarded the elderly, the young, the disabled, and the mentally ill. You could say for "reasons of state," except that there is no reason in it.

We built the welfare state for reasons of defence against the cupidity, rapacity, and recklessness of corporations, which were them-selves growing ever larger, thus requiring ever more activity to keep them in check, but we did not build a counter-balancing check on government spending. We did not understand that we were creating a national debt of mammoth proportions by adopting and maintaining a high-interest-rate policy, which multiplied our burden. Faced with

*the cold figures produced before us every year at budget time, we
resigned ourselves to allowing governments to take an axe to the social
system. We told ourselves that there was really no alternative.*

*The groups who are at the sharp end of this turnaround are the
groups who cannot do much about it: the young, the old, the ill, the disabled, the mentally disadvantaged, the people of Canada's First
Nations, and the poor.*

One group that should concern us most, because they represent
our future, are the children. Quite a few thousand Canadian
children do not have enough to eat every day; many are homeless and many are abused. But we mustn't become indignant or
sentimental on this subject because, as the Fraser Institute
reminds us:

> Children in Canada are hungry, abused, unloved, and dys-
> functional for reasons that have absolutely nothing to do with
> inadequate incomes . . . If we want children to get a good and
> healthy start in life, what we need more than anything else is
> responsible parents.[1]

I think we can all agree with this statement. A child born, let us
say, on a reserve in northern Manitoba to a single mother who
has four other children — a mother who has been destroyed by
drugs, alcohol, and sexual abuse — should be able to pull himself out of the mire and become, in this land of unlimited
opportunity, the president of a bank. Well, he may have a little
trouble getting the right schooling, and may fall behind in his
studies when he has the bejabbers kicked out of him from time
to time, but if this child has any complaint, it should be directed
where it belongs — at the parents.

The evidence suggests that children who start in a poor way
are at a disadvantage. As a recent study explains:

> Undernutrition triggers an array of health problems in chil-
> dren, many of which can become chronic. It can lead to

extreme weight loss, stunted growth, weakened resistance to infection, and, in the worst cases, early death . . .

. . . Inadequate nutrition can also disrupt cognition — although in different ways than were previously assumed. At one time, underfeeding in childhood was thought to hinder mental development solely by producing permanent, structural damage to the brain. More recent work, however, indicates that malnutrition can impair the intellect by other means as well.[2]

So, the good news is that, the way things are going, the labouring class is not likely to be serious competitors for the BMW crowd. The bad news is that we are adopting, as the latest economic gospel, policies that produced a shudder of revulsion more than a century ago. We say that it won't do much good for the state to intervene, providing adequate housing, decent food, education, and all those expensive fripperies of welfarism. The Fraser Institute has set us right:

Indeed, tens of billions of dollars have been spent in recent years on so-called anti-poverty programs, the net result of which is more dependency, more single parent families, and more problem children. And if we listen to the social planners, we now have more poverty than ever. Why should we then give the state even more money?

The reason this writer, economist Chris Sarlo, author of the Fraser Institute's publication *Poverty in Canada*, refers to "so-called anti-poverty programs" is because the institute claims that there is not much real child poverty in Canada — that's just a rumour put out by interested parties. I particularly like the logic of the argument that, despite all the money spent, we have more poor children than ever. It reminds me of the kid who was drowning 10 feet off the dock; someone threw a 6-foot length of rope towards him, but he went under anyway. Next day when there were two kids drowning 12 feet off the dock, no one wanted to waste more rope.

These views used to be the preserve of a small group of extremists in this country, but what makes them important today is that they have become mainstream. These are not the views of fanatics; they are the serious opinions of people who are consulted by the highest in the land. No mainstream politician is going to declare, as Sarlo does, that the claim that there were 1.4 million poor children in Canada in 1994 is "clearly an exaggeration." What the mainstream politicians say, over and over again, is that child poverty in Canada is a disgrace and that it must be remedied.

Then these same politicians cut the support plans that try to apply the remedy. In 1989 the House of Commons passed a unanimous resolution pledging to eliminate child poverty in Canada by the year 2000.[3] There were, at that time, 934,000 poor children in Canada, according to the most commonly accepted measure, Statistics Canada's Low Income Cutoff. A report released in November 1997 by Campaign 2000, a group of sixty agencies that took the 1989 pledge seriously, listed the results of these efforts:

- the number of poor children has increased to 1,472,000, a jump of 58 per cent;
- the number of children living in families whose parents are experiencing unemployment is up 47 per cent;
- the number of children living in "unaffordable" rental housing — housing that costs more of the family income than makes economic sense — is up 48 per cent.
- the number of children living in families who need social assistance is up 48 per cent; and
- the number of children living in families where the income is less than $20,000 a year is up 45 per cent.

Especially hard hit were children who were already at a disadvantage because of their race. Among Canada's First Nations, for example, the infant mortality rate is about double the national average, the death rate for preschool children is four times the national average, and suicide among adolescents is six times the national average.

These figures, which indicate the utter failure of government to live up to the promise made in 1989, are not really surprising. Both Ottawa and the provinces cut welfare rates, made it more difficult to qualify for benefits in welfare and in unemployment insurance (now called employment insurance, in a nice Orwellian twist), and withdrew funding from support groups. The Institute for the Prevention of Child Abuse, an organization recognized around the world for its research into child abuse, and for training social workers and police officers who have to deal with the problem, closed its doors in August 1995 when the province of Ontario withdrew its funding. Both levels of government also drew back on the provision of day care, which enables single and poor parents to work. Of course, having a job no longer means escaping poverty. Thanks to our competitive wages — competitive, we hope, with Mexican peons — we have a higher proportion of working poor than ever. Over half of Canada's poor children live in families in which one parent works; one-third live in families where this employment is full time or the equivalent of full time. They are still poor.[4]

Linda Goyette of the *Edmonton Journal* neatly summarized what happened:

> Back in 1989, after a unanimous resolution in Parliament, Canada promised the United Nations that it would work tirelessly to eradicate child poverty by the year 2000.
>
> In their curious wisdom, Ottawa and the provinces decided to reach this goal by cutting billions of dollars out of health, education and social programs; reducing the employment insurance and welfare payments to families; replacing the Canada Assistance Plan with a watery substitute; and abandoning the promise of a national day-care program.[5]

Probably the most severe blow was the change to block funding for transfer payments to the provinces, accompanied by $7 billion in cuts. At the same time, the Canada Assistance Plan, the law that required the provinces to meet "basic requirements" and provide "adequate support," became a dead letter. Then federal funding for the Community Action Program for Children, which provided funds to "innovative collaborations to assist children six and under," was cut by 52 per cent annually.[6]

In some provinces, the scramble to save a buck on the backs of children hit harder than in others. Almost everywhere, Children's Aid Societies found themselves in trouble because of overwork, impossible caseloads, inadequate funds, and the replacement of experienced workers by newer, and cheaper, help. Case after case of child abuse was not detected until it was too late. In Alberta, our richest province, where the number of abused children requiring social service jumped by 14 per cent in 1996–97, the system became so overwhelmed that abused and neglected children were put on waiting lists for protection. Only those seen to be in immediate danger received "prompt intervention."[7] In the oil patch, kids who are just moderately abused must wait their turn.

The widening gap between rich and poor in this country adds its own special flavour to the mix. Although many of us live in affluence unimaginable in many parts of the world, and Canada ranked first of 174 nations on the United Nations Human Development Index for 1996 (which measures such things as education, literacy, and health services), a poor child in Canada is worse off — because there is now less government help — than in ten other industrialized countries, and the gap between rich and poor children is the most marked in the industrialized world. In Canada, as elsewhere, the number of millionaires and the number of children living in poverty keep rising in lock-step. The combined wealth of the richest fifty Canadians now exceeds $39 billion, which means that these fifty individuals have more money than five million low-income Canadians.[8]

Unseen and unnoted, changes have been made in the economic underpinnings of our disadvantaged which are bound to widen the gap still further. Consider one, apparently minor, change. To accommodate the cry for competitive rates, the minimum wage has sunk, slowly but certainly, during the last two decades. In 1976 the minimum wage in every province but Ontario returned an income that was above the Low Income Cutoff — the poverty line. If you lived in Saskatchewan and earned the minimum wage, your pay was 118 per cent of the poverty line.[9] Twenty years later, the minimum wage in every province was well below the poverty line and the federal minimum wage was about half the poverty line. As Tony Clarke and Maude Barlow point out: "In short, people earning the minimum wage rate in this country today are already consigned to a life of poverty."[10]

When we ensure that a large sector of the economy is occupied by the working poor, we can hardly be astonished that we have more poor children than ever. When we reduce the benefits available, we compound the problem. We are coasting on the accomplishments — what the Fraser Institute would call the waste — of past years. A poor child in France gets about 50 per cent more support than in Canada, and thus has a much better chance of escaping the poverty trap. We now have enough poor children to form a province that would be the fifth in population in the nation. Six of ten children in single-parent families in this country live in poverty. Among young families, child poverty has increased by 39 per cent since 1989, and has almost doubled in the last decade.[11] It does not take a trained social worker to reckon what this will mean to us in social terms. Children from poor families are more likely to use drugs, have problems with alcohol, or come into conflict with the law than those in what we used to call the middle and upper classes (we have now abolished the classes and have "median income" and "higher income" groups). The death rate due to fires, drowning, accidents, suicides, and homicides is up to ten times higher for poor children than for the general population.[12]

How do we expect these children to behave when they reach maturity? Will they not feel a certain resentment, a certain sense that perhaps they have not been fairly dealt with, a certain distance from the bumper stickers that tell them to shun drugs, work hard, and trust Jesus to sort things out? We are creating the population that will swell our jails, courts, and mental institutions. We are doing this to save money, and, at the same time, we are signalling our willingness to spend tax funds on the jails, alarm systems, and private police we need to protect ourselves from this rising crime base rather than on social programs to ease the problem. We think we can afford Band-Aids, so that is what we choose to provide. But we do not count the higher costs to come.

Wiping out welfare

The children were first in line as sacrifices to the new economic gods; next came welfare recipients in general. Money to serve them became scarce; regulations to keep them from receiving aid became plentiful; and then, because it is mean to keep hacking the handouts to the underprivileged in a society that is constantly creating more and more millionaires, we discovered — rediscovered, pardon me — that it was all their fault. Once we relearned the lessons of the Elizabethan Poor Law — that there were two classes of poor, the deserving and the undeserving — we could see our way forward.

Make the bastards hustle for their supper. The fact that workfare, which is what we call this approach, was tried in the Great Depression and proved disastrous, did not matter. We don't know our own history, anyway. What we discovered at that time was what every serious study has shown since: people want to work. Except for a tiny, measurable share of misfits, everyone wants gainful employment. Forcing us to perform makework tasks doesn't produce money, dignity, or reform; all it produced in the Great Depression was a series of nasty riots among the coerced. Never mind, we have forgotten all that. Workfare was presented to us as something new, untried, and worthwhile.[13] It was the elixir that would cut government spending, end welfare dependence, and set the economy back on track; as side benefits, it would also cure unsightly blemishes, gout, rheumatism, warts, and female troubles.

Workfare was pulled back onto the front burner of policy debate in the United States in the 1980s by a group of critics led by Charles Murray.[14] These critics were concerned that, in many American cities, welfare was sometimes inherited. Certain families had a fifth or sixth generation of welfare recipients. To break the cycle, it was necessary to get the adults into, or back into, employment. Since retraining programs and other incentives didn't seem to work, the only way to accomplish the goal was to give them a stark choice: work or starve. The plan was not put in these words, but that was the intent, and it was certainly the effect. It could be argued that the reason the retraining programs and other aids didn't work was that the programs needed far more money, not less, to be successful. Nobody was willing to spend any more money, so the alternative was taken: a population of poorly fed, uneducated, abused, diseased, and despairing people would get to work if they got hungry enough.

All across the United States, welfare rates were cut and new rules were imposed. The result was a sharp drop in welfare cases. This decrease proved that the remedy worked — just as, if you make it impossible for many to collect unemployment insurance, you can claim a great victory, even though the practical effect is not to create more jobs but more paupers. Workfare swept across the largest undefended border, like everything else, and is now the official law in Ontario, and likely to become so across the country. The federal government embraced workfare in 1994, but quietly and behind the scenes. The Department of Human Resources Development discussion paper *Improving Social Security in Canada* recommended cutting unemployment benefits to frequent claimants, and this policy became the law in 1997, making income support "conditional on their willingness to participate in programs that make them more employable."[15]

Unemployment insurance was supposed to be just that — insurance. To start applying workfare conditions to payments makes no more sense than insurance companies refusing to pay out on fire-damage policies unless their customers take courses in fire-fighting. However, if employment insurance is just a government handout to a bunch of bums who would rather loaf than work, then the new approach can be justified. Toronto allocated $3.32 million annually to a new Citibank scheme to prevent fraud through use of fingerprinting techniques. Actually, this technique can only prevent the fraud of one person applying for two or more cheques, about 3 per cent of total fraud cases, according to the Ontario Ministry of Community and Social Services. The point is not to stamp out fraud, but to be seen to be tough on welfare bums — unless they are corporations, of course.

The toll of Canadians deprived of benefits by simple rule changes is staggering. The number of unemployed Canadians receiving payments plunged from 89 per cent in 1990 to less than 50 per cent in 1996.[16] The money saved is spectacular: the employment insurance fund was running a surplus, in September 1997, of $13 billion, while nearly one employable person in ten was out of a job.[17] When their benefits run out, the still unemployed will be shoved from the insurance fund onto workfare, but the new jobs that are to be created there are all "entry level," or, to put it less politely, they are at or below minimum wage. The hope is that those who take them will move on to better jobs; the likelihood is that we will simply add to the large and increasing pool of Canadians who are counted among the working poor.

In New Brunswick, welfare support for single people was set at 24 per cent of the poverty line, ensuring that anyone who didn't want to starve would take whatever work was offered, under whatever conditions. In many municipalities in Nova Scotia, young, able-bodied males who went on strike, or who were locked out by employers, were denied any assistance whatever.[18] Both provinces were then able to show that they had worked an economic miracle: fewer folks on welfare.

The question put by Charles Murray was pretty simple: "Why should one person give *anything* to a stranger whose only claim to his help is a common citizenship?"[19] We used to answer that common citizenship was a perfectly sufficient reason, at least in Canada. Now we are not so sure. In the end, the real argument about workfare comes down to our view of humanity. If we think that most of our fellow humans are lazy louts who won't work unless forced to by the threat of starvation, then cutting welfare and replacing it by workfare makes sense. If we think that most of us want to work for the dignity, self-worth, sociability, and other advantages it provides, and that the money is only a small part of the mix, then we will be more eager to reach for the chequebook than the whip.

Targeting women

Women have become the particular victims of the cutbacks in quite a different way. We are just a little shamefaced about the way we have made women the target of downsizing. Pay equity, while laudable, is not practical right now. Day care, while it has been promised for several elections running, is beyond our reach because of all these other demands on the budget.

Seventy per cent of Canadians living in poverty are women and children.[20] Twice as many older single women than men live in poverty.[21] Aboriginal women face unemployment rates of 20 to 80 per cent.[22] The unemployment rate for women with disabilities is 16.6 per cent, and of those who could find work, only 45 per cent have full-time jobs; another 23 per cent work as volunteers, without any pay. And the percentage of women living in poverty has increased by 50 per cent in the past two decades.[23] No one boasts about these facts, or about the cuts to disabled transport, the abandonment of day-care promises, or the withdrawal of funding from many of the groups that have provided support in the past. But we are told, time after time, that the cuts have been forced on us by circumstance. If cutting the deficit is our first priority, then that is what we must do, even if it results in a few thousand kids going hungry or the odd bum freezing to death on city streets.

No one set out to coop Pearl Miller, seventy-nine, in her Toronto home; it just happened. Mrs. Miller, a widow who suffers from asthma, osteoporosis, and collapsed vertebrae in her spine, was able to get around with the help of Wheel-Trans, a service of the Toronto Transportation Commission which picks up disabled people at their homes and takes them where they need to go for ordinary transit fares. The province cut $8 million from the TTC; the TTC then applied new rules to Wheel-Trans to get rid of 9,200 riders like Pearl Miller, on the grounds that anyone who can actually get to a TTC station or bus stop doesn't need help. Mrs. Miller has a rotary walker. The province said the TTC could have cut something else, and kept Wheel-Trans as it was; the TTC said it had nothing else left to cut.[24] When the *Toronto Star* ran a story, everybody promised to think things over. In the meantime, 9,199 other disabled people who didn't make the paper are out of luck.

In Smith Falls, Ontario, not far from Ottawa, a man named Clayton Bratrud, suffering from terminal cancer, was sent a bill for not dying quickly enough. Bratrud went into the Perth and Smith Falls District Hospital in October 1996, bedridden and in need of constant nursing care. He was not expected to last long. However, he kept on going, and, in January 1997, new rule changes mandated by the province came into force. Before that time, patients in long-term care were given a sixty-day grace period before they began to be charged what is called a "chronic care co-payment." This payment had been jumped from $26.00 to $40.29 a day — a 54 per cent hike — but it wasn't being collected for the first sixty days. When the province wiped out the grace period, the hospital had no choice but to send Bratrud a bill. A hospital spokesperson explained: "Unfortunately, in the case of cancer patients, even though they have been designated terminal, they can live for a considerable period of time."[25]

The food banks that have sprung up around the nation are the most prominent symbol of the acceptance of the new economics. They should not exist, if welfare payments were sufficient to allow people to buy their own food. We hear a good deal, these days, about the need for personal dignity, but anyone who has watched the operation of a food bank for a few hours knows there is nothing so hostile to personal dignity as forcing people to line up to get food for their children. The food banks measure the failure of recent economic and social policy. They were established, as a temporary measure, to tide us over the recession, to serve the small population of unfortunates who fell through the cracks of the system. Now the food banks are trying, with shrinking resources, to handle a much wider segment of the population. They are being called on to serve the needs of people who used to be middle class and no longer have enough to eat. A survey in Toronto showed that 4,400 families using the food banks had given up their houses because they couldn't keep up the payments; 10,350 families had sold their cars. In all, 80 per cent of food-bank clients had given something up to raise money; the other 20 per cent had nothing left to give up. In Toronto 50,000 families collect food hampers every month, but demand has caught up with the supply and, at many food bank locations across the country, the shelves are empty.[26]

Another way to curb expenses is to cut the funds for one kind of support while promising another kind of support to take its place. The second level of support is then forgotten. When the Ontario government decided to "de-institutionalize" the mentally ill because they would be better off in the community than in sterile institutions, the change was accompanied by a promise to provide community help. But this help was never forthcoming in adequate amounts. Instead, the mentally ill were turned loose to wander at large, and if they forgot to take the pills that were required to keep them functioning, well, too bad. The plan was first tried in Toronto when the Lakeshore Psychiatric Hospital closed 300 beds in 1979. Most of those who were discharged settled in the Parkdale area because it was close to the Queen Street Mental Health Centre. Some of them died, some committed suicide, some turned violent, and some survived.[27] The province was so pleased with the money it saved that it kept closing beds. In the 1960s, Ontario had 16,000 psychiatric beds; by 1998, only 5,300 were left, and the Health Services Restructuring Commission was planning to cut 2,000 of these.[28] This plan backfired when stories began to appear of released psychiatric patients shoving people off subway platforms, getting shot by the cops, and in other ways disturbing the tranquility of the province. A moratorium was announced "on the closing of psychiatric beds until adequate community services were created." Thus, Ontario did not close four-fifths of its psychiatric beds, only two-thirds of them. At least the Tories put some money into community health services — $23.5 million. The NDP, party of the socially conscious, hacked $60 million out of the budgets of provincial psychiatric hospitals without investing a dime in community services.[29]

In October 1997 a report to the Health Services Restructuring Commission by the Metropolitan Toronto Council's Advisory Committee on Homeless and Socially Isolated Persons commented on how well this experiment had worked out over the years: the patients are winding up in city hostels. As the *Globe and Mail*'s social policy reporter, Margaret Philip, put it:

> Three decades after people with psychiatric illnesses were sprung from mental institutions, a growing number are landing on the streets, at the doors of crowded homeless shelters, and in cramped rooming and boarding houses run by private landlords who are in the business, first and foremost, to make a living.
>
> And as beds in psychiatric institutions and hospital wards continue to disappear, as subsidized apartments grow scarce, as crack cocaine becomes a mainstay on Toronto streets, people with diagnosed mental illnesses have turned to hostels where overworked staff have scant time or professional credentials to deal with the serious psychiatric disorders in their midst.[30]

The report on which Philip based her story estimated that at least 600 people with serious mental illnesses were living in

Toronto hostels, more than in the city's two main psychiatric institutions.

In late 1997 scores of mentally ill patients were being held in jail — illegally — simply because there were no psychiatric hospital beds available for them.[31] Surely a society that decides to turn loose its mental patients in the hopes of saving money is working from a perverted set of rules.

The same sort of bait-and-switch tactics are being applied elsewhere as well. A physiotherapist explained to me that she no longer has time to help her clients as she used to do:

> When the cuts came, the promise was that the money saved by moving people out of hospitals before they were really ready to go would be devoted to helping them at home. Which made perfect sense. Then our staff was cut. Then more and more patients were added to our work-load. Not a penny of new money was ever put into the system, that we could see. The end result is that we are run off our feet, and we are not doing an adequate job, and people are suffering because of it.

It is hard to escape the notion that at least some of the hacking and hewing is inspired by motives that have nothing to do with saving money and more to do with attitudes and prejudices. Consider the case of Operation Beaver, one of the most efficient organizations in the nation for working with First Nations' people. Frontiers Foundation/Operation Beaver builds and renovates houses, churches, and other community projects in some of the poorest parts of Canada. People who never touched a hammer in their lives find themselves clinging to ladders and banging in nails all over the nation — and even as far away as West Africa, South America, and the Caribbean.[32]

This tight-fisted organization pulls together a small army of volunteers every year and scrabbles around for funds to finance the building. Most of its projects in Canada provide decent housing for aboriginals who live off reserves, and it does the work for about 20 per cent of what it would cost through one of the state's dwindling housing programs. In Canada alone, since its founding in 1964, Operation Beaver has built or renovated more than 2,000 homes, thirty adult training centres, a tannery, three schools, a fishery co-op, two hockey arenas, three recreation parks, three youth camps, a sports centre, and six churches. It has worked its miracles with close to 3,000 volunteers representing seventy different nations, along with helpers from seventeen Canadian First Nations. In turn, the group has sent Canadians abroad to help others in the same way.

This multinational, multilingual, multicultural group builds housing, and bridges to understanding, for very little cost. Just as important, the handful of professionals associated with each project passes on skills and training to all the other participants. Yet the federal and provincial governments have slashed their support to the foundation to the point where its very survival is threatened.

Of course, it's cheaper still if you just leave the homeless and disadvantaged to shift for themselves. With the money saved, the politicians go out and make speeches calling for the voluntary sector, which they have just gutted, to make up the difference.

The Road Back

What this country wants more than anything
else is a fool-killer.
— Sir William Van Horne, 1891

Choices

What we are seeing today is a depressing level of
anti-government and anti-social rhetoric. There is
a gradual dissolution of the bonds that hold us
together as a society, a dissolution of collective
responsibility.

— Jonathan Murphy, University of Alberta, 1997

The decision to cut off the oxygen for Margaret Lamanna, a seventy-four-year-old pensioner who lives in Scarborough, Ontario, was not taken lightly. She had been receiving oxygen without cost because she has difficulty breathing. Her doctor filled in the necessary forms because there was sufficient medical reason for her to receive this help. But the province of Ontario decided that to qualify for free oxygen, it was not enough that a person have difficulty breathing. Under the new criteria, if you get out of breath when you move, but you can breathe normally when you sit still, you buy your own oxygen. In this way, the province was able to cut 2,000 people from the free-oxygen program during 1997, bringing the total recipients down to 18,000 from 20,000.

Margaret Lamanna was upset by the ruling. She told Art Chamberlain, a Toronto Star *reporter, that she was now trapped in her condo: "I'm so embarrassed because I huff and puff when I move. I pray, literally pray, that no one sees me when I go out across the lobby."[1] What we all have to understand is that government can no longer* *afford to coddle people. It has to ask itself exactly how much trouble they have breathing when they move: just gasping for breath or falling right down? We have to be careful with public funds these days. It costs the province roughly $2,750 per person per annum to pay a private company to supply the oxygen. Knock 2,000 people off the list and you save $5.5 million, enough to pay the green fees for the whole cabinet and more. Lamanna was sent a bill for $2,658.27 for service after the government stopped paying. The Ontario taxpayer is spared this expense. Every little bit helps when you are trying to meet other priorities.*

In the case of Ontario, for instance, the province agreed during 1997, the same year in which it cut these 2,000 heavy breathers off the public oxygen supply, to increase the money paid to doctors by about $600 million a year. That money has to come from somewhere. Admittedly, some of it was taken from the province's day-care workers, who were asked to take pay-cuts averaging $4,500, but that still leaves a lot of leeway to make up.

If the doctors get unhappy about their pay, they can make it really uncomfortable for the party in power, whereas Margaret Lamanna doesn't count for much in terms of power. So we cut off her oxygen.

We have come far enough now to set out a little chart, so we will know what things we can afford in this up-to-date society and what things we must drop from our list of state responsibilities — or, at the very least, cut back.

Things we can afford	Things we cannot afford or must cut back
private health care	universal health care
fixing the "Millennium Bug"	adequate day care
hockey salaries up to $8 million; bank pay up to $10 million;	pay equity
private drug testing	public drug testing
lawsuits without number	free legal aid
Registered Retirement Savings Plans,	Canada Pension Plan
toll roads	maintenance of the national highway system

several hundred new models of cars annually	public transit
expense account lunches	school lunches
corporate subsidies	welfare programs
private schools	public schools
product research	scientific research
condos on pleasure liners, starting at $1.7 million*	public housing
stock bonuses	unemployment insurance
$594 million in pay raises for Ontario doctors	pay for nurses
Porsches for stockbrokers	air traffic controllers for many cities
$100.9 billion for corporate mergers	pharmacare
charity casinos	mines inspectors
$3 billion on Bre-X shares	securities watchdogs

And so it goes. If it is public, we must be prepared to make sacrifices and cut it back, owing to hard times. If it is private, we can afford it and we must have it, whatever it costs. Take the matter of fixing the Millennium Bug. It turns out that when the geniuses who design and sell computers and software programs were setting up their programs, they decided to represent years by two digits: 98, not 1998. It saved time and storage space. But they forgot one little drawback: the computer program, faced with 00 to represent 2000, will think it is dealing with 1900 and act accordingly. Financial instruments, passenger jets, elevators, and other implements of modernity may all well come to a standstill as we bring in the new year on January 1, 2000. A few years ago some companies began hiring expensive professionals to solve the problem, and in mid-1997 the *Wall Street Journal* estimated the cost of fixing all the computer programs that needed attention. It came to US$600 billion.[2] The Canadian Press thought that this figure was too low: "Solving the millennium bug — often referred to as the Y2K problem — is expected to cost between $600 billion and $2 trillion (U.S.) globally."[3]

---

*A company called ResidenSea is offering luxury floating condominiums in a ship called The World, which will spend its time circling the globe. *Toronto Star*, January 31, 1998, G2.

A whole new industry is springing up to deal with the Millennium Bug, which is not, please note, a government-created glitch. The Canadian share of the bill is estimated to be around $12 billion in our funds. No one is saying we can't afford to get the calendar working again. All our best and brightest minds agree that we can't afford *not* to do it. Jean Monty, president of BCE Inc. and chairman of the Canadian Task Force Year 2000, has expressed concern that fewer than 10 per cent of Canadian firms are spending serious money on the problem. "Frankly, I'm very worried," he said.[4]

The costs of all this fixing are a business expense and thus are tax deductible against the profits of the firms that need to make the changes. Thus the taxpayer gets to share in the task — up to 58 per cent in the case of wealthy corporations that haven't worked out a sufficient dodge to avoid taxes altogether. The money has to come from somewhere, right?

That US$600 billion figure, properly invested, could provide safe drinking water, sanitation, primary education, health care, and family planning to all the world's poorest people.[5] A mere $38 billion annually would cover those costs.[6] In other words, all the people who now suffer from shortages so monumental that they are already causing wars could be looked after on the income from the money we are going to blow on the Millennium Bug.

But if we look on the bright side, the US$600 billion, or the $12 billion we will spend in Canada, becomes a positive number when we calculate our gross domestic product. If the money is spent within Canada, it becomes part of the GDP, helps our economy to look better, and persuades foreign investors to bring us their money. The same $12 billion represents almost twice the money Ottawa has chopped so far from its social transfers to the provinces. If we put the same money into refurbishing medical care in this country, while it would also show up as a positive part of the GDP, it would add to government spending, increase our deficit, and persuade foreign investors to keep their wallets in their pockets.

In the current philosophy, public is bad, private is good. A liposuction treatment on the overly developed haunches of a citizen, to restore that svelte appearance, is an economic good; oxygen for Margaret Lamanna is a waste of public funds, for we are already overcommitted.

The Canada Pension Plan hoax

The Canada Pension Plan, we're told, is in dire straits and is in the process of being revived by transfusions of new money. Everyone with a paying job, and everyone who hires anyone, is laying out more to keep the CPP from sinking into the mire. Some people don't like it. The younger generations argue that they are being hit hard in the wallet to allow the retirees to live in style on up to $740 a month. As they see it, the old busters created the problem by allowing the CPP fund to get into this mess in the first place.

That is one way to look at it. Another way is to suggest that the entire crisis was invented as part of the crusade to convince us that we were headed down the tubes and the time had come for some of that short-term pain for long-term gain we hear so much about. In September 1997 Finance Minister Paul Martin announced a series of changes to the premiums paid to support the plan. Over six years, these premiums will be boosted by 73 per cent, from $945 per year in 1997 to $1,635 per year in 2003. An employee who earns $38,500 or more, the maximum salary covered under the plan, will be paying $1,635 in premiums in 2003, and his employer will pay the same. Put another way, the premiums were 5.85 per cent of earnings when Martin rose in his place in the House of Commons; when he sat down again, they were 6 per cent as of January 1, 1997 (retroactively), rising to 9.9 per cent seven years later.[7]

Without these severe hikes, Martin said, the result would have been "financial chaos." Canadians who came to collect from the national sock in future years would have found nothing at the bottom but a lump of coal. The CPP has been spending more than it takes in, and nothing lies ahead but ruin. Because of this looming shortfall, the maximum pension available will be cut by $144 a year, and disability and survivor benefits will be reduced. Sorry, but the money is gone.

Oh, yes, Martin said while he was on his feet, he is giving us a new CPP investment board composed of twelve appointed professionals, who will invest the funds of the plan "at arm's length from governments."[8] The Quebec Pension Plan has a pension board that is allowed to invest more widely than the CPP, and does, chiefly through the Caisse de dépôt et placement. Ottawa is off down this same track. So, Finance has privatized the funds, and the board can go play in the global markets with the pension money. That should be fun. But what pension money? Are we not broke? Not quite. There is about $40 billion in the fund at the moment — $5 billion in cash, and the other $35 billion held by the provinces in the form of bonds.

The way the plan was set up, the premiums went into the fund and were invested — usually by way of loans to the provinces at interest rates equal to the rate of twenty-year Government of Canada bonds. At the end of 1996 this money was earning about 11 per cent per annum. Nice. The income is used to pay off the claims of beneficiaries. If there is a surplus, we hang onto it. If there is a shortfall in any given year, the money comes out of general revenue or the fund gets reduced. Between 1966, when it was established, and the end of 1993, the Canada Pension Plan showed savings that ranged as high as $2.8 billion, in 1982. The QPP made $914 million that year. Then both plans began to lose money; the CPP lost $1.2 billion in 1994, and the QPP lost $600 million in 1995. Bad show, but hardly a cause for panic. Overall, we took in $40 billion more than we spent between 1966 and 1995 under the CPP.[9]

However, we stand to lose more and more each year as the baby boomers of the 1950s come into pensionable age, and that will lead to a charge against the fund or against general government revenues. Still, in the ordinary way, there is no reason to get alarmed here unless we look at the CPP as if it were a private company pension plan.

In the private, occupational pension plans, the law requires full funding: there must be enough in the pool of investments to cover the cost of pensions for all retired employees and for all current employees. There is no guarantee that the company will still be here a few decades from now, so the rule in private plans is "Show me the money!"

Governments are in a completely different situation. Barring calamity dreadful to contemplate, the federal government will stay in business. If it needs more money to meet its obligations under the CPP, it can raise it. Looked at another way, if the federal government had to cover every dollar contemplated as future spending by the CPP, it would need, according to a calculation performed by the chief actuary in the Office of the Superintendent of Financial Institutions, $556 billion in the sock.[10] This calculation makes no sense because it presumes a situation that will never happen, and then works backwards.

However, driven by a series of unfounded myths promulgated by our native neocons — that the plan is broke, that it is lending out the funds at bargain-basement rates, and that there won't be any money in the plan when the time comes for younger Canadians to retire — the process has been turned into a huge tax hike and a pool of investment for the private market. By the federal government's own figures, the CPP will, under its new regime, break even on an annual basis in 2003. It will then begin to pile up cash until, by the year 2007, the fund will stand at $126 billion. Of this total, $30 billion will be needed to meet obligations, and $90 billion will be available for investment.[11] So we are hiking rates dramatically, cutting pension payments, and reducing disability and survivor benefits to create huge commissions for security sales persons.

The National Council of Welfare has been saying, for at least seven years, that there was no need for this panic. Let the premiums rise very slowly, it advised, widen the contributory base, and improve the old age pension itself.[12] Our senior citizens need more money, not less. More of them live in poverty than ever before; don't make them the victims. When the plan was set up in 1966, Ottawa and the provinces agreed to look at the contribution rates, which have always been much lower than those for comparable plans in Europe and the United States, every five years. The first such review took place in 1991, twenty-five years into the plan. Now, in a spasm of remorse for this neglect, we appear to be intent on piling up billions we don't need. The CPP has become part of our preoccupation with the deficit, part of our conviction that we are bankrupt as a nation. The council says the reason we are following this mad regime is clear:

> Despite the many advantages of the Canada Pension Plan, it has been the object of continuing attacks by the radical right. Some people have even espoused a Chilean-style system of compulsory individual registered retirement savings plans as an alternative to the CPP.[13]

The only part of this analysis I find difficulty with is the comment about the radical right. It is not the radical right that wants to push the state out of the pension business but a Liberal government that has swallowed the nostrums of the radical right and made them into policy. The CPP is being savaged for reasons that have nothing to do with accountancy or economics and everything to do with our perception that governments cannot be trusted to do anything for us. When this line of thinking leads us to cut survivor benefits to find fun money for an investment board carefully removed from government control, I give up.

Fortunately, there are others more cheerful than I, men and women who believe we can, and will, turn things around again. Among the experts I talked to while researching this book was Penny Richmond, a senior official with the Canadian Labour Congress in Ottawa. She told me that although the unions were picking up signs of social breakdown and widespread fear from the media, there was room for optimism:

> In the United States and even in this country there are things that go on that are not reflected in the media or reported. I think about the women's "March against Poverty," where we started off in the Yukon and Newfoundland, New Brunswick and Vancouver, to march on Ottawa. We were in ninety different communities, some very tiny, some massive rallies, and the national press virtually ignored it until we started getting closer to Ottawa. We were talking about the need for government to continue to play its role, and we thought we were talking to ourselves until one day we were marching through Barry's Bay, a small town near Algonquin Park in Ontario, and there was this old boy standing on the sidewalk, he must have been at least eighty, and as we went by, he raised his hand and shouted, "Go for it girls, the feet have hit the street!" I thought, by God, there's something happening out there, even if the media don't see it.[14]

David Ross, the executive director of the Canadian Council on Social Development, also thinks the pendulum, having swung thus far to the right, may be ready to move back in the other direction, as it does from time to time:

I don't feel as gloomy now as I did two or three years ago, when it looked as if the issue of the deficit was going to go on forever. The governments made a serious effort and, by the turn of the century or even before, it will be yesterday's news. I'm greatly encouraged not only by what I observe but by the opinion polls, which are now saying we cut too hard, too fast. I mean, we're not American, that's the good news, and that is the thing that has restrained governments . . .

. . . I really think what we've gone through is a shift of the pendulum to the right. Now, the neocons are more and more being depicted as boobs. This is a big change. Starting in 1984, the only thing our politicians ever talked about was the deficit. Ministers, even when they were opening a dam, would talk about the damn deficit.

But now the provinces are running a surplus and the federal government will be running a surplus soon and people are saying, "Now wait a minute, why are we tightening our belts?" Because the deficit's done with and because the GDP is growing, the debt is going down as a percentage of GDP, that's all falling into place. Now the issue is, "What happened to all the hospitals you closed? What happened to the social services you took away from us? What happened to the environmental controls?"

I don't think Canadians, or at least the majority of Canadians, ever deserted what we like to feel is our chief Canadian characteristic, that we are more collective in solving problems than the more individualistic approach of the Americans. We never went as far into the welfare state as the Europeans. Maybe we're the third way.[15]

I bring these two cheerful commentators forward because I hope they are right. But if they are, we are going to have to take at least three positive steps to get to where they think we may be heading.

1. We must have a realistic assessment of government spending

We have not been overindulging ourselves for years. Rather, we have been paying excessive interest costs, which is quite a different matter. You don't need to close hospitals to curb interest charges; you need to keep interest rates down. When we did that, the economy bounced back, just as expected. In the real world, budgets at all three levels of government are drawn on the basis of previous budgets. One item goes up a little, another comes down a little, and then the pushing and shoving takes place among the interested parties, both within the government and outside. It's unfair, or at least naive, to hope that the money we save by not buying helicopters will be switched over to health care. It doesn't work that way.

Still, every so often we have a "program review," where everything is up for grabs and every expenditure by every department is called into question. Recent program reviews have been more like pogroms — exercises in massacre rather than judicious pruning. We need a new program review, starting from the premise that what the politicians say on the campaign trail has at least a minimal validity. We are not Americans; we do believe in a more interventionist state than they do; we cherish our social welfare network; and we simply do not believe that it is necessary to turn mental patients loose in the community with no support to balance our books.

Consider a couple of items in our national accounts. In 1955, as table 6 of the appendix sets out, Canadian corporations were paying 43 per cent of all the income tax collected in Canada, and individuals just more than half. By the end of 1995, individuals were paying nearly 90 per cent, and corporations just over 11 per cent. This contrast represents a transfer of financial obligations of more than $30 billion annually from the corporate sector to private persons. In 1955 total income taxes collected by the federal government came to $11.4 billion, of which corporations paid $4.9 billion and individuals paid $5.9 billion. (There were also some other payments to this account, to make up the $11.4 billion.) Forty years later, the total income tax take was $96.7 billion, of which corporations paid $11.2 billion and individuals paid $87.4 billion. Our share of the burden went up by $81.5 billion ($87.4 billion paid in 1995, minus $5.9 billion paid in 1955); their share, by $6.3 billion ($11.2 billion minus $4.9 billion); in current dollars, the corporations are actually paying a good deal less now than they were four decades ago.

If the two groups had paid the same proportion in 1995 that they did in 1955, the corporations would have paid $41.6 billion in tax in 1995 (43 per cent of the total $96.7 billion), which is $30.4 billion more than they did in fact have to pay. We could have drastically reduced individual income tax or, given how much the corporations complained about the accrual of public debt, used the extra $34.8 billion we collected from them to wipe out the deficit.

If you look at the table again, you will see that, in 1980, when we first began to get really excited about debt, the corporate tax bill was $12.6 billion; by 1994, when the hue and cry about the federal deficit reached its climax, the corporate tax bill had *dropped* to $7.4 billion, a savings to them of $5.2 billion, while individuals were paying $37 billion more than in 1980. Revenue Canada got a little more from them in 1995.

If the deficit was such a danger to the public weal, why didn't we keep the corporate tax level and wipe out our debt decades ago?

There is an economic argument to be made that taxing corporations doesn't make much sense anyway, since they simply pass on the costs to their customers. Besides, if we don't give our corporations all the goodies American corporations do, they will depart. Well, it's an argument, but not one that comes up when the budget comes down. The massive transfer of fiscal responsibility from corporations to individuals has taken place, year by year, largely at the instance of a lobbying system that now rivals the one in Washington.

If Canadians had been told, "Look, we are running into financial trouble, so we have decided to take the national hatchet to our hospitals in order to give the money to corporations," it might have been a hard sell. As it was, we never saw it as a choice. We were told, literally, that we had no choice. It was chop or perish.

Again, consider the way a change was made in financing the public debt. In 1975 the Bank of Canada and government accounts held 20.8 per cent of our public debt.[16] When the Bank of Canada holds debt, it pays the interest to itself, subtracts its own administrative costs, and hands over the difference to the receiver general of Canada. If it makes $2 billion in interest, it holds back the $200 million it costs to run the institution and sends the receiver general a cheque for $1.8 billion. The effect, according to calculations done by Ruben C. Bellan at the University of Manitoba, is that we pay less than 1 per cent per annum in interest on money held this way.[17]

With privatization, we threw in everything, including the public debt. By October 1995 the percentage of public debt held by the Bank of Canada and government accounts had plummeted to 6.5 per cent.[18] Most of the difference was taken up by the commercial banks. Instead of borrowing money at an effective rate of less than 1 per cent, we are now paying the Bank of Montreal and others five to seven times that percentage every year. William Henry Pope, author of *All You MUST Know about Economics*, calculates that this represents "an annual subsidy" to the commercial banks of $3.5 billion a year.[19]

Suppose Paul Martin were to stand up in the House of Commons and say, "By the way, fellas, we are giving the chartered banks an extra $3.5 billion every year because we think they deserve it. We plan to get the cash from the block transfer payments to the provinces." How do you think that would affect his plan to become prime minister?

Another example: the government of Canada decides to invest $700 million in help to companies, very profitable companies, who are exploiting the tar sands of Alberta. This may be a very good idea, but it should be compared with, say, investing the same amount of money in cutting tuition fees, which will undoubtedly return at least as big a dividend — and last longer.

We are making these choices every day, but we don't know it. Year after year we have taken money from the funds that defend the old, the young, the poor, the sick, and the disadvantaged; year after year we have given equivalent funds to groups of people who are more skilful and more demanding in extracting it, including and especially our large corporations.

This exchange is possible only because we have no notion that it is going on. All we need to do is to wake up.

2. We must change the way we look at government spending

First, if we want to know how deeply in debt we are, we must have some realistic estimate of our assets, not just our liabilities. Calculating the cost of the entire system of air traffic control which we put in place over decades at $1, and then showing a drop in the federal deficit of $1.5 billion when we sell it at a loss, is simple-minded madness.[20] We must recalculate the national debt on the basis of assets and liabilities, not fake $1 assets and real liabilities. I have no idea where such a realistic assessment would leave us, but I strongly suspect that we would find that, overall, we are not in debt at all. We are a very rich nation in the eyes of everyone on the planet but Canadians. Maybe others are looking at us more intelligently than we do ourselves.

Second, when we look at matters like the Canada Pension Plan, we should be guided by common sense, not ideology. The same applies to privatization, to hospital economies, to education, to the environment. A system which tells us that money spent on computer games for kids is well spent, but that money invested in defending the environment is wasted, is badly out of kilter.

3. We must find Canadian solutions for Canadian problems

We behave as if we had elected Newt Gingrich to lead us, and we have swallowed whole the collection of bumper-stickers that makes up current American political policy. We have been putting ourselves through this self-immolation for reasons that have no justification in recent Canadian history. How can we take pride in the fact that we are, at one and the same time, creating more millionaires and more paupers than ever before? We spent decades putting in place a social safety net we were proud of; now we have shredded it in the name of a frontier philosophy that comes from Daniel Boone and Jay Gould rather than from ourselves.

The downsizing exercise we are still going through has had some positive benefits; for example, the Harris government of Ontario, in lancing the swollen boards of education, did us all a favour. The school boards were formed in the first place to keep an eye on public spending on education, not to absorb most of the money. The board headquarters of the Region of Durham, in Whitby, just west of Toronto, cost $21 million and looks like a cathedral. Now that the board has been downsized, maybe they can rent the building out for a crusade.

This example — and it would not be hard to multiply — suggests that what we are in need of is not simply an exercise to reinflate the state. The muscular anarchy of the Harris government of Ontario, and the Klein government of Alberta, among others, informs us that there is still plenty of power left in the hands of government. In those provinces, the entire educational systems have been turned on their heads and medical care systems have been disembowelled by laws passed with too much haste and too little care. What we need is not more government, but more responsive government. We need to reclaim the territory that has been taken from us by the Business Council on National Issues, the Fraser Institute, and their like, and to re-establish the notion that public policy ought to be directed towards the greatest good of the greatest number — not just campaign contributors.

When the federal government produced the first balanced budget in twenty-eight years on February 24, 1998[21] (the last time was in 1969–70), Paul Martin nearly fractured his arm patting himself on the back. The budget documents showed, however, that what worked the miracle was not the "sacrifices" he and his colleagues had exacted from the nation, but the expansion of the economy that resulted from a number of factors, chief of which was the reversal of the high-interest rate policy that produced our run of deficits.[22] One of the things the budget documents revealed was how little grasp of the matter Martin and his minions had. They were working on a budget deficit for this period of $17 billion; instead, the economy produced a *surplus* of at least $3 billion. It was never acknowledged as a surplus, for that would have led to demands to spend it, so it was stuck away in a contingency fund — rainy day money. On a budget of $147.5 billion, the Finance wizards guessed wrong by $20 billion, but because they took in more, rather than less, than planned, their ineptitude was greeted with spasms of joy from almost every editorial pulpit in the land. The finance minister could have restored every cut made, and still have been billions of dollars ahead of his projections. But instead of asking why we were still being put through savage savings that we now knew to be excessive, we were to attribute success to the shrewd fiscal planning of a group that didn't know, within $20 billion, how much it had to spend.

The good news was still drying on the front pages of the nation's newspapers when the Business Council on National Issues had its say. The BCNI, which represents the "chief executives of 150 major Canadian corporations"[23] controlling assets of $1.7 trillion (most of the large ones are actually the Canadian ends of foreign corporations), fired off a memo to Prime Minister Jean Chrétien entitled "Building on Strength towards a More Competitive and Socially Progressive Canada." For those who don't understand the language, "building on strength" means "keep cutting taxes," "more competitive" means "lower wages," and "socially progressive" means "keep cutting taxes." The eight-page, single-spaced memo congratulated the prime minister on the balanced budget, but spent most of its time warning him not to stop the cuts: "A determined assault on the level of the national debt is required to ensure a steady reduction in the amount of tax revenue required for debt service," it claimed. "This in turn will allow Canadians to enter the new millennium convinced that every year, they can expect their total tax burden to fall rather than to rise."[24]

The goal of government, then, is not to provide services, ensure national independence, or maintain a balance between the more- and less-favoured of society, but to keep those taxes falling, year after year, no matter what.

The BCNI is perhaps the most powerful lobby in the nation, and when it talks, even if it talks nonsense, politicians listen. Two governments, one Conservative, the other Liberal, bought almost entirely the BCNI's campaign for "free" trade, and there is no reason to suppose it will be any less successful in this campaign to put tax cuts ahead of restoring services on the government agenda in the years to come. The only recourse is for Canadians who don't control $1.7 trillion in assets, but who do control votes, to take action.

The notion that the federal Liberal government, now that it has beaten the deficit into submission, will put money back into social spending is akin to the notion that if we all clap our hands at once, Tinkerbell will fly again. Linda McQuaig, in her new book, *The Cult of Impotence*, makes two key points that relate to this argument. The first is that public opinion is firmly on the side of restoring government programs and creating jobs; the second is that the people who run the nation intend to pay absolutely no attention to this feeling. As she puts it:

> Yet, even as we reach the promised land of deficit-free nir-
> vana — the place where, we are told, the world will once again
> be our oyster and even the Finance minister claims we can
> make our own decisions — there are certain things we appar-
> ently still can't have, like jobs and social programs. [25]

Our decision makers respond with alacrity to the BCNI, the C.D. Howe Institute, and other outposts of orthodoxy for the astoundingly simple reason that they all chum together, down at the Albany Club, and that the corporations of Canada con-tribute a lot more to the campaign funds of the decision makers than does your local food bank. This situation has produced a misanthropic and misleading reaction among Canadians — What's the use? — which overlooks the fact that the ballot is, in the end, mightier than the bank book.

This is not the time to turn against the political parties because "they're all the same." It is the time to reinvade the par-ties on behalf of ordinary Canadians, rather than the elites who now run them. We who do not attend the BCNI clambakes, or the Fraser Institute seminars, still have the power, collectively, to reverse the trend of the last decade or so. You and I and Tom D'Aquino, president and CEO of the BCNI, have one vote each. All we have to do is use it.

This does not mean hiring more bureaucrats and loosening spending controls on governments. One thing we have learned from all the cuts is that some of them were necessary and that some of our institutions had grown too fat and too lazy. "Efficient public service" is not an oxymoron but a necessity.

But much of the downsizing has been both mean-spirited and wrong-headed, and most of it was utterly unnecessary. Not long ago it was the custom to poke fun at left-wingers who thought you could solve any problem by throwing money at it; now we think we can solve any problem by taking the money away. It makes even less sense. You cannot cure child poverty by cutting welfare benefits; you cannot buy social peace by widening the gap between rich and poor; you cannot make this nation greater by taking an axe to its underpinnings and a bazooka to its self-esteem.

We are a rich nation, much richer by far than we were when Tommy Douglas opened the Radville Hospital in 1947. We are also, alas, much poorer in spirit. Almost all our problems, when you think about them, are matters of perception. We are tearing ourselves apart over a poverty that does not exist, except in our own minds. To begin to reverse the process, we need to look at our history and accomplishments, not American propaganda. We need to begin the trek back to the responsive state we built, not so very long ago, when we believed in ourselves as a people of care, common sense, and compassion.

Appendix

TABLE 1
How Poor Are We?

Canada's Gross Domestic Product in Millions of Constant (1996) Dollars

1980:	$613,860	1990:	$756,498
1985:	$627,076	1995:	$791,825

Change 1986–95:   +29 per cent
Population growth, 1980–95:   23 per cent

The GDP has grown faster than the population over this period. As a nation, we produced 6 per cent more per capita in 1995 than in 1980, measured in constant dollars — that is, with the effects of inflation removed.

Another way to look at this is to measure personal expenditure on consumer goods and services:

Personal Spending in millions of Constant (1996) Dollars

1980:	$348,280	1990:	$451,230
1985:	$387,049	1995:	$475,289

Change 1980–95:   +36 per cent
Population growth, 1980–95:   23 per cent

We have more money than ever, and we spend more money than ever, measured in constant dollars.

Now, let's look at the revenues of all levels of government over the same period:

Revenues of All Levels of Government, in Millions of 1996 Dollars

1980:	$625,980	1990:	$756,497
1985:	$627,076	1995:	$791,824

Change 1980–95:   + 26 per cent
Population growth, 1980–95:   23 per cent

Government income, too, is higher than it was in 1980, although only very slightly when measured on a per capita basis. We had a good deal more money, measured in the same dollars, in 1995, for every Canadian, than we did in 1961.

How, then, did we manage to convince ourselves that we were poor?

Sources: Calculated from Statistics Canada, *Canadian Economic Observer, Historical Supplement, 1995–96* (Ottawa: Industry Canada 1996), tables 1 and 3; *Canadian Global Almanac, 1997,* 236

TABLE 2
Employees in Public Administration, All Levels of Government, 1976–95

Year	Employees	Population of Canada	Number of Canadians per Civil Servant
1976	701,000	22,933,000	33
1981	793,000	24,343,000	31
1986	829,000	25,309,000	30
1991	873,000	27,297,000	31
1995	810,000	29,606,000	37

Note: Canada's population increased by 29 per cent during this period, while the number in public administration increased by 15 per cent.

Sources: Statistics Canada, *Canadian Economic Observer, Historical Supplement, 1995–96,* table 8, and population tables from the *Canadian Global Almanac, 1997*

TABLE 3
Interest Charges and the National Debt, 1955–97
(in $*billions)

Year	Federal Government Revenues	Program Spending	Interest Charges	Increase in Federal Debt*
1955–64	65	57	7	-1
1965-74	159	150	19	10
1975–84	414	434	107	127
1985–94	956	944	314	302
1995–97	389	340	134	85
Total	**1,983**	**1,925**	**447**	**525**

*In these forty-two years, the federal debt increased by $525 billion, the increase that has put us in a financial straightjacket today. Program spending — the outlay on welfare, education, transfer payments, etc. — was actually lower than revenues; the damage was done by interest charges, without which the debt, which stood at just under $16 billion when the process began, would have been wiped out long ago. Of the $525 billion increase, $447 billion, or 85 per cent, was added to the bill by interest charges.

Sources: Statistics Canada, *Canadian Economic Observer*, table 3; *Budget Plan, 1997*, introduced in the House of Commons on February 18, 1997, tables 3.6, 3.7, and 3.8

TABLE 4
Where the Medical Money Goes
(in $ billions)

Year	Physicians	Hospitals	Other Institutions	Drugs	Other Health Professionals	Other Costs*	Total
1975	1.840	5.512	1.124	1.073	0.902	1.804	12.255
1980	3.287	9.395	2.536	1.877	1.906	3.395	22.396
1985	6.046	16.384	4.076	3.789	3.312	4.593	38.200
1990	9.258	23.870	5.720	6.903	5.179	10.722	61.652
1995	10.799	25.944	7.252	10.560	6.467	7.709	74.306

Note: In the two decades shown here, the consumer price index went up by 295 per cent, and the gross domestic product by 452 per cent. What this table shows is that, in this same period, pay to doctors went up 586 per cent; hospital costs went up 470 per cent; and drug costs went up 984 per cent.

*Other costs includes public health, capital costs, and miscellaneous costs.

Sources: *National Health Expenditures in Canada, 1975–1996*, table 4; Statistics Canada, *Canadian Economic Observer*, table 1; and *National Health Expenditures in Canada, 1975–1996*, Health Canada Fact Sheets (Ottawa, June 1997)

TABLE 5
Government Spending on Culture and Heritage
(in $ millions)

Area	Federal	Provincial	Municipal	Total
arts education	4	81	–	85
broadcasting	1,509	217	–	1,726
film & video	240	77	–	317
heritage				
instruction	435	367	49	851
libraries	47	755	1,053	1,855
literary arts	167	21	–	188
multicultural aid	7	40	–	47
nature parks	190	67	–	257
performing arts	115	140	62	317
sound recording	5	4	–	9
visual arts	13	41	–	54
other activities	94	124	249	467
TOTALS	**2,827**	**1,933**	**1,413**	**6,173**

Sources: Statistics Canada, *Canada's Culture, Heritage and Identity, A Statistical Report* (Ottawa: Industry Canada, December 1995), table 2.5A

TABLE 6
The Share of Income Tax
(in millions of constant 1986 dollars)

Year	From Individuals	From Corporations	Total	Individual Tax as Percentage of Total	Corporate Tax as Percentage of Total
1955	5,974	4,960	11,428	52.3	43.4
1965	11,308	7,026	18,340	58.8	36.5
1970	24,739	9,945	35,408	69.7	28.0
1975	39,450	12,186	52,657	74.9	23.1
1980	41,570	12,666	55,548	74.8	22.8
1985	55,362	10,465	69,670	79.5	15.0
1990	77,595	12,247	91,168	85.1	13.4
1994	78,366	7,419	86,952	90.1	8.5
1995	84,503	10,867	96,698	87.4	11.2

Note: During this period, the personal share of all income taxes collected from Canadians went from just over 50 per cent to 87 per cent. The corporate share went from just under 50 per cent to 11 per cent. This represents a transfer of tens of billions of dollars a year in tax obligations from corporations to individuals. If corporations had paid the same proportion of taxes in 1995 as they did in 1955, their share of this burden would have been $41,966 million instead of $10,867 million — a difference of more than $31 billion.

Source: Derived from "Income Taxes Collected from Individuals and Corporations," in the *Canadian Global Almanac, 1998*, 237. The table includes federal and provincial income taxes, and, in the case of corporations, old age security tax.

Endnotes

1 The Slow Rise and Swift Fall of the Responsive State

1 Speech to U.S. publishers, New York, 1957.
2 Quoted in Pierre Berton, *The Great Depression* (Toronto: McClelland & Stewart, 1990), 132.
3 National Archives of Canada, Bennett Papers, vol. 11, 50359, Sir Charles Gordon to R.B. Bennett, January 6, 1934.
4 Alvin Finkel, *Business and Social Reform in the Thirties* (Toronto: Lorimer, 1979), 88.
5 R.B. Bryce, "The Canadian Economy in the Great Depression," in his *Interpreting Canada's Past* (Toronto: Oxford University Press, 1993), vol. 2, 481.
6 Quoted in James Struthers, "Shadows from the Thirties," in *The Canadian Welfare State*, ed. Jacqueline S. Ismael (Edmonton: University of Alberta Press, 1987), 10.
7 Max Beloff, *Wages and Welfare in Britain, 1914–1945* (London: Edward Arnold, 1984), 263ff.
8 Blair Fraser, *The Search for Identity* (Toronto: Doubleday, 1967), 18–19.
9 Struthers, "Shadows from the Thirties," 13.
10 J. Harvey Perry, *A Fiscal History of Canada: The Postwar Years* (Toronto: Canadian Tax Foundation, 1989), 160–61.
11 Struthers, "Shadows from the Thirties," 4.
12 Tom Kent, a key policy maker during the Pearson years and into the early Trudeau years, has an excellent description of the genesis of these plans in his book *A Public Purpose* (Kingston and Montreal: McGill-Queen's University Press, 1988), 129ff.
13 Kenneth Bryden, *Old Age Pensions and Policy-Making in Canada* (Montreal: Queen's University Press), 5.
14 Kent, *A Public Purpose*, 316.
15 "The Welfare State in Historical Perspective," *European Journal of Sociology* 2 (1961): 228.

16 John Maynard Keynes, *The General Theory of Employment, Interest and Money* (New York: Harcourt, Brace, 1936).
17 *The 1997 Canadian Global Almanac*, 204.
18 Quoted in Linda McQuaig, *The Wealthy Banker's Wife: The Assault on Equality in Canada* (Toronto: Penguin, 1993), 14.
19 Linda McQuaig, *Shooting the Hippo: Death by Deficit, and Other Canadian Myths* (Toronto: Viking, 1995), 152–53.

2 Goddam Guvmint

1 *Globe and Mail*, January 29, 1998, A10.
2 *Toronto Star*, December 17, 1996, A3.
3 *Toronto Star*, September 24, 1996, A22.
4 *Globe and Mail*, October 21, 1996, A1, A6.
5 Interview, Ottawa, April 10, 1996.
6 Statistics Canada, *Canada Year Book, 1963–64*, 160.
7 Statistics Canada, January 16, 1998.
8 *Ottawa Citizen*, January 26, 1997, A1.
9 John Ralston Saul, *The Unconscious Civilization* (Toronto: House of Anansi, 1995), 76.
10 *Globe and Mail*, December 24, 1997, B1.
11 *Report of the Auditor General of Canada*, November 1995, chapter 9.
12 *Toronto Star*, November 3, 1997, A6.
13 Ibid.
14 *Globe and Mail*, January 2, 1997, A1, A2.
15 Interview, Public Service Commission, April 11, 1997.
16 *Toronto Star*, August 23, 1997, E2.
17 Christopher Schenk and John Anderson, eds., *Re-shaping Work* (Toronto: Ontario Federation of Labour, 1995), 37.
18 Statistics Canada, *Microdata File of Economic Families* (Ottawa 1996).
19 Ibid.
20 Schenk and Anderson, eds., *Re-shaping Work*, 39.
21 Linda Duxbury, *Study of Public Sector Works in Ottawa Region*, cited ibid., 36.
22 Public Service Alliance of Canada, Technology Adjustment Research Programme, *Report*, 47.
23 "OPS Moves from 'Rowing to Steering the Boat,'" *Topical*, published by Management Board Secretariat, August 22, 1997, 1.
24 Ibid.
25 David Zussman, "Government's New Style," *Financial Post Weekly*, October 18/20, 1997, 4. Micromedia accession number: 3972662.
26 Ibid.
27 Jan Borowy and Theresa Johnson, "Unions Confront Work Reorganization and the Rise of Precarious Employment," in Schenk and Anderson, eds., *Re-shaping Work*, 23.
28 Statistics Canada, *National Income and Expenditure Accounts, First Quarter, 1997*.

29 Quoted in Harry Pope, *All You MUST Know about Economics* (Toronto: Comer, 1996), 24.

30 *Budget Plan 1997* (Ottawa: February 18, 1997) table 3.8, Public Debt Charges.

31 *Report of the Auditor General of Canada* (Ottawa: October 1995), 9–15.

32 *Toronto Star*, December 8, 1997, A6.

33 Department of Finance, *Budget Plan, 1997*, tables 3.6, 3.7, and 3.8.

34 *1997 Ontario Budget Papers*, 62, table B1.

35 *Toronto Star*, December 27, 1997, B1.

36 *The Crisis in Child Welfare Campaign: Children and Families at Risk, Membership Survey Results* (Winnipeg: Canadian Union of Public Employees, December 10, 1996), 8.

37 *Winnipeg Free Press*, December 11, 1996, A1.

38 H.W. Arthurs, "Mechanical Arts and Merchandise: Canadian Public Administration in the New Economy," *McGill Law Journal* 42 (February 1997): 40.

3 Medicare: The Sick System

1 Canadian Press newswire, February 19, 1997.

2 *Calgary Herald*, November 3, 1996, A1.

3 Canadian Press newswire, February 25, 1996.

4 *Toronto Star*, January 26, 1997, A1.

5 *Maclean's*, December 2, 1996, 45.

6 Ibid., 67

7 *Toronto Star*, September 15, 1997, B1.

8 Ibid., A1.

9 Hilda Neatby, *Quebec: The Revolutionary Age* (Toronto: McClelland & Stewart, 1977), 239.

10 Quoted ibid., 283, note 36.

11 Esdras, Minville, "Labour Legislation and Social Services in the Province of Quebec," *Report of the Royal Commission on Dominion-Provincial Relations* (Ottawa: King's Printer), 1939, 45–46.

12 Alvin Finkel, *Business and Social Reform in the Thirties* (Toronto: James Lorimer, 1979), 81.

13 Ontario *Legislature Debates*, December 19, 1868.

14 Grace MacInnis, *J.S. Woodsworth* (Toronto: Macmillan, 1953), 53, 64.

15 Lewis H. Thomas, *The Making of a Socialist: The Recollections of T.C. Douglas* (Edmonton: University of Alberta Press, 1982), 7.

16 Finkel, *Business and Social Reform*, 97.

17 J. Harvey Perry, *A Fiscal History of Canada* (Toronto: Canadian Tax Foundation, 1989), 624.

18 Canada, Dominion-Provincial Conference, *Report* (Ottawa: King's Printer, 1946), 89-94.

19 Perry, *A Fiscal History of Canada*, 636.

20 Ibid., 640.

21 *Maclean's*, December 22, 1996, 58.

22 Perry, *A Fiscal History of Canada*, 641.

23 Peter Newman, *The Distemper of Our Times: Canadian Politics in Transition, 1963–68* (Toronto: McClelland & Stewart, 1968), 412.

24 *Report of the Royal Commission on Canada's Health Services* (Ottawa: Queen's Printer, 1964), chapter 12, 1.

25 Ibid., Conclusions and Recommendations, 1.

26 Tom Kent, *A Public Purpose* (Kingston and Montreal: McGill-Queen's University Press, 1988), 367.

27 Perry, *A Fiscal History of Canada*, 645.

28 Ibid., 655.

29 Ibid., 657.

30 Health Canada, *National Health Expenditures in Canada, 1975–1994* (Ottawa: January 1996).

31 Perry, *A Fiscal History of Canada*, table 22.1.

32 Larry Bryan, *A Design for the Future of Health Care* (Toronto: Key Porter, 1996), table 2.2, 2.3, and 2.4. The figures were originally complied by the American College of Surgeons.

33 The higher figure is the estimate used in Linda McQuaig's *The Wealthy Banker's Wife: The Assault on Equality in Canada* (Toronto: Penguin, 1993), 135.

34 Canadian Health Coalition, *A Prescription for Plunder* (Ottawa: 1997), 4–5, 20.

35 "Our ability to change our patent law is defined by these obligations," Industry Minister John Manley told a House of Commons committee. *Toronto Star*, February 18, 1997, A12.

36 Queen's Health Policy Research Unit, *The Economic Impact of Bill C-91 on the Cost of Pharmaceuticals in Canada* (Kingston, January 17, 1997), 16.

37 Saint John *Telegraph Journal*, August 27, 1997, A9.

38 Canadian Health Coalition, *A Prescription for Plunder*, 17.

39 Statistics Canada, *Canada Year Book, 1997*, 101, 103.

40 Kevin Taft, *Shredding the Public Interest* (Edmonton: University of Alberta Press, 1997), 3.

41 Ibid., table F.

42 Ibid., 14.

43 Ibid., 51, 108.

44 *Calgary Herald*, December 22, 1996, A1.

45 Statistics Canada, Cansim databases, update, January 1996.

46 KPMG Consultants, *Health Care System Benchmarking, Project Report*, March 29, 1996, cited in Taft, *Shredding the Public Interest*, 95.

47 Gordon Laird, "Barn-Raising at the Alberta Summit," *Globe and Mail*, October 6, 1997, A15.

48 Perry, *A Fiscal History of Canada*, 447.

49 Canada, House of Commons, *Fifth Report of the Standing Committee on Financing* (Ottawa 1997), 118–19.

50 Ibid.

51 *Toronto Star*, July 24, 1997, A18.

52 *Chatelaine*, September, 1997, 76, 96ff.

53 *Toronto Star*, May 18, 1997, A4.

54 *Globe and Mail*, June 2, 1997, A2, and Ontario Ministry of Health.

55 Health Canada, *National Health Expenditures in Canada, 1975–1996*, 2.

56 Canadian Press newswire, May 6, 1997.

57 *Toronto Star*, September 22, 1997, A20.

58 Kent, *A Public Purpose*, 370.

4 The New Three Rs: Retrenching, Retreating, and Retailing

1 Hilda Neatby, *Quebec: The Revolutionary Age, 1760–1791* (Toronto: McClelland & Stewart, 1977), 242.

2 Ibid., 246.

3 Fernand Ouellet, *Lower Canada, 1791–1840* (Toronto: McClelland & Stewart, 1980), 71.

4 Neatby, *Quebec*, 246.

5 Ouellet, *Lower Canada*, 165.

6 Gerald M. Craig, *Upper Canada: The Formative Years, 1784–1841* (Toronto: McClelland & Stewart, 1979), 25.

7 Ontario Department of Public Records and Archives, *Sixth Report*, 1909, 66–67.

8 Ibid., 56.

9 Ontario Archives, *Ninth Report, Journals of the Assembly, 1812*, 19.

10 Craig, *Upper Canada*, 182.

11 Quoted ibid., 182.

12 Ibid., 183.

13 Ibid., 187.

14 W.S. MacNutt, *The Atlantic Provinces: The Emergence of Colonial Society, 1712–1857* (Toronto: McClelland & Stewart, 1965), 165.

15 Ibid., 166.

16 Ibid., 167.

17 Quoted in ibid., 169.

18 Phillip McCann, "The Newfoundland School Society, 1823–1836," lecture to the Newfoundland Historical Society, St. John's, January 27, 1976, 4.

19 Ibid., 8.

20 The actual wording in the Act provides that no provincial government could take any action "which would prejudicially affect any Right or Privilege with respect to Denominational Schools which any Class of Persons have by Law in the Province at the Union."

21 Samuel Martin, *An Essential Grace* (Toronto: McClelland & Stewart, 1985), 64.

22 Donald Creighton, *Canada's First Century* (Toronto: Macmillan, 1970), 5–6.

23 Quoted in J.M.S. Careless and R. Craig Brown, eds., *The Canadians, 1867–1967* (Toronto: Macmillan, 1967), 164.

24 *Globe and Mail*, September 3, 1997, A1.

25 Careless and Brown, eds., *The Canadians*, 405, 407.

26 J. Harvey Perry, *A Fiscal History of Canada* (Toronto: Canadian Tax Foundation), 779, table 29.9.

27 "Education Financing in Canada — An Update," *Canadian Tax Journal*, 43, 1 (1995): 222.

28 *Social Indicators of Development, 1996* (Baltimore and London: World Bank Book, 1997), tables 1, 13.

29 Ontario, Ministry of Education and Training, *Putting Students First: Ontario's Plan for Education Reform* (Toronto 1997).

30 *Globe and Mail*, October 11, 1997, A1.

31 Ontario, Ministry of Education, *Putting Students First*; 1; *Toronto Star*, October 25, 1995, A10.

32 Ontario, Ministry of Education, *Education in Ontario: Facts and Figures*, (Toronto, 1997), *Canadian Global Almanac* (Toronto: Macmillan, 1988).

33 Victoria Board of Education, *Auditors' Report, 1996*.

34 Ontario, Ministry of Education, *Putting Students First*, 6.

35 *Toronto Star*, September 26, 1996, A46.

36 Maude Barlow and Heather-jane Robertson, *Class Warfare: The Assault on Canada's Schools* (Toronto: Key Porter, 1994), 163.

37 *Toronto Star*, December 8, 1997, A18.

38 Ontario, Ministry of Education, *Putting Kids First* (Toronto 1997), 50.

39 Ontario, Ministry of Education, *Report of the Advisory Panel on Future Directions for Post Secondary Education* (Toronto, December 1996), 4.

40 Statistics Canada, quoted in *Globe and Mail*, September 30, 1997, A3.

41 *Dalhousie Gazette*, January 30, 1997, 1.

42 Statistics Canada, August 26, 1997.

43 Ibid., phone interview, December 9, 1997.

44 *Toronto Star*, February 5, 1998, A2.

45 Naomi Klein, ibid., April 28, 1997, A19.

46 Ibid.

47 John Ralston Saul, *The Unconscious Civilization* (Toronto: House of Anansi, 1995), 65.

48 Alberta Education, *Charter Schools Handbook* (Edmonton 1995), 2.

49 *Vancouver Sun*, March 18, 1996, A1.

50 Anne Daltrop, *Charities* (London: B.T. Batsford, 1978), 27.

5 How Much Justice Can We Afford?

1 Speech to the County of Carleton Law Association, November 15, 1991. See *Policy Options* 13 (November 1992): 3–6.
2 *Edmonton Journal*, October 19, 1996, A1.
3 *1997 Ontario Budget*, table B4, 64.
4 *Toronto Star*, January 15, 1997, A19.
5 Ibid., October 1, 1996, A1, A24.
6 Ibid.
7 Ibid., September 24, 1996, A1, A20.
8 Ibid., December 5, 1996, A6.
9 Ibid., January 17, 1997, A19.
10 *Globe and Mail*, January 15, 1997, A15.
11 Interview, August 17, 1997.
12 David A. Stager with Harry W. Arthurs, *Lawyers in Canada* (Toronto: University of Toronto Press, 1990), 219.
13 Owen Lippert, "Legal Aid in Ontario: What Went Wrong," *Canadian Lawyer*, January 1997, 15–16.
14 Statistics Canada, *Legal Aid in Canada: Resource and Caseload Statistics*, 1995, 44.
15 Lippert, "Legal Aid in Ontario," 15.
16 *Globe and Mail*, April 7, 1997, A4.
17 Interview, August 12, 1997.
18 *Globe and Mail*, September 12, 1997, A14.
19 Statistics Canada, *National Income and Expenditure Accounts*, 1995, table 52.
20 The new choppers have a starting rate of $525 million each, plus another $31.5 million in development costs (*Globe and Mail*, September 12, 1997, A1), assuming that they come in at cost. The total tab: $8.355 billion, or approximately thirteen times the nation's total legal aid bill.
21 Ontario Provincial Correctional Services Estimate.
22 *A Super-Jail for Lindsay-Ops*, Questions and Answers, undated pamphlet.
23 Solicitor General Canada, Correctional Service of Canada, *The Universal Almanac 1997*, edited by John W. Wright (Kansas: Andrews and McMeel, 1996), 232.
24 *The Justice Data Factfinder*, Statistics Canada, September 1996, 16.
25 House of Commons, Justice Committee, *Report of the Task Force* (Ottawa 1996), 3.
26 *Toronto Star*, June 22, 1997.
27 Statistics Canada press release, March 5, 1997.
28 Richard Swift, "Rush to Punishment," in *New Internationalist Magazine*, August 1996, 7–11.

29 *Toronto Star*, June 22, 1997, F2. The council's recommendation persuaded the Liberals to pledge to allocate another $30 million a year to crime prevention, but there was no sign of the money two years later.
30 Canadian Centre for Justice Statistics, "Private Security and Public Policing in Canada," *Juristat* 14, No. 10 (March 1994): 3.
31 Ibid., table 1.
32 *Winnipeg Free Press*, June 18, 1997, A1.
33 Paul Palango, "Mountie Misery," *Maclean's*, July 28, 1997, 10–16.

6 Defanging the Watchdogs

1 Morton Mintz, *At Any Cost: Corporate Greed, Women and the Dalkon Shield* (New York: Pantheon, 1985), 177, 197.
2 Walter Stewart, *Belly Up: The Spoils of Bankruptcy* (Toronto: McClelland & Stewart, 1995), 200.
3 Canada, House of Commons, *Debates*, April 3, 1986, 17,787.
4 Lee Brown, a letter writer to the *Toronto Star*, October 21, 1997, A21, logged onto the Web site and complained that the department "raises its funds from the very companies it is supposed to regulate. No wonder the department now views drug companies and other health industry participants as its clients, rather than the people of Canada."
5 Juanne Nancarrow Clark, *Health, Illness and Medicine in Canada* (Toronto: Oxford University Press, 1996), 378–83.
6 Peter Richards, *The Westray Story: A Predictable Path to Disaster*, Report of the Mine Inquiry, December 1, 1997, Introduction.
7 *Globe and Mail*, October 31, 1997, A10.
8 House of Commons, *Debates,* September 26, 1997, 1124.
9 *Toronto Star*, October 21, 1997, A3.
10 Laboratory Science Review, "Keeping Faith with Canadians: More Effective Health Protection through Federal Laboratory Science and Testing."
11 *Globe and Mail*, May 28, 1997, A1–A8.
12 Memorandum, Dr. M. Brill-Edwards to Michèle Jean, deputy minister, Health Canada, January 19, 1996.
13 Canadian Health Coalition, *A Prescription for Plunder* (Ottawa 1987), 16.
14 These examples are all culled from a memo written to Allan Rock by his own scientists and leaked to the Canadian Health Coalition in late 1997.
15 *The Main Estimates: Estimates Part II* (Ottawa: Minister of Supply and Services, 1996) 10–4.
16 Ministry of Natural Resources press release, "New Regulations Guide Activities on Crown Land," November 5, 1997.

17 Canadian Institute for Environmental Law and Policy, *Ontario's Environment and the Common Sense Revolution: A Second Year Report* (Toronto, July 1997), 107.

18 Interview, Toronto, August 21, 1997.

19 Martin Mayer, *The Greatest Ever Bank Robbery: The Collapse of the Savings and Loan Industry* (New York: Macmillan, 1992); 92–93, 97.

20 James O'Shea, *The Daisy Chain* (New York: Pocket Books, 1991), 44, 218.

21 James Ring Adams, *The Big Fix: Inside the S&L Scandal* (New York: Wiley & Sons, 1991), 283.

22 Nick Leeson, *Rogue Trader* (London: Little, Brown, 1996), 262, 253ff.

23 Reuters Newswire, July 19, 1995.

24 *Report of the Inquiry into the Collapse of CCB and Northland Bank* (Estey Report) (Ottawa: Supply and Services Canada, 1987), 12.

25 A number of books have been written about this farrago of fraud, the best of which is *Private Money, Public Greed* by Terence Corcoran and Laura Reid (Toronto: Collins, 1984).

26 Estey Report, 12.

27 Arthur Johnson, *Breaking the Banks* (Toronto: Lester, Orpen & Dennys, 1986), 244, 212.

28 *Canadian News Facts*, September 1–15, 1985, 3310.

29 Estey Report, 501–2.

30 Ibid., 5.

31 Ibid., 502.

32 *Maclean's*, December 1, 1986, 36.

33 Annual Report of the Inspector General of Financial Institutions, 1994, 1, 13.

34 James Ring Adams and Douglas Franz, *A Full-Service Bank: How BCCI Stole Billions around the World* (New York: Pocket Books, 1992), 348, 11.

35 *New York Times*, December 18, 1987, A1.

36 Adams and Franz, *A Full-Service Bank*, 134, 292.

37 *The Times*, July 21, 1991, A1.

38 *Financial Times*, July 24, 1991, 1.

39 *Washington Post*, August 6, 1991, 1.

40 *Globe and Mail*, September 27, 1993, B3.

41 Reuters Newswire, December 10, 1996.

42 The figures were given in a speech by John Palmer, the Superintendent of the OSFI, to a joint session of the Canadian and Empire Clubs in Toronto, April 4, 1995.

43 *Toronto Star*, July 31, 1995, E6.

44 Ibid., January 6, 1998, C1.

45 Ibid., November 27, 1997, A12.

46 Peter Newman, *The Canadian Revolution, 1985–95: From Deference to Defiance* (Toronto: Viking, 1995), 135.

47 *Toronto Star*, November 27, 1996, A23.

48 *New York Times*, January 29, 1982, 14.

49 Ministry of Consumer and Corporate Relations, New Directions in Public Safety Program Delivery, 1997 (press release).

50 Canadian Institute for Environmental Law and Policy, *Ontario's Environment and the "Common Sense Revolution"* (Toronto 1997), 118.

51 Interview, August 21, 1997.

52 Canadian Institute for Environmental Law and Policy, *Ontario's Environment*, 117, 121.

53 Canadian Labour Congress, *Women's Work: A Report* (Ottawa 1997), 41.

54 Susan J. Tolchin and Martin Tolchin, *Dismantling America* (Boston: Houghton Mifflin, 1983), 276.

7 Let the Environment Look After Itself

1 *Globe and Mail*, August 5, 1997, A1.

2 *Report of the Auditor General of Canada*, May 1996, chapter 2.

3 Minister of Finance, *Budget Plan, 1997*, 143.

4 *Report of the Auditor General of Canada*, May 1995, chapter 2.

5 *Globe and Mail*, January 13, 1997, A15.

6 *Toronto Star*, May 12, 1997, A23.

7 The Commission for Environmental Co-operation, press release, July 30, 1997.

8 Environmental Science Workshop, *The Urgent Need to Sustain Long-Term Econological Research and Monitoring in Canada* (1997), 4.

9 Donella H. Meadows et al., *The Limits to Growth: A Report for the Club of Rome's Project on the Predicament of Mankind* (Washington, DC: Potomac Associates, 1972).

10 World Commission on Environment and Development, *Our Common Future* (Oxford: Oxford University Press, 1987).

11 There is a good precis of this argument in Jim MacNeill, Pieter Winsemius, and Taizo Yakushiji, *Beyond Interdependence: The Meshing of the World's Economy and the Earth Ecology* (New York: Oxford University Press, 1991), 19–27, an update and explanation of *Our Common Future*. To declare my interest, I was one of a number of people consulted on an early draft of this book.

12 *Vital Signs*, the annual produced by Worldwatch Institute, became a once-a-year nag, with reports showing ever-increasing carbon releases and ever-mounting global temperatures.

13 *Vital Signs 1996* (New York: W.W. Norton, 1997), 69.

14 See Charles Caccia, the former environment minister, "Implementing Sustainable Development," *Policy Options*, November 1991, 27–28.

15 *United Nations Framework Convention on Climate Change* (Geneva 1992).

16 *Toronto Star*, October 23, 1997, C2.

17 Ibid.

18 *Winnipeg Free Press*, June 18, 1997, D10.
19 *Globe and Mail*, November 4, 1997, A8.
20 *Toronto Star*, October 23, 1997, C2.
21 Canadian Association of Petroleum Producers, advertisement, *Globe and Mail*, November 6, 1997, A33.
22 Robert Thomas, Department of Economics, University of Washington, in *The Attack on Corporate America: The Corporate Issues Sourcebook*, Law and Economics Centre, University of Miami School of Law (Coral Gables, Florida: McGraw-Hill, 1978), 14–15.
23 This argument was put forward by the Institute for Research on Public Policy in a number of papers during the early 1990s, but was not supported by Jim MacNeill, who ran the institute's environmental policy section. See the discussion in *Beyond Interdependence*, especially 105–6.
24 *Toronto Star*, November 6, 1997, A29.
25 *Globe and Mail*, December 11, 1997, A1.
26 *Policy Options*, November 1990, 5.
27 This material is derived in the main from an article by two scientists, Al Davidson and Tony Hodge, based on a two-year international study conducted by the Conservation Foundation in the United States and the Institute for Research on Public Policy in Canada. It appeared in the October 1989 issue of *Policy Options*, "The Fate of the Great Lakes," on pages 19–26.
28 International Joint Commission, *Eighth Biennial Report on Great Lakes Water Quality* (Washington 1996), 7.
29 Interview, September 11, 1997.
30 Interview, August 21, 1997.
31 Ministry of the Environment and Energy Budget Reductions, press release, April 11, 1996.
32 *Globe and Mail*, March 15, 1997, A1.
33 Interview, August 27, 1997.
34 *Globe and Mail*, October 6, 1997, A1, A7.
35 Canadian Institute on Environmental Law and Policy, *Ontario's Environment and the "Common Sense Revolution"* (Toronto 1997), 81.
36 *Toronto Star*, November 20, 1997, A12.
37 Sergio Marchi, *Strengthening Environmental Protection in Canada: A Guide to the New Legislation* (Ottawa: Environment Canada, 1997).
38 *Toronto Star*, October 25, 1997.
39 Interview, August 21, 1997.

8 Curbing Culture

1 Interview, May 28, 1997.
2 Interview, May 28, 1997.
3 Jean-Philippe Tebet, director of Training, Cultural Human Resources Council, quoted in *The 1997 Budget and Beyond*, 77.
4 Statistics Canada, *Focus on Culture*, summer 1996, 6.

5   *Crown Corporations and Other Corporate Interests of Canada, Annual Report, 1997* (Ottawa: Minister of Public Works, 1997), A-42.

6   *Quarterly Bulletin for the Culture Statistics Program* 8, (autumn 1996): 8.

7   "Strangers in the House," Great North Productions, National Film Board of Canada and Vision TV, documentary broadcast December 17, 1997.

8   Mel Hurtig, *At Twilight in the Country: Memoirs of a Canadian Nationalist* (Toronto: Stoddart, 1996), 463.

9   Tony Clarke and Maude Barlow, *MAI: The Multilateral Agreement on Investment and the Threat to Canadian Sovereignty* (Toronto: Stoddart), 1997, 137.

10 Statistics Canada, *Canada's Culture, Heritage and Identity: A Statistical Perspective* (Ottawa 1996), 24.

11 Hurtig, *At Twilight in the Country*, 466.

12 *Quarterly Bulletin for the Culture Statistics Program* (autumn 1996): 2.

13 Statistics Canada, *Focus on Culture*, summer 1996, 6.

14 Wilfred Kesterton and John S. Moir, "Communciations," in *The Canadians, 1867–1967* (Toronto: Macmillan, 1967), 540.

15 This section is based on — though in quite different language from — Frank W. Peers, *The Politics of Canadian Broadcasting, 1920–1951* (Toronto: University of Toronto Press, 1969).

16 Sandy Stewart, *From Coast to Coast: A Personal History of Radio in Canada* (Toronto: CBC Enterprises, 1985), "How God Created the CBC." It is a good read, even though Sandy is my brother.

17 *Report of the Royal Commission on Radio Broadcasting* (Ottawa: F.A. Acland, Printer to the King's Most Excellent Majesty, 1929), 6.

18 Quoted in Walter Stewart, *Uneasy Lies the Head: Canada's Crown Corporations* (Toronto: Collins, 1987), 173.

19 Letter, February 5, 1997.

20 *CBC Annual Report*, 1996–97, 42.

21 Quoted in Clarke and Barlow, *MAI*, 129.

22 Marci McDonald, *Yankee Doodle Dandy* (Toronto: Stoddart, 1996), 162.

23 Ibid., 173.

24 Clarke and Barlow, *MAI*, 131–33.

25 Ibid., 180.

26 Ibid., 187.

27 Ibid., 131.

28 Ibid., 132.

29 Figure supplied by the Canadian Magazine Publishers Association, March 1997.

30 Clarke and Barlow, MAI, 133–34.

31 *Metropolitan Toronto Reference Library News* 23, Nos. 1,2, and 3.

32 *Canada's Culture*, 49.

33 *Toronto Star*, December 8, 1997, A15.

34 Canada Council, Annual Reports.

9 The National Dream Just Went Off the Track

1 John N. Jackson, *Welland and the Welland Canal* (Belleville, Ont.: Mika Publishing, 1975), 39.

2 Both quotes are from G.C. Patterson, *Land Settlement in Upper Canada, 1783–1840*, 209 (pamphlet in Metropolitan Toronto Reference Library).

3 The remark, from John Galt, the land promoter, is quoted in Gerald M. Craig, *Upper Canada: The Formative Years, 1784–1841* (Toronto: McClelland & Stewart, 1979), 156.

4 Quoted in Walter Stewart, *Uneasy Lies the Head: Canada's Crown Corporations* (Toronto: Collins, 1987), 46.

5 Craig, *Upper Canada*, 157.

6 The term was coined by Merritt's son. Ibid., 159.

7 A breathless, and bitter, account of these goings-on is to be found in the reprint of Gustavus Meyers' muckraking volume, *A History of Canadian Wealth* (Toronto: James, Lewis and Samuel, 1972), 170–205.

8 Roger Orshinger, *Banks of the World* (London: Macmillan, 1967), 3–8.

9 Myers, *A History of Canadian Wealth*, 186.

10 W.S. MacNutt, *The Atlantic Provinces, 1712–1857* (Toronto: McClelland & Stewart, 1965), 243.

11 Ibid., 246.

12 J. Bartlet Brebner, *Canada: A Modern History* (Ann Arbor: University of Michigan Press, 1960), 308.

13 Pierre Berton, *The National Dream* (Toronto: McClelland & Stewart, 1970), 353.

14 Herschel Hardin, *A Nation Unaware* (Vancouver: J.J. Douglas, 1974), 57.

15 Berton, *The National Dream*, 104.

16 *Canadian Monthly*, November 1872.

17 House of Commons, *Debates*, 1890, I: 1718.

18 Kenneth McNaught, *The History of Canada* (New York: Praeger, 1970), 197.

19 K.W. Studnicki-Gizbert, "Transport," in *The Canadians, 1867–1967*, edited by J.M.S. Careless and R. Craig Brown (Toronto: Macmillan, 1967), 507.

20 Canadian National Railway, Corporate filing, Financial Post Datagroup, November 19, 1997, 7–8.

21 Hardin, *A Nation Unaware*, 75.

22 Max Ward, *The Max Ward Story* (Toronto: McClelland & Stewart, 1991), 219.

23 Quoted ibid., 221.

24 Ibid., 223.

25 Statistics Canada, *Canada Year Book*, 1997, 385.

26 Ward, *The Max Ward Story*, 315.

27 Dominion Bureau of Statistics, *Highway Statistics*, Annual.

28 Governments spent a total of $16.8 billion: $11.3 billion on roads, and $5.5 billion on everything else. Transport Canada, *Transportation in Canada, Annual Report* 1997 (Ottawa: Minister of Public Works, 1997), 2.

29 Statistics Canada, *Canada Year Book, 1997*, 385.

30 *Directions: The Final Report of the Royal Commission on National Passenger Transportation* (Ottawa 1996), 3: 130.

31 *Toronto Star*, January 4, 1997, E1, E5.

32 Stewart, *Uneasy Lies the Head*, 136.

33 See Walter Stewart, *Paper Juggernaut* (Toronto: McClelland & Stewart, 1979), for the details on Mirabel spending.

34 Interview, April 8, 1997.

35 National Transportation Agency, Annual Report, 1994, 211.

36 Statistics Canada, *Rail in Canada*, 1995, 15.

37 National Transportation Agency, *Annual Report*, 1994, 99–101.

38 Canadian National Railway Company, *Financial Post Datagroup*, 6.

39 *Western Producer*, March 20, 1997, 7.

40 *Toronto Star*, February 8, 1997, A23.

41 Office of the Provincial Auditor, *1996 Annual Report*, 236.

42 Government of Ontario, Ministry of Transportation, *Municipal Transit Backgrounder*, January 1997.

43 Transport 2000, April 1997.

44 Transport Concepts, *External Costs of Truck and Train* (Ottawa 1997), table 1 and passim.

10 Curiosity Killed the Budget

1 Atomic Energy of Canada Limited, TASCC, undated bulletin, 1.

2 Atomic Energy of Canada Limited, *Annual Report, 1995–1996*, 4.

3 Atomic Energy of Canada Limited, *FusionCanada: Fusion, Energy for the Future* (Chalk River 1991), 1.

4 AECL, *TASCC*, 11.

5 Ibid.

6 AECL, *Annual Report, 1996–1997*, 11.

7 Interview, September 1, 1997.

8 National Research Council, *Report to Parliament, 1995–1996*, 7.

9 Interview, November 18, 1997.

10 Council of Ontario Universities, *Financial Position*, 1995, 23.

11 These phrases recur in the past three NRC annual reports.

12 NRC, *Report to Parliament*, 1995–1996, 15.

13 Interview, Chalk River, November 26, 1997.

14 *NRC Annual Report, 1996–1997*, 1.

15 The quote is from the National Research Council Act, and is cited in every annual NRC report.

16 NRC, *Annual Report, 1996–1997*, 32.

17 The National Research Council Act, introduction.

18 Quoted in J.M.S. Careless and R. Craig Brown, eds., *The Canadians*, (Toronto: Macmillan, 1967), 550.

19 George C. Laurence, *Early Years of Nuclear Energy Research in Canada* (Chalk River: AECL, 1991), pamphlet.

20 Dr. Henry Friesen, president of the MRC, on CBC Radio News, October 30, 1997.

21 Dr. Henry Friesen, speech, Calgary, Alberta, December 3, 1997, quoted on CBC Radio, December 4, 1997.

22 David Crane in the *Toronto Star*, December 3, 1997, D2.

23 *Toronto Star*, October 5, 1997, A5.

24 Quoted ibid.

25 *Toronto Star*, October 20, 1997, A3.

26 Ibid., May 5, 1997, A19.

27 Ibid., November 3, 1997, A16.

28 Speech from the Throne, September 23, 1997.

29 *Budget Plan*, 1997, 98.

30 *Toronto Star*, April 21, 1997, A17.

31 *Budget Plan*, 1997, 99.

32 *Vancouver Sun*, December 31, 1996, A12.

33 Ibid.

34 Statistics Canada, *Canada Year Book*, 1994, 399.

35 *Toronto Star*, January 28, 1997, D2.

36 Press release, Industry Canada, December 1996.

37 NRC, *Annual Report, 1996–1997*, 8. The NRC does not break out the numbers by firm, or even by project.

38 Interview, September 10, 1997.

39 *Quirks and Quarks*, CBC Radio, November 22, 1997.

11 The New Robber Barons

1 Douglas Goold and Andrew Willis, *The Bre-X Fraud* (Toronto: McClelland & Stewart, 1997), 14.

2 *Globe and Mail*, May 5, 1997, A9.

3 Matthew Josephson, *The Robber Barons* (New York: Harcourt, Brace, 1934), 141–48.

4 Ibid., 32.

5 Ibid., 15.

6 Stuart Holbrook, *The Age of the Moguls* (New York: Harmony Books, 1985), 140–41.

7 See, for example, John S. McGee, *In Defense of Industrial Concentration* (New York: Praeger, 1971), and Maury Klein, *The Life and Legend of Jay Gould* (Baltimore: Johns Hopkins University Press, 1986).

8 Frederick Lewis Allen, *The Great Pierpoint Morgan* (New York: Harper, 1949), 206.

9 Josephson, *The Robber Barons*, 149.

10 *Globe and Mail*, February 5, 1997, B10.

11 Josephson, *The Robber Barons*, 318.

12 Quoted in Holbrook, *The Age of the Moguls*, 346.

13 Eric Kierans and Walter Stewart, *Wrong End of the Rainbow* (Toronto: Collins, 1988), 79.

14 Josephson, *The Robber Barons*, 15.

15 *Time*, May 24, 1993, 12.

16 William Greider, *One World, Ready or Not: The Manic Logic of Global Capitalism* (New York: Simon & Schuster, 1997), 337–46.

17 *Washington Post*, May 11, 1993, A25

18 *Financial Post Daily*, May 13, 1993, 8.

19 Greider, *One World*, 338.

20 ABC TV News, July 20, 1993.

21 The $100.9 billion figure, from Statistics Canada, is cited in the *Globe and Mail*, January 29, 1998, B1.

22 *Globe and Mail*, January 24, 1998, B1.

23 Allen, *Morgan*, 161.

24 Josephson, *The Robber Barons*, 367.

25 *Globe and Mail*, April 10, 1996, B1, B4.

26 *Time*, November 11, 1996, 42.

27 *Wall Street Journal*, April 9, 1997, B10.

28 *Toronto Star*, July 30, 1997, A15.

29 Ibid., November 12, 1997, D1.

30 Richard Thompson, president of the Toronto Dominion Bank, quoted in Walter Stewart, *Bank Heist: How Our Financial Giants Are Costing You Money* (Toronto: HarperCollins, 1997), 17.

31 Statistics Canada, December 23, 1997.

32 The citation, from a speech Galbraith made in Ottawa in 1987, quoted in Dalton Camp's column, *Toronto Star*, July 30, 1997.

12 The High Cost of "Free" Trade

1 Paul A. Samuelson and Anthony Scott, *Economics*, 2nd Canadian edition (Toronto and New York: McGraw Hill, 1968), 744–49.

2 Quoted in Donald Creighton, *John A. Macdonald, Vol. 2: The Old Chieftain* (Toronto: Macmillan, 1955), 215.

3 See Eric Kierans and Walter Stewart, *Wrong End of the Rainbow* (Toronto; Collins, 1987), 161–71.

4 *Toronto Star*, October 21, 1989, D5.

5 Press release, Canadian Labour Congress, December 1989.

6 Mel Hurtig, *At Twilight in the Country: Memoirs of a Canadian Nationalist* (Toronto: Stoddart, 1996), 455.

7 In 1989 just over 2 million Canadians were employed in manufacturing; in 1993, fewer than 1.6 million. Statistics Canada, *Canada Year Book 1997* (Ottawa: 1997), 353.

8 Statistics Canada, *Canadian Economic Observer, 1996*, table 1.

9 *Toronto Star*, January 12, 1998, A12.

10 William Greider, *One World, Ready or Not: The Manic Logic of Global Capitalism* (New York: Simon & Schuster, 1997), 494.

11 *Globe and Mail*, February 24, 1997, A24.

12 Royal Commission on the Economic Union and Development Prospects for Canada, *Report* (Ottawa 1985), 1: 311.

13 William Henry Pope, *All You MUST Know about Economics* (Toronto: Comer, 1996), table 8-4.

14 Lawrence B. Krause, "Managed Trade: The Regime of Today and Tomorrow," *Journal of Asian Economics* 3, 2 (1992): 112.

15 Gordon Ritchie, *Wrestling with the Elephant: The Inside Story of the Canada–U.S. Trade Wars* (Toronto: Macfarlane Walter & Ross, 1997), 272–73.

16 John Maynard Keynes, *Collected Works* (Cambridge: Macmillan, 1978), 13: 128.

17 Royal Commission on the Economic Union and Development Prospects for Canada, *Report* (Ottawa: Minister of Supply and Services, 1985), 1: 301.

18 Linda Diebel in the *Toronto Star*, September 26, 1997, A13.

19 Ibid., August 6, 1997, A13.

20 Greider, *One World*, 64–67.

21 *Toronto Star*, February 11, 1998, D14.

22 Ibid., January 12, 1998, A12.

23 United Nations, *Human Development Report* (New York 1996), 3.

24 Reuters, November 10, 1997.

25 An excellent discussion of this still-in-process agreement appears in Tony Clarke and Maude Barlow, *MAI: The Multilateral Agreement on Investment and the Threat to Canadian Sovereignty* (Toronto: Stoddart, 1997).

26 The actual wording in the draft treaty reads: "Each Contracting Party shall accord to investors of another Contracting Party and to their investments, treatment no less favourable than it accords (in like circumstance) to its own investors and their investments with respect to the establishment, acquisition, expansion, operation, management, maintenance, use, enjoyment and sale or other disposition of investments." Clarke and Barlow point out that there is nothing to prevent a nation from treating the corporations of another country better than their own; they just can't treat them worse.

27 *Toronto Star*, November 23, 1997, F3.

28 Clarke and Barlow, *MAI*, 108.

29 Linda McQuaig, *The Cult of Impotence: Selling the Myth of Powerlessness in the Global Economy* (Toronto: Viking, 1978), 23, 284.

13 Private Parts

1 Saint John *Telegraph Journal*, August 27, 1997, 9.
2 Ibid., August 15, 1997, 1.
3 Quoted, ibid., August 22, 1997, 7.
4 *London Free Press*, February 15, 1997, A1.
5 Robert Reich, *The Next American Frontier* (New York: Penguin, 1984), 233. Reich was then teaching business and public policy at Harvard.
6 For a detailed description of how the Little Egypt Bump worked, see Walter Stewart, *Too Big to Fail* (Toronto: McClelland & Stewart, 1993), 119–21.
7 *Globe and Mail*, October 22, 1985, A1.
8 *Report of the Auditor General of Canada*, May 1996, chapter 1.
9 *Globe and Mail*, August 5, 1997, B2.
10 *Maclean's*, December 30, 1996, 18.
11 *The Canadian Global Almanac 1998*, 171–74.
12 Canadian National Railway Company, Corporate Report, December 17, 1997, *Financial Post Datagroup* 2, 10, and 1.
13 *Toronto Star*, February 11, 1998, D1, D8.
14 *Transport Action*, 19, 2 (1997): 4.
15 *This Magazine*, December 1996, 14.
16 Ibid., 15.
17 Paul McKay, *Electric Empire* (Toronto: Between the Lines, 1983).
18 Department of Energy and the Environment, Ontario Hydro, *Direction for Change*, 1997.
19 See Allan Levine, *The Exchange: 100 Years of Grain Trading in Winnipeg* (Winnipeg: Peguis, 1987).
20 Canadian Wheat Board, *Corporate Abstract*, 1997 (Winnipeg, 1997).
21 *Toronto Star*, January 14, 1998, A19.
22 David Griesling and Laurie Morse, *Brokers, Bagmen and Moles: Fraud and Corruption in the Chicago Futures Markets* (Chicago: Wiley, 1991), 126.
23 Quoted in Walter Stewart, *The Golden Fleece: Why the Stock Market Costs You Money* (Toronto: McClelland & Stewart, 1992), 151.
24 See Walter Stewart, *Uneasy Lies the Head* (Toronto: Collins, 1987), 201–8.
25 David Orchard, *The Fight for Canada* (Toronto: Stoddart, 1993), 61.
26 *Globe and Mail*, October 17, 1996.
27 "Privatized Water," *the fifth estate*, CBC TV, January 7, 1997.
28 *Sunday Sun*, November 17, 1996, 4.
29 *The Times*, May 3, 5b.
30 *Winnipeg Free Press*, June 8, 1997, A10.
31 Interview, Ontario Savings Office, Toronto, January 29, 1998.
32 Air Canada, *Annual Information Form*, April 30, 1997, 4, "The Corporation."
33 Ibid., 10.

34 LCBO *Annual Report, 1996–1997,* 1 and 39.

35 *Public Accounts of Canada,* 1995–1996, 181.

36 *Globe and Mail,* December 18, 1997, A1.

37 Statistics Canada, *Canada Year Book,* 1988, 26.

38 *Economic Reform,* July 1997, 6.

39 Ibid., October 1996, 1.

40 *Public Accounts of Canada, 1995–96,* volume 1, 1.17.

14 Suffer, Little Children

1 Fraser Forum, January 1997, 28.

2 J. Larry Brown and Ernest Pollitt, "Malnutrition, Poverty and Intellectual Development," *Scientific American,* February 1996, 36.

3 House of Commons, *Debates,* November 27, 1997, 2382.

4 Campaign 2000, *Mission for the Millennium,* November 1997.

5 *Edmonton Journal,* November 27, 1996, A14.

6 *Child Poverty in Canada, 1996* (Toronto: Campaign 2000, 1997).

7 *Globe and Mail,* October 17, 1997, A6.

8 Ed Finn, "Child Poverty Keeps Rising, and—Surprise!—So Does the Number of Millionaires," *Canadian Forum,* March 1997, 6–7.

9 National Council on Welfare figures, January 1998.

10 Tony Clarke and Maude Barlow, *MAI: The Multilateral Agreement on Investment and the Threat to Canadian Sovereignty* (Toronto: Stoddart, 1997), 69–70.

11 *Child Poverty in Canada,* 1997.

12 The figures in this paragraph are from *Child Poverty in Canada,* 1994, and are derived in turn from Statistics Canada, the National Council of Welfare, Human Resources Development Canada, and the Centre for International Statistics.

13 *Workfare: Does It Work? Is It Fair?,* edited by Adil Sayeed for the Institute for Research on Public Policy in 1995, contains four essays, three of which argue that it does work and that it is fair. The fourth is not so sure. There is no reference whatsoever to the experience of the Great Depression.

14 Charles Murray, *Losing Ground: American Social Policy, 1950–1980* (New York: Basic Books, 1984).

15 Human Resources Development Canada, *Improving Social Security in Canada* (Ottawa 1994), 44.

16 Employment Canada, December 19, 1997.

17 *Financial Post,* September 6/8, 1997, 1, 2.

18 Pat Dodson, "Disappearing Act," *New Maritimes,* September/October 1996, 4.

19 Murray, *Losing Ground,* 197.

20 National Action Committee on the Status of Women, *Women in Canada after Beijing: Left Out, Left Over, Left Behind!* (Ottawa: September 1997), 3.

21 National Council on Welfare, December 1997.

22 *Women in Canada*, 5.

23 Canadian Labour Congress, *Women's Work* (Ottawa, 1997), 5, 3.

24 *Toronto Star*, November 29, 1996, A4.

25 Ibid., January 3, 1997, A1.

26 Ibid., April 2, 1994, A.4.

27 *the fifth estate*, CBC TV, January 14, 1997.

28 Ontario Ministry of Health, January 23, 1998.

29 Elizabeth Witmer, minister of health, in a letter to the *Toronto Star*, February 9, 1998, A15.

30 *Globe and Mail*, October 11, 1997, A1.

31 *Toronto Star*, January 24, 1998, A6.

32 This material is from a series of articles I wrote about Operation Beaver over the years; the most recent appeared in the *Toronto Sun*, on February 17, 1997.

15 Choices

1 *Toronto Star*, December 24, 1997, A1.

2 Cited in *Globe and Mail*, May 28, 1997, B10.

3 *Canadian Press* newswire, February 2, 1998.

4 *Toronto Star*, December 9, 1997, D1.

5 Earthscan, *The Realities of Aid* (London 1996), 8.

6 United Nations estimate, quoted ibid.

7 See House of Commons, *Debates*, October 6, 1997, 495–520, for details and the debate on the changes.

8 *Toronto Star*, September 26, 1997, A34.

9 Statistics Canada, *Canadian Economic Observer*. Historical Supplement 1995/1996 (Ottawa: Minister of Industry, 1997), table 3.

10 The calculation was made on behalf of the National Council of Welfare, a government body. The $556 billion figure was calculated as of the end of 1995; it would be much higher now. National Council of Welfare, *Improving the Canada Pension Plan*, (Ottawa 1996), 3.

11 *Toronto Star*, September 26, 1997, A34.

12 National Council of Welfare, *A Pension Primer* (Ottawa 1996), and *Improving the Canada Pension Plan*, 1.

13 Interview, Ottawa, April 7, 1997.

14 Interview, Ottawa, April 8, 1997.

15 *Bank of Canada Review*, winter 1995–96, table G-5.

16 Ruben C. Bellan, *ER* magazine, March 1996, 6.

17 *Bank of Canada Review*, table G-5.

18 William Henry Pope, *All You MUST Know about Economics* (Toronto: Comer Books, 1997), 54.

19 Canada, Department of Finance, *Budget Plan 1997* (Ottawa 1997), 60.

20 *Building Canada for the 21st Century: The Budget in Brief 1998*, Hon. Paul Martin, minister of finance (Ottawa, February 24, 1998).

21 BDO Dunwoody, Chartered Accountants, a grave and conservative gaggle if ever there was one, put it this way in their *Federal Budget Report*: "While spending cuts have contributed to the deficit fight, the elimination of the deficit ahead of schedule has been mainly due to booming tax revenues and historically low interest rates."

22 Business Council on National Issues, *News Release* (Ottawa, March 25, 1998).

23 BCNI, *Memorandum for the Right Honourable Jean Chrétien, P.C., M.P. Prime Minister of Canada*, March 12, 1998, 2.

24 Linda McQuaig, *The Cult of Impotence: Selling the Myth of Powerlessness in the Global Economy* (Toronto: Viking, 1998), 6.

Index